December 2012

W9-BUZ-382

Dear Reverend Lloyd
& Church of the Holy Apostles,

Thank you as always
for your matchless hospitality.
We are blessed to be neighbors!

In christ alone,

Jo, Chy Howard,
Kim & Matt

Praise for *Red Letter Revolution*

"I don't know Shane but after reading this, I want to . . . As regards Tony Campolo, it's always been an embarrassment to me that the Preacher is more radical than any rock star. I don't love all that I read in this . . . some of it makes me uncomfortable. I think that's why they wrote it."

—Bono

"This book, by a young and an elderly Christian, will help you decide how we Christians could change the world if we took the 'red letter' words of Jesus literally and seriously."

—President Jimmy Carter

"Jesus did not mince words and neither do Shane and Tony. The Good News of the Gospels is that Jesus guides us with lessons that are abundantly clear; there are no ambiguities, no rationalization of war, oppression, wealth, or of the disgraceful economic divide that threatens to consume us. In *Red Letter Revolution* the uncompromised truth of Jesus' teachings are given voice by two modern-day Christian leaders who do more than preach this Good News. They walk the talk and lead the way."

—Archbishop Desmond Tutu

"I started reading this book and couldn't stop. Now *Red Letter Revolution* travels with me everywhere I go—Rome, Ukraine, Jordan, Lebanon. I read it as a book of spiritual guidance, and urge others to do the same. Thank you, Tony and Shane . . . Thank you for this book. May the movement spread around the world. I thank you for expressing yourselves with inclusive views of our Christianity without any kind of compromising the power of the Lord's message."

—Abuna Elias Chacour, Melkite Catholic Archbishop of Galilee

"The conversation between Shane Claiborne and Tony Campolo, well known for their clear evangelical witness on the front lines of poverty, justice, discrimination, and economics in America, is a generous invitation to us to join their conversation as they take the words of Jesus serious, literally, and obediently. *Red Letter Revolution* is an adrenaline-producing conversation with prophetic bite."

—Eugene H. Peterson, professor emeritus of spiritual theology, Regent College, and author of *The Message* Bible

"I cannot over-emphasize or exaggerate the richness of this book of conversations. Between them, Claiborne and Campolo have given us some of the wisest discussions I have seen to date on a number of subjects, particularly on war, violence, Hell, Islam, and the liturgy, not to mention some of their remarkably keen insights into the history of many of the changes effecting westernized Christianity today."

—**Phyllis Tickle**, author of *Emergence Christianity*

"Our capacity for continually missing Jesus' message is rather astounding. But worse, we historically replaced it with harmless cultural religion that often was directly at odds with the staggering change of perspective that Jesus offered both individuals and institutions. In this courageous and well crafted book, we have a return to the core message of the Gospel from two Christians who first tried to live it themselves—and only then spoke."

—**Fr. Richard Rohr, O.F.M.**, Center for Action and Contemplation

"Shane Claiborne and Tony Campolo are two of the most significant prophetic voices in the Christian world, and *Red Letter Revolution* is such an exciting and brilliant book that it should be read by people of all faiths and by secular humanists as well. Their interpretation of Jesus' message closely aligns with that of many Jews who are now reclaiming our Jewish prophet from Nazareth as one of our inspiring teachers. Make sure you get this book in the hands of anyone who wants to repair America's economic and political mess—it will give them a spiritual foundation for the healing we desperately need."

—**Rabbi Michael Lerner**, editor of *Tikkun Magazine* (tikkun.org)

"Muslims revere Jesus as a messenger of God. In *Red Letter Revolution*, Shane Claiborne and Tony Campolo demonstrate how Jesus' words and example apply to our broken world today. Claiborne and Campolo remind us that Jesus was the champion of the poor, the despised, and the outcast, rather than the powerful or the wealthy. Muslims have a deep respect for Jesus, and we know the world would be a better place if Christians took his words seriously. This book does just that."

—**Sami Rasouli**, Muslim Peacemaker Teams, Najaf, Iraq

"Shane and Tony? Talking freely and honestly about almost everything under the sun—telling stories, quoting stats, giving insights? Seriously? Now that's a book I'd give my friends . . ."

—**Rob Bell**, author of *Love Wins* and *Velvet Elvis*

"Few people have touched the conscience of the church—or that of myself and my own family—like Tony Campolo and Shane Claiborne. But the passion that flows through them that matters most is the passion of Jesus for so many on the margins of life who are urgently loved by the One who—though He was rich—yet He became poor for our sakes. I am grateful for their work and thought and lives. May the words of Jesus grip the world once more with the urgent conviction of impatient love."

—**John Ortberg**, senior pastor of Menlo Park Presbyterian Church, Menlo Park, California, and best-selling author of *The Me I Want to Be* and *The Life You've Always Wanted*

"In their own unique ways, Shane Claiborne and Tony Campolo have reinvigorated the debates around life, politics and theology. This is an exciting collaboration and conversation between two people truly committed to living out what Jesus teaches in the Scriptures, and in *Red Letter Revolution*, they are challenging us to do the same. Both Tony and Shane are friends I deeply respect and admire. This is a must-read book for anyone who is seeking to take Jesus' call on their lives seriously."

—**Jim Wallis**, founder and editor of *Sojourners* magazine

"I urge every Christ-follower to read my friends'—Tony and Shane—new book *Red Letter Revolution*. If you think they are radical in their thinking about some of the most critical issues of our day, wait until you learn where they have drawn their inspiration . . . from the Red Letter words of Jesus of Nazareth himself."

—**Noel Castellanos**, CEO, Christian Community Development Association

"What's the most hopeful movement within evangelical Christianity? Let Shane Claiborne and Tony Campolo introduce you . . . it's a conversation about issues that really matter today, rooted in the Church's rich history, taking the Bible seriously, and enthralled at every turn with the words and ways of Jesus. If you ever wished you could eavesdrop on a conversation with two of the world's most interesting and inspiring Christians, just turn to page one."

—**Brian D. McLaren**, author/speaker (brianmclaren.net)

"Radical, relevant and urgently important. Good Christians will argue about this or that concrete application. But every Christian should embrace *Red Letter Revolution*'s powerful call for Christians to live what Jesus taught."

—**Ronald J. Sider**, president, Evangelicals for Social Action and professor of theology, Palmer Seminary

"What an excellent reminder that the Gospels, among other things, are radical and subversive—Jesus demands that we love our neighbors, and that leads us into the middle of very real life. Shane Claiborne and Tony Campolo do a superb job of making it clear how we can live up to those demands—not easily, but joyfully!"

—**Bill McKibben**, author of *The Comforting Whirlwind: God, Job, and the Scale of Creation*

"Shane and Tony have interpreted well what the gospel really is. They have shown wisdom in choosing the 26 themes and making each one personal. Their sense of humor comes through in their conversations. The book is easy to read, down-to-earth and folksy, but it is not just a surface treatment of important issues. The authors reach down into the depths and make us want to go deeper with them in the spiritual search. This book has done an outstanding job in alerting us to the importance of our ushering in Christ's new society that lives more faithfully under the true gospel. The time for that new society is now."

—**Rev. N. Gordon Cosby**, cofounder of the Church of the Saviour, Washington, DC

"By recording their dialogue with one another, Shane and Tony are offering the church a desperately needed fresh perspective on some of the weightiest theological and sociopolitical issues that Christians wrestle with, positioned within a framework of biblical clarity, simplicity, and pragmatism. For Christians, this opens up a new form of access to 'deep' or 'complicated' spiritual questions, whether ancient and timeless or uniquely modern. Shane and Tony provide something that is applicable in any context, by cutting to the heart of what Jesus Christ actually did and said, so we can understand how to model Christ in our own daily lives. They do this deftly, with insight and relevance, and a tremendous amount of integrity. This may very well provide the push that many of today's Christians need to reignite their authentic, personal relationship with the person of Christ."

—**The Reverend Luis Cortés, Jr.**, president, Esperanza

"Reading two of my favorite authors banter back and forth about Jesus and the set-apart life challenged me in all the best ways. What does it mean to honor Jesus' legacy on the mean streets of this world? And how can I be as winsome as Jesus? This book frames a new way of walking out our Christianity and invites us to be different."

—**Mary DeMuth**, author of *Everything: What You Gain and What You Give to Become Like Jesus*

RED LETTER REVOLUTION

WHAT IF JESUS *REALLY MEANT* WHAT HE SAID?

SHANE CLAIBORNE
and TONY CAMPOLO

THOMAS NELSON
Since 1798

NASHVILLE   DALLAS   MEXICO CITY   RIO DE JANEIRO

© 2012 by Tony Campolo and The Simple Way

All rights reserved. No portion of this book may be reproduced, stored in a retrieval system, or transmitted in any form or by any means—electronic, mechanical, photocopy, recording, scanning, or other—except for brief quotations in critical reviews or articles, without the prior written permission of the publisher.

Published in Nashville, Tennessee, by Thomas Nelson. Thomas Nelson is a registered trademark of Thomas Nelson, Inc.

Published in association with the literary agency of Mark Sweeney & Associates, Bonita Springs, Florida 34135.

Thomas Nelson, Inc., titles may be purchased in bulk for educational, business, fund-raising, or sales promotional use. For information, please e-mail SpecialMarkets@ThomasNelson.com.

Unless otherwise noted, Scripture quotations are taken from HOLY BIBLE: NEW INTERNATIONAL VERSION®. © 1973, 1978, 1984 by International Bible Society. Used by permission of Zondervan Publishing House. All rights reserved.

Scripture quotations marked KJV are from the KING JAMES VERSION of the Bible.

Scripture quotations marked NRSV are from NEW REVISED STANDARD VERSION of the Bible. © 1989 by the Division of Christian Education of the National Council of the Churches of Christ in the U.S.A. All rights reserved.

Scripture quotations marked ESV are from THE ENGLISH STANDARD VERSION. © 2001 by Crossway Bibles, a division of Good News Publishers.

Scripture quotations marked ISV are from the INTERNATIONAL STANDARD VERSION of the Bible.

Scripture quotations marked NLT are from *Holy Bible*, New Living Translation. © 1996. Used by permission of Tyndale House Publishers, Inc., Wheaton, Illinois 60189. All rights reserved.

ISBN 978-1-4002-7507-6 (IE)

Library of Congress Cataloging-in-Publication Data

Claiborne, Shane, 1975–
  Red letter revolution : what if Jesus really meant what he said? / Shane Claiborne and Tony Campolo.
    p. cm.
  Includes bibliographical references.
  ISBN 978-1-4002-0418-2
  1. Christianity. 2. Christian life. I. Campolo, Anthony. II. Title.
  BR121.3.C54 2012
  230'.04624—dc23

Printed in the United States of America

12 13 14 15 16 QG 6 5 4 3 2

To all of us, young and old, who want a
Christianity that looks like Jesus again

Contents

PART III: RED LETTER WORLD

INTRODUCTION

Why This Book?

Whenever the word *evangelical* is used these days, a stereotype comes to mind. Whether or not that image is justified can be debated, but there is little argument that the word *evangelical* conjures up an image of Christians who are anti-gay, anti-feminist, anti-environmentalist, pro-war, pro-capital punishment, and conservative Republican. There are many of us, however, who are theologically evangelical, but who defy that image. Trying to escape that definition, a group of us gathered together to adopt a new name for ourselves: Red Letter Christians.

Starting in 1899, Bibles have been published that highlight the words of Jesus in red. We adopted the name Red Letter Christians not only to differentiate ourselves from the social values generally associated with evangelicals but also to emphasize that we are Christians who take the radical teachings of Jesus seriously and who are committed to living them out in our everyday lives.

We can't be sure of the extent of this new movement's outreach or of how many theologically evangelical Christians will adopt the new label for themselves. And even if they do, we have no way of knowing how seriously they will live out the teachings of Jesus as a countercultural lifestyle. But we have high hopes.

For more than forty years, Ron Sider, the author of *Rich Christians in an Age of Hunger*[1]; Jim Wallis, the founder of *Sojourners*; and I have been trying to make clear that it is imperative for followers of Jesus to serve the needs of the poor and oppressed. Lately, however, a new generation of young leaders has taken up the baton we've been carrying and are articulating the same themes of social justice in fresh and relevant ways. A standout among them is the coauthor of this book, Shane Claiborne. His book *The Irresistible Revolution*, his itinerant ministry, and, most of all, his life lived among the poor, have made him an icon for young Christians who want more than a belief system. They're looking for an authentic lifestyle that embodies the teachings of Jesus. Shane, a onetime student of mine at Eastern University, has become a representative of the Simple Way, an intentional community committed to environmental responsibility and, most important, putting into practice the teaching of Jesus about what we should do with the money we have.

Shane and I have had long discussions about how to live out those red letters of the Bible, and, separated in age by four decades, we have done so differently. We are aware that while we agree for the most part on theology and social ethics, living out what we believe has taken different forms for each of us.

As Shane and I have discussed our commonalities and our differences, we have come to believe that it would be helpful for others to listen in on what each of us has to say to the other. We want to share with you how our differing expressions of being followers of Jesus have evolved over the years.

As an example, most of us who grew up in the 1950s and 1960s did not even think about living in intentional community. During those socially tumultuous decades, the countercultural lifestyles of many of those who were called "hippies" were lived out in communes. The positive aspects of these communes, however, were often marred by the extensive smoking of marijuana and the use of psychedelic drugs. Furthermore, the pervasive, permissive sexual behavior of many communal hippies was scandalous to the general public and deemed highly immoral by evangelical Christians. Such negative reactions kept us from giving serious consideration to living in those kinds of intentional communities.

The intentional communities in which many young Red Letter Christians are living today are very different. If you are familiar with Shane and those who have identified with the lifestyle he has embraced, you are already aware that many in his generation are looking for intentional community as a way to create the kind of loving fellowship that strives to imitate what is described in the second chapter of Acts.

There are many other ways Shane and I differ in living out the biblical red letters. For instance, we are both committed to taking action to stop wars, defy unjust political structures that oppress the poor, speak out for the oppressed who have no voice, and endeavor in general to change society into something more like what God wants for it to be. But while Shane's generation does not see politics as the primary way to make justice a reality, my generation did.

Jim Wallis's *Sojourners* magazine has been overtly political, and many would claim that Jim himself argues for left-of-center policies. Ron Sider is the founder of Evangelicals for Social Action, an organization that advocates for justice and organizes Christians to lobby for legislation that addresses the concerns of the poor. In my own case, I ran as a candidate for the US Congress from the Fifth District of Pennsylvania in 1976 in order to work within the political process for Christian social change.

As you will find in your reading of this book, Shane and his generation of Red Letter Christian radicals have been, for the most part, disengaged from the political process, preferring instead to employ more direct ways of implementing the justice requisites of Jesus. For instance, when the Second Gulf War broke out, Shane and several other young Christians flew to Jordan, rented vans, and drove out across the desert to Iraq. They wanted to be in Baghdad to work in the hospitals and minister to those who would be casualties of the American bombings they knew were coming. We older Red Letter

Christians, on the other hand, tried to raise awareness here at home of the immorality of the war, hoping that those in positions of power in Washington, DC, would stop the war when they felt the pressure for peace we were trying to generate. Both generations of Red Letter Christians held the same beliefs about the war, but our styles of responding to it were very different.

When it comes to the church, both Shane's generation and mine recognize how greatly some things have changed for the better over the past forty years. Having come of age prior to Vatican II—and the ways that this church council opened up Catholicism to being more ecumenical and evangelical—we older evangelicals held distorted and negative views of Roman Catholics. We were sure that they had missed out on the doctrine of justification by faith and were propagators of a "works salvation." Religiously, we would have little to do with Roman Catholics, and they would have little to do with us. The idea that there was something for us to learn about spirituality from Catholics was unthinkable, and any suggestion of our trying to worship with them was extremely suspect.

The younger generation of Red Letter Christians cannot imagine the hostilities that existed between Catholics and Protestants back then, since things are different today. Shane's generation of Red Letter Christians has no difficulty worshiping with Catholics; indeed, many Red Letter Christians are members of Catholic churches. They appreciate the liturgies of Catholic worship and don't mind calling holy Communion the eucharist, and many are delving into the spiritual disciplines of ancient Catholic saints. All of this is new to some of us.

Younger Red Letter Christians are teaching older ones like me whole dimensions of the Christian faith that go back centuries before the Reformation. And it seems that there's a growing movement of young Christians like Shane who are aware that even though God is doing something fresh, we can still follow in some great footprints of those who blazed a revolutionary path and prepared the way. That's why this intergenerational conversation is so important. Our goal has not been to homogenize but rather to harmonize our dreams. As the Scriptures say, "Your young men will see visions, your old men will dream dreams" (Acts 2:17).

This is why Shane and I wrote this book as a dialogue. We want you to grasp the ways in which each of us is learning from the other and critiquing the other as we seek to work out our own salvation (Philippians 2:12) and live out what we read in the red letters of the Bible.

Our hope is that our conversation provides you with insight as you seek to live the teachings of Jesus. We invite you to join us in the conversation at www.redletterchristians.org. But more important, we invite you to join the Red Letter Revolution.

—Tony Campolo

PART I

RED LETTER
THEOLOGY

Dialogue on History

Very truly I tell you, whoever believes in me will do the works I have been doing, and they will do even greater things than these, because I am going to the Father.

JOHN 14:11–12 UPDATED NIV

SHANE: Tony, why do you think we need a new term like *Red Letter Christianity*? What happened to the terms *fundamentalist* and *evangelical*?

TONY: Christians with orthodox beliefs have, over the past century, adopted a couple of different names to distinguish themselves from those whom they thought had strayed from the historic teachings of the church.

During the late 1800s, scholars in Germany created a critique of the Bible that really tore traditional beliefs about the Bible to shreds. They raised questions about who the authors of Scripture were and suggested that much of the Bible was only the rehashing of ancient Babylonian myths and moral codes. In addition, theologies came out of Germany from the likes of Friedrich Schleiermacher, Albrecht Ritschl, Ernst Troeltsch, and others who raised serious doubts about such crucial doctrines as the divinity of Christ and his resurrection from the dead.

There was a reaction to all of this "modernism"—the name given to this recasting of these new Christian teachings that were attempts to be relevant to a rational and scientific age—and a collection of scholars from the United States and England got together and published a series of twelve books called the Fundamentals of the Christian Faith. These books were an intelligent defense of the traditional doctrines that we find outlined in the Apostles' Creed.

It was in reaction to those books that Harry Emerson Fosdick, a prominent liberal preacher in New York City, preached a sermon called "Shall the Fundamentalists Win?" which was printed and circulated throughout the country. Thus the term *fundamentalism* was born.

The label *fundamentalism* served us well until about 1928 or 1929. From that time on, and especially following the famous Scopes trial in which William Jennings Bryan argued against Darwin's theory of evolution, fundamentalism began to be viewed by many as being anti-intellectual and naïve. Added to this image of anti-intellectualism was a creeping tendency among fundamentalists toward a judgmentalism, by which they not only condemned those who deviated from orthodox Christian doctrine but any who did not adhere to their legalistic lifestyles, which were marked by condemnation of such things as dancing, smoking, and the consumption of alcohol.

By the time the 1950s rolled around, the word *fundamentalist* carried all kinds of negative baggage, and many wondered whether we could use the word anymore in a positive manner. About that time Billy Graham and Carl Henry, who was then the editor of *Christianity Today* magazine, began using a new name: *evangelical*. Again, orthodox Christians had a word that served us well, and did so right up until about the middle of the 1990s. By then, the word *evangelical* had lost its positive image with the general public. Evangelicals, to a large extent, had come to be viewed as married to the religious Right, and even to the right wing of the Republican Party.

When preachers like you and me go to speak at places like Harvard or Duke or Stanford and are announced as evangelicals, red flags go up and people say, "Oh, you are those reactionary Christians! You're anti-woman; you're anti-gay; you're anti-environmentalist; you're pro-war; you're anti-immigrant; and you're all in favor of the NRA." Defending ourselves, we say, "Wait a minute! That's not who we are!" I think evangelicalism also has been victimized by the secular media, which is largely responsible for creating the image by treating evangelicalism and the religious Right of the Republican party as synonymous.

It was in this context that a group of us, who were sometimes referred to as "progressive evangelicals," got together and tried to figure out how to come up with a new name for who and what we are. We kicked around various names and eventually came up with the name Red Letter Christians. We wanted people to know that we are Christians who make a point out of being committed to living out, as much as possible, what those red letters in the Bible—the words of Jesus—tell us to be and do. We're not into partisan politics, though we have a bias for political policies that foster justice for the poor and oppressed, regardless of which party espouses them.

Christianity Today magazine published a full-page article critiquing our new name, saying, "You people act as though the red letters in the Bible are more important than the black letters." To that we responded, "Exactly! Not only do *we* say that the red letters are superior to the black letters of the Bible, but *Jesus* said they were!" Jesus, over and over again in the Sermon on the Mount, declared that some of the things that Moses taught about such things as divorce, adultery, killing, getting even with those who hurt you, and the use of money had to be transcended by a higher morality.

When Jesus said he was giving us new commandments, I believe they really were new commandments. They certainly went beyond the morality prescribed in the black letters that we read in the Pentateuch. Furthermore, we don't think you can really understand what the black letters in the Bible are telling you until you first come to know the Jesus revealed in the red letters. This in no way diminishes the importance of those black letters; we believe that the Holy Spirit directed the writers of Scripture so that all of Scripture was inspired by God.

Shane, I know what you believe about those red letters in the Bible. As I have listened to you over these past few years, I've noticed that you make a big point out of the fact that the time has come for Christians to take the teachings of Jesus seriously, to take the Sermon on the Mount seriously.

SHANE: We clutter, explain away, jazz up, and water down the words of Jesus, as if they can't stand on their own. I once heard someone say, "I went to seminary to learn what Jesus meant by the things he said. And then I learned in seminary that Jesus didn't really mean the stuff he said." That's sad! Sometimes we just need to enter the kingdom as a kid, as Jesus said—with innocence and simplicity.

As theologian Søren Kierkegaard said back in the 1800s, "The matter is quite simple. The Bible is very easy to understand. But we Christians . . . pretend to be unable to understand it because we know very well that the minute we understand, we are obliged to act accordingly."[1]

There comes a moment when we return to that innocence. We read the Bible again, without all the commentaries, and ask, *What if he did really mean this stuff?* I'm not as concerned with figuring out every minute theological question as much as I am reading the simple words of Jesus and trying to live my life as if he meant them. If I can be a little more faithful today than yesterday to love my neighbor, pray for my enemies, and live like the lilies and the sparrows, I'm doing well.

It's important to note that Red Letter Christians are not, as someone once told me, "Christocentric," meaning we emphasize Christ so much that we are not trinitarian. I've been called worse things than "Christocentric," but that's not what we're up to.

We believe the God revealed in Jesus is the God of the Hebrew Bible. With all the ancient creeds, we know that the trinitarian God is one—Father, Spirit, Son. Nevertheless, as you read the Hebrew Scriptures, you encounter some troubling things. Just look at Judges 19 when a nameless concubine is cut into pieces and mailed to the twelve tribes of Israel. It can be confusing. And that is why Jesus is so wonderful. Jesus came to show us what God is like in a way we can touch, and follow. Jesus is the lens through which we look at the Bible and the world; everything is fulfilled in Christ. There are plenty of things I still find baffling, like the Judges 19 concubine thing, but then I look at Christ, and I get a deep assurance that God is good, and gracious, and not so far away.

TONY: There is a whole different feel about God when we move from the black letters in the Old Testament to the red letters of the New Testament. While Red Letter Christians believe that the Old Testament is also the inspired Word of God, it's hard to ignore that there is a contrast between the image of God that many people get from what they read in the Old Testament and what they find in the teachings of Jesus. Some early Christians even thought they were dealing with two different gods. Of course, they weren't, but it's easy to see why some Christians back then thought that way.

SHANE: This is precisely the beautiful thing about the incarnation. Jesus shows us what God is like with skin on—in a way we can see, touch, feel, and follow. My Latino friends have taught me that the word *incarnation* shares the same root as *en carne* or *con carne*, which means "with meat." We can see God in other places and at work throughout history, but the climax of all of history is Jesus, revealed in those red letters.

TONY: Again, this does not mean the black letters of Scripture are not divinely inspired—they are! Theologian G. Ernest Wright said that what we know about God is through what we discern in God's mighty acts in history. In his little monograph called *The God Who Acts* (1952), he says that unlike the Koran and unlike the Book of Mormon, our God does not come down and dictate word for word what's in the Bible. Instead, our God is revealed by what he does, and the Bible is the infallible record of those mighty acts. Those black letters that make up the words of the Old Testament are the record of those mighty acts in which we see God revealed.

The ancient Greeks used words like *omnipotent*, *omniscient*, and *omnipresent* to describe God, but these words just don't appear in the Old Testament. The ancient Jews never would have talked about God in those abstract Greek terms. If you had asked the ancient Jews to describe God, they would have said, "Our God is the God who created the world, who heard our cries when we were enslaved and led us out of the land of Egypt and into the promised land. Ours is the God who defeated the armies of Sennacherib. The God we worship enabled us to rise above the threatening powers of the world that would have destroyed us. We worship the God who acted in the lives of Abraham, Moses, and Jacob." What the ancient Jews knew about God, they knew through the things God did. It was the mighty acts of God in history that enabled them to begin to understand what God is like.

In the New Testament, we read that God, who in times past was revealed in diverse manners and in diverse places, has been, in these last days, fully revealed in Jesus Christ (Hebrews 11:1–2). The Bible is the account of those events in history through which we gain progressive insights into the nature of God; but in the end, it's in Jesus that we get the full story.

The Gospels are a declaration of how to live as a kingdom people, working to create the kingdom of God in this world. In the red letters of the Gospels, Jesus spells out for us specific directives for how his followers should relate to others and what sacrifices are required of them if they are to be citizens of his kingdom.

SHANE: Over the past few decades, our Christianity has become obsessed with what Christians believe rather than how Christians live. We talk a lot about doctrines but little about practice. But in Jesus we don't just see a presentation of doctrines but an invitation to join a movement that is about demonstrating God's goodness to the world.

This kind of doctrinal thinking infects our language when we say things like, "Are you a believer?" Interestingly, Jesus did not send us into the world to make believers but to make disciples. You can worship Jesus without doing the things he says. We can believe in him and still not follow him. In fact there's a passage in Corinthians that says, "If I speak in the tongues of men or of angels, but do not have love, I am only a resounding gong or a clanging cymbal. If I have the gift of prophecy and can fathom all mysteries and all knowledge, and if I have a faith that can move mountains, but do not have love, I am nothing. If I give all I possess to the poor and give over my body to hardship that I may boast, but do not have love, I gain nothing" (1 Corinthians 13:1–3 author's paraphrase).

At times our evangelical fervor has come at the cost of spiritual formation. For this reason we can end up with a church full of believers, but followers of Jesus can be hard to come by.

TONY: The Gospels provide us a prescription for a kingdom lifestyle, and the other books of the New Testament provide us with a solid theology. Red Letter Christians need both. We don't want to minimize the theology of justification by faith. We declare that we are saved by grace, through faith and not of works, lest any person should boast (Ephesians 2:8). We surrender our lives to Christ and don't trust in our own righteousness and good works for salvation. We trust in what Christ has done for us on the cross as a basis for salvation. But at the same time we declare that Christ has called us to live a lifestyle that is specifically defined for us in the Sermon on the Mount and in other red-letter passages of Scripture.

And just as we need to declare the doctrines of the faith, as the apostle Paul articulated with such clarity in his epistles, we also need to live out the lifestyle that Jesus modeled for us in the Gospels.

SHANE: A few years ago, Willow Creek Community Church in Chicago, one of the most influential megacongregations in the world, conducted a fascinating study. It was an attempt to measure the progress of their mission to raise up "fully devoted followers of Christ," and they surveyed their congregation to see how they were doing at that.[2] There is no question they have been phenomenal at reaching unchurched people and leading people into new faith commitments to Jesus. Their question was, do their lives look different? Do the social networks and consumption patterns of folks change as they become believers? And what they found was heartbreaking. Willow Creek, with courage and humility, released the study called *Reveal*, which was almost a confession as it showed that we may be good at making believers, but we have a long way to go when it comes to forming disciples.[3] Studies like this continue to show that our Christianity has become a mile long but an inch deep.

And I want to be clear: I have a deep respect for Willow Creek. I think they have consistently raised the bar on what membership means. I worked there for a year, and we always used to joke that if you complained about something at Willow, you had just volunteered yourself to help solve whatever was wrong. I remember hearing at Willow that "90 percent commitment still falls 10 percent short."[4]

What Willow Creek so courageously unveils through their own confession is that we have much work to do in most of our congregations when it comes to forming fully devoted followers of Jesus, not just believers.

If our gospel is only about personal salvation, then it is incomplete. If our gospel is only about social transformation and not about a God who knows us personally and counts the hairs on our heads, then it, too, is incomplete.

TONY: Because I am not yet living up to what Jesus expects me to be in those red letters in the Bible, I always define myself as somebody who is saved by God's grace and is on his way to becoming Christian. As Philippians 3:13 to 14 says, "Forgetting what is behind and straining toward what is ahead, I press on toward the goal to win the prize for which God has called me heavenward in Christ Jesus." Being saved is trusting in what Christ did for us, but being Christian is dependent on the way we respond to what he did for us.

SHANE: As the old saying goes, "I'm not saved because I'm good, but I'm trying to be good because I'm saved." Good works do not earn our salvation. They prove and demonstrate our salvation. If we have truly tasted grace, we become more gracious people. Grace makes us gracious. If we really become a new creation in Christ, that should transform how we act, who we hang out with, how we look at money and war and politics, and why we are here on earth. Indeed, all things become new.

One of the challenges we have is the concept that where everything is Christian, nothing is Christian. By that I mean that we live in a Christianized civilization wherein God-talk is heard everywhere, but with little attention given to what we're actually saying or what's implied in what we're saying. So when our money says, "In God we trust," that's quintessentially taking the Lord's name in vain when it is used to buy heroin in my neighborhood, or guns or bombs or pornography, or whatever. It would be better if it said, "In God sometimes we trust" or "In God we hope to trust." But then, when God-talk is used thoughtlessly and carelessly, it inoculates us. It's like getting a small dose of something that's real, but not getting hit with the full force of it—you become immune to the real thing. No one wants Christianity because of the little bit they've experienced.

TONY: I remember reading somewhere that Søren Kierkegaard, the Danish philosopher, told this wonderful story about how he was learning to swim. He remembers being in the swimming pool with his father standing on the edge of the pool, urging him to let himself go and trust the water to keep him afloat. He remembers splashing with his hands, kicking in the water with one foot, and yelling to his father, "Look! I'm swimming, I'm swimming!" But all the time, he said, "I was hanging onto the bottom of the pool with my big toe."

That describes me. I want to yell out to the Lord, "Look how I'm obeying you! Look how I'm fulfilling your will! I've let go of the things of the world!" But I really haven't. I'm holding on, so to speak, with my big toe. There's something in each of us that holds onto the things of this world. We hope we can let go and let Jesus have his way with us, but most of us can't pull that off as well as we should.

SHANE: So the litmus test of whether or not something is Christian is the question, Does it look more and more like Jesus? There are some folks who would say they are Christian, but they are looking less and less like Jesus. And there are some folks who would never claim to be Christian, yet their hearts and their passions are slowly moving closer and closer to Jesus' heart. It's up to God to sort all that out. Being more like Jesus is what we are trying to do as Red Letter Christians; it's where we're coming from, and where we're going.

Dialogue on Community

For where two or three come together
in my name, there am I with them.

MATTHEW 18:20

TONY: Shane, you have become an icon for many young people around the world who seem to be tired of what they consider to be inauthentic Christianity because you represent something that's refreshing to them. You, more than most of us, appear to be living out this Red Letter Christianity stuff by faithfully taking Jesus seriously. Because of this, many have called you a representative of postmodern Christianity—postmodern in the sense that while holding to the traditional doctrines of Christianity, you embrace a view of God's love and grace that extends beyond the parameters evangelicals tend to establish about who is "in" and who is "out" in God's family.

To a large extent, I think one of the reasons for your popularity as a writer and a speaker is that you represent how God's Spirit is moving in these times. You seem to suggest that God is creating a new consciousness among young people who seem to be craving a Christianity that is different from the one that I grew up with.

SHANE: People today want a Christianity that looks like Jesus again. The good news is that Jesus has survived the embarrassing things that we Christians have done in his name, as found in the dark side of the history of fundamentalism, the messiness of the religious Right, and even more recently, in folks who burn the Koran and hold signs that say "God Hates Fags," all in the name of Christianity. What's remarkable is that young people know there is more to Christianity than that, and that such destructive acts don't represent Jesus.

In the same way, African American friends have said that the fact that the Black church survived or that Native Americans still love Jesus is one of the greatest signs that God is at work in the world that we can ever imagine, considering the hideous, terrible things that we have done in his name.

Young folks have also grown up with a ton of questions, but they aren't always looking for somebody to answer their questions. Sometimes they are looking for people to question the answers, because the answers they've been given are not substantial. They are looking for people to ask the questions with them, and to sit with them in the brokenness of the world that we have. And through the Internet and other technology, folks are aware that the world we've been handed is fragile— and if our faith is only promising people life after death and not asking if there is life *before* death, we are going to lose them.

There's a ton of energy right now behind thinking about what Jesus has to say about things like economics, about violence. Because these are things we see everywhere right now—poverty and war, for example. The good news is that Jesus had a lot to say about these things. He wasn't just talking about what happens after we die. He was talking about how we live right now. He was talking about widows and orphans, laborers and wages—the exact same things that young people are talking about today.

TONY: This new group of young people that you sometimes call "ordinary radicals" includes some who are living in the intentional community called the Simple Way. Together, you live in one of the derelict sections of Philadelphia and are struggling with the issues you have mentioned.

I am not surprised that young people today are asking questions that were seldom asked by my generation. I saw this coming. Back when I was teaching at the University of Pennsylvania some thirty-five years ago, I remember a young Jewish man who became a convert to Christianity who, having read the Sermon on the Mount, asked me whether or not I had an insurance policy and a retirement fund.

When I answered, "What kind of question is that?" he said, "Well, I was just reading in Matthew that you're to take no thought for the future as what you need to eat and what you need to be clothed. Jesus said you shouldn't concern yourself about these things."

I almost felt like saying, "What do you want me to do, live like the birds of the air and the flowers of the field?" I didn't say that because he would have said, "That's what Jesus told you to do, so why don't you?"

Here I am, an old guy, living on my pension, social security, and 401(k) that I've set aside for my old age, and I'm asking myself how to explain all that while claiming to be a follower of Jesus who said, "Lay not up for yourself treasures on earth, where moth and rust doth corrupt, where thieves break through and steal" (Matthew 6:19 KJV), I did exactly what Jesus told me *not* to do. I have laid up treasures for myself here on earth.

As young people like yourself come along and challenge me about such things, I really am having to review my lifestyle in light of the words of Jesus. It's one thing to talk about the radical lifestyle that Jesus prescribes, but I am asking myself, *Do I have the faith to live out that radical lifestyle?* I'm constantly struggling with this. I'm calling myself a Red Letter Christian. I'm promoting this movement, but to what extent am I actually living out those red letters? My only defense is that I'm not as unfaithful today as I was yesterday.

One of my students once told me, "I know non-Christians who

are living more Christ-like lives than you're living!" My response was, "If they're so wonderful without Jesus, can you imagine how much *more* wonderful they would be *with* Jesus? And if you think that I'm so bad with Jesus, can you imagine what I would be like without Jesus?" Don't judge me in terms of what I am, but how far I've come, and in terms of where I hope to go in life. I hope to go a far greater distance toward living a Christ-like life from where I am right now.

SHANE: One of the things people seem to identify with in my journey is that I've been working really hard on the log in my own eye. I came out of a Bible Belt culture that was very suffocating, with racism and sexism, and I was handed a lot of answers that just didn't work for me. You know, "God and Country," and all those things. I was steeped in guilt and bitterness, and confused about what was right. In the same way I've been working on that, I think there are a lot of people who have logs in their own eyes that are similar to the one in my eye. They are figuring that out too.

I'm not a big fan of guilt. In John 10:10, Jesus says he has come to give us life to the fullest, not guilt to the fullest. So I'm interested in that life—and so are a lot of other folks—because we often settle for something far short of life to the fullest. We opt for survival, security, and comfort rather than the cross and suffering love of Jesus. We choose the American dream instead of the gospel dream. But the freest people I know are the folks who have learned to live like the lilies and the sparrows. Once a reporter said to Mother Teresa that he couldn't do what she did if he was paid a million dollars. She answered, "Yes, for a million dollars I wouldn't do it either."[1] I think Jesus is showing us that there is a pearl, a prize, worth leaving everything for. So it's not about what you've left, but it's about what you've found.

One of the things that's been really helpful for me is being

surrounded by folks like you, Tony, and others who keep push-
ing me to risk more. I wouldn't have imagined taking off my
shoes and putting them on someone who's homeless until I
saw my buddy Chris do it. I wouldn't have thought of offsetting
the carbon impact when I go speak by asking the people I'll be
talking to if they would commit to not driving their cars for a
week until my friend Will started doing that. So I think that's
where community is really clutch—because it keeps daring us
to move further than we already have. We look toward folks
who are a little further along, and they take us with them.

When we started our community, we had a real Franciscan
sense of the love of poverty, and the desire to get rid of everything. We still believe that we don't need the stuff of earth
that moths can destroy and rust can kill (Luke 12:33). But that
doesn't mean that we're left without any providence or security. We have an alternative security, and it comes from God
and from a community that believes in bearing each other's
burdens. So when someone has a financial need, like the early
church, we are going to pool our money together and meet
that need. Some of that has more structure now, fifteen years
after we started the community. We have ways of taking care
of medical bills when they come up. We have ways of taking
care of someone's house if it catches on fire.

For the early church, it wasn't that they were being sent
out with no extra food, no extra clothes, just to suffer on the
streets; they were learning about this new kind of community.
When they went into a town, people were going to welcome
them into their homes. The early Christians discovered that
even if they did not own houses, they had homes everywhere
they went. And that's what I've found when I've traveled: there
is enough. And the hope is that there will be enough daily
bread for this day. We've found that as we hold less and less
for tomorrow, there's more and more for today for everyone.

TONY: Your concept of community is so crucial to our discussion because there's an extreme sense of individualism that pervades our society. From a historical point of view, Plutarch, a Greek philosopher, is considered by many to be the man who sowed the seeds that gave birth to the Renaissance because he was the first one to lift up the concept of individualism and to make fulfilling individual potential the primary goal of human existence. But some of us Red Letter Christians contend that this heightened individualism can be called a Christian heresy. Jesus did not call us into individualism as much as he called us into community. It is in the context of community, according to Scripture, that we discover our individual gifts and callings and discover how we are to make our unique contributions to the well-being and blessing of all.

Back to that University of Pennsylvania student who was converted from Judaism to Christianity and then asked me about my lifestyle and "laying up treasures here on earth" in anticipation of my retirement. I asked him, "Well, who's going to take care of me in my old age? If I get sick and don't have an insurance policy, who is going to take care of me? Who is going to take care of my wife and kids should I get hit by a truck tomorrow morning?"

He looked at me with sheer surprise and said, "Well, the church! Right? You belong to the church, don't you? Doesn't the community of Christians take care of its people? Doesn't the church meet the needs of its individual members?"

I took a deep breath and said, "You know what? The church as described in Acts 2 seldom exists, and it certainly doesn't exist for me. I have had to function as an individual rather than being a part of a community that will take care of me when I need help."

Granted, I go to some churches where I can glean a few good feelings and say, "Oh, those churches gave me a deep, warm sense of belonging." But that's not community. Such churches provide a little bit of warm fellowship, but community is where people, as Paul writes so graphically in the book of Galatians, "bear one another's burdens, and so fulfill the law of Christ" (6:2 KJV). I don't belong to that kind of community, but I think the world is hungry for it.

Conversely, there's communism. If heresy is an exaggeration of a distorted biblical truth, I would say that communism falls into that category. We all know what communism strove to do—create community. Of course, it didn't! It was horrible and dictatorial. You cannot create community by imposing it on people politically. Community has to emerge out of a oneness of spirit, which is what the early church had. That is what's very rare in today's world. It's community that you and your friends in the Simple Way are endeavoring to create.

SHANE: Community is exactly what the early church had, and it was an imperfect community too. But the more you look at it, you can see that their sharing wasn't a *prescription* for community but a *description* of community. It wasn't that they had community because they shared; they shared because they had community. So it's not a system—"if you share everything then you're instantly a community." It was natural outgrowing because they believed they were born again. Why should someone have less when someone else has more? In fact, as one historian (who wasn't a Christian) described the early Christians, "Every one of them who has anything gives ungrudgingly to the one who has nothing. If they see a traveling stranger, they bring him under their roof. They rejoice over him as over a real brother, for they do not call one another brothers after the flesh, but they know they are brothers in the Spirit and in God. If they hear that one of them is imprisoned or oppressed for the sake of Christ, they take care of all his needs. If possible they set him free. If anyone among them is poor or comes into want while they themselves have nothing to spare, they fast two or three days for him. In this way they can supply any poor man with the food he needs."[2]

There are many precedents for that. John Wesley, in a sense, fasted. He lived off a poverty wage and said, "If I leave behind me ten pounds . . . you and all mankind bear witness against me, that I lived and died a thief and a robber."[3]

TONY: And Wesley did die with only five British pounds in his pocket. All he had to his name was a Bible and five pounds. He had given away what he didn't need. Lenny Bruce, who was known for being a foul-mouthed comedian, said, "Any man who calls himself a religious leader and owns more than one suit is a hustler as long as there is someone in the world who has no suit at all."[4] I wish he had been able to meet John Wesley.

Most of us know John 3:16. Many Christians memorize that verse. But few of us memorize 1 John 3:17, which reads basically "If you have this world's goods, and you know of a brother or sister who is in need, and you keep what you have while that person suffers, how can you say, 'I have the love of God in my heart?'" That verse raises the question, How can I claim that I have the love of God in my heart if I could help someone who's in need, but I keep what I have while that person suffers?

SHANE: Martin Luther, the champion of those saved by grace alone not works, said: "There are three conversions necessary: the conversion of the heart, mind, and the purse."[5] And Baptist evangelist Charles Spurgeon once said, "With some [Christians] the last part of their nature that ever gets sanctified is their pockets." We need to realize that community and radical economics are at the heart of the Christian faith. Even John the Baptist insisted as he preached repentance from sin, "If you have two tunics give one away" (Luke 3:11). Rebirth comes with responsibility and causes us to hold our possessions loosely. We are to live simply so others may simply live.

Dialogue on the Church

*I pray also for those who will believe in me through
their message, that all of them may be one,
Father, just as you are in me and I am in you.*

JOHN 17:20–21

TONY: There's a lot of talk these days about a "religionless Christianity" that claims that being a member of a local congregation is not a necessity for a Christian. You must be aware that many young people who are attracted to Red Letter Christianity are Christians who often drop out of church. Every sociological study done of late indicates that young adults are becoming more and more spiritual but less and less religious, that institutionalized religion is a turnoff for them.[1] Because your community, the Simple Way, isn't affiliated with a denomination, do you see a need for a local church?

SHANE: I certainly understand the spiritual hunger and the discontentment that many young Christians have with the church. Fifteen years ago, when folks asked me if the Simple Way was Protestant or Catholic, I would say, "No, we are just followers of Jesus." There was an innocence in that answer, but I also began to see that it is pretentious to think we can be Christian without the church. So now when people ask me if we are Protestant or Catholic, I answer by saying, "Yes." And I do mean that. We have Protestants and Catholics and Pentecostals and Quakers, and we have found that rather than trying to throw out our traditions, we need to bring them back to life. Instead of complaining about the church we've experienced, we are working on becoming the church that we dream of.

In the third century, the Bishop of Carthage, Saint Cyprian, put words to the conviction held by the early Christians: "If we don't accept the Church as our Mother, then we cannot have God as our Father." Now I don't think that means we have to leave her the way she is. In fact, just the opposite. We need to love her and help her recover, and never give up on her.

God is restoring all things. Institutions like the church are broken just like people, and they are being healed and redeemed. So I think of the church kind of like a dysfunctional parent. It's been famously said, "The church is a whore, but she's my mother."

The church needs discontentment. It is a gift to the kingdom, but we have to use our discontentment to engage rather than to disengage. We need to be a part of repairing what's broken rather than jumping ship. One of the pastors in my neighborhood said, "I like to think about the church like Noah's Ark. That old boat must have stunk bad inside. But if you try to get out, you'll drown."

Just as we critique the worst of the church, we should also celebrate her at her best. We need to mine the fields of church history and find the treasures, the gems. We need to celebrate the best that each tradition can bring—I want the fire of the Pentecostals, the love of Scripture of the Lutherans, the roots of the Orthodox, the mystery of the Catholics, and the zeal of the evangelicals. We want to discover the best saints and heroes from our different histories.

At the Simple Way, we didn't want to end up like the seed that Jesus described that falls on the ground and sprouts up, but dies because it has no roots (Matthew 13), so we are careful to see our communities as little cells that are part of a big body. Cells are born and cells die, but the body goes on living. We are community planters, not church planters. We want to join together the local congregations in our neighborhood, like cells in a body. In this way we are not parachurch; instead, we are prochurch. We are a part of restoring the congregations around us.

TONY: What, specifically, does this look like for your community?

SHANE: Every long-term member of our communities is encouraged to be a part of some local congregation. Incidentally, this is why many folks see what we are doing as reminiscent of monasticism, because we live in communities where we pray and work together every day, and we are a part of the local parish on Sundays. We go to worship at Catholic mass and at the storefront Pentecostal church. The inner city doesn't need more churches; it needs a Church—a body of people united together to do God's work.

One of the redemptive things going on in Philly and connected to us at the Simple Way is a flag football league called Timoteo, which is "Timothy" in Spanish. It's committed to mentoring young men, connecting them to other good male role models, and introducing many of them to Jesus and to the faith. There are about two hundred guys in the league now, on a dozen teams. But here's the cool part: every team is sponsored by a local congregation. One of the goals is to connect youth to local congregations. The great thing about the football league is that it is bringing the church together in a common mission, and getting folks out of the buildings and into the neighborhood. Pastors who might not agree on theology or politics can work together toward the same end.

Jesus' longest prayer in John was that we would be one as

God is one (17:22). With more than 36,000 Christian denominations, we have a long way to go. As one pastor in our neighborhood
said, "We've got to get it together because Jesus is coming back.
And he's coming back for a bride—not a harem."

TONY: Yes, the church is often the unfaithful bride of Christ. It has
been unfaithful in many ways—the ways it spends its money, the
ways it often tries to evade the hard sayings of Jesus, and the ways it
fails to be the church that Acts 2 leads us to expect it to be. But we
also have to acknowledge that we wouldn't have the Scriptures if it
weren't for the church. Through the Dark Ages, it was the monks of
the church who laboriously copied the Scriptures by hand, preserv-
ing the Word from generation to generation, right down to our own.

Would we even know who Jesus is if it weren't for the church?
Isn't it in a church fellowship that each of us first encounters the living Christ? Would any of us be Christians today without the church?

As the apostle Paul wrote, "We have this treasure in earthen ves-
sels" (2 Corinthians 4:7 KJV). In spite of all its inadequacies, the church
has been the vessel that has carried Christ into our lives. Yes, that vessel
needs renewal. That's what Red Letter Christians, along with other
renewal movements, are trying to bring about. We want others to join
us in living out the teachings of Jesus as we find his expectations
recorded in God's Word and, in doing so, renew the church.

SHANE: Church renewal is an important conversation these
days. A decade or so ago, folks talked a lot about the "emerging church." If we aren't careful, much of the post-evangelical
scene ends up also becoming sort of post-Christian or post-
church. That's dangerous and lonely. It is also true, however,
that the mainline congregations, traditional denominations,
the institutional church itself is in intensive care, hemorrhaging in almost every way. It desperately needs fresh vision
and imagination. One of the most promising things that has

come out of the emerging church has been folks looking back and reclaiming the best of their traditions, seeing that it's not an either/or but a both/and—God is doing something ancient and something new. Phyllis Tickle calls it "hyphenated denominations"—Presby-mergence, Bapti-mergence; Luther-mergence—because what they are doing is renewing and building on what was. Many of the Salvation Army folks and Mennonites are looking back as they move forward. They are remembering the best of their traditions that have kept alive the peace tradition of the faith—the simple living, deep community, and restorative justice are just as relevant today as they were a few hundred years ago. We need a new Anabaptist renewal to help us combat the myths of our culture that happiness must be purchased or that war can bring peace. The Mennonites were some of the best countercultural Christians in history. They went to jail and got killed for their uncompromising faith. I had a friend tell me it's the difference between being in a canoe and a rowboat. In a canoe you look forward as you row, but in a rowboat you look back as you move forward.

Frankly, one of the most disconcerting things to me as a Methodist was reading John Wesley. I started to wonder if any Methodists still read John Wesley—he was a wild brother! I was just talking to some Methodist bishops, and I asked them, "If Wesley was alive today, would he be a Methodist?" We all laughed awkwardly. It's a good question though, as it can be so easy to forget our roots.

Likewise, by the end of his life, Saint Francis was not a Franciscan. The Franciscan order had left Francis and diverged from his original vision, as it grew to 30,000 members in roughly twenty years. In his final years Francis experienced terrible sadness and regret for how his holy order had decayed as well as anger at the friars who betrayed the order's founding standards and principles. Here is how one Franciscan scholar,

Paul Sabatier, describes Francis' thinking at the end of his life: "'We must begin again,' he thought, 'create a new family who will not forget humility, who will go and serve lepers and, as in the old times, put themselves always, not merely in words, but in reality, below all men.'"[2]

Saint Francis is an interesting figure, especially when it comes to discontentment with the church. He lived in a time when the church had gotten very sick, infected with the materialism and gluttony of the Middle Ages in the midst of the Crusades and holy wars. There was a moment in Francis' life where he just could not take it anymore, and he began to read the Gospels with fresh eyes. While he did not hold back on his relentless critique of the church that had sold out, he ultimately remained humbly committed to restoring her dysfunction rather than giving up on her. He heard God whisper, "Repair my church, which is in ruins."[3] Of course, Francis took that literally and started picking up bricks and rebuilding the old San Damiano chapel. But he did not give up on the church; he even ended up preaching at the Vatican. But his deepest critique of what was wrong was the practice of something more beautiful. His best sermon was his life.

Legend has it, the first time he preached at the Vatican, the pope told him to go preach to the pigs. But later the pope had a vision: the corner of the church was collapsing, and little Francis and the youth of Assisi were holding it up. Arguably that youth movement was one of the most powerful restorations of church history. Every few hundred years our church gets a little sick and needs another reformation. Maybe we are living in one of those moments now.

TONY: While Saint Francis recognized the church's failures and hypocrisies, he still saw it as a community of faith where Christ could be encountered. When young people say to me, "I can't be a part of the church because the church is full of hypocrites," I always say, "That's why you are going to feel right at home among us."

I go on to tell them that if they feel that the church is full of hypocrites, they really should go and join them. They will probably end up saying, "My kind of people!" In the end, we are all hypocrites. But as Red Letter Christians, we should be trying to overcome our hypocrisy through the power of the Holy Spirit and through the influence of gospel preaching.

When I left the University of Pennsylvania, one of my faculty colleagues, E. Digby Baltzell, said to me, "You are going to be working in the life of the church, and that's beautiful. Early on, however, you need to define the limits of your hypocrisy."

I was stunned. But as I thought about it, we are all hypocrites. There are always inconsistencies between who we really are and our public personas. It's easy for me to recognize those inconsistencies in my life, and I am sure you can do the same. But there have to be limits to those hypocrisies. There has to be a point that, if crossed, is so intolerable that you have to just stop everything and say, "I need to go off by myself and take a good look at myself, and ask God to help me overcome my inconsistencies." As Christians, we should always strive toward eliminating all hypocrisy, but we have to start with limits.

SHANE: Here's what I've come to realize: people do not expect Christians to be perfect, but they do expect us to be honest. The problem is that much of the time, we have not been honest. We've pretended to be perfect and pointed fingers at other people. So then when we get caught doing the same things we have called others out on, we are doubly guilty. There really is something to this idea of "Judge not, that you not be judged" (Matthew 7:1 NKJV). When we preach about how wrong it is to smoke, and then we get caught smoking, naturally people are ticked. The question isn't whether or not we are hypocrites. The question is, is there room for another hypocrite? And are my own hypocrisies a little less today than they were yesterday?

TONY: I remember that shortly after Jim Bakker of television's *PTL Club* was exposed for his sexual improprieties and then put on trial for financial fraud, I went to speak to a conference of Presbyterian ministers. The moderator of that group, prior to introducing me, said, "We must learn to distance ourselves from the likes of Jim Bakker, lest the world out there think that we are all like him."

When I got up to speak, I said, "First of all, this is no time to distance ourselves from Jim Bakker. This is a time to embrace a Christian brother who is suffering. If we don't do that, we negate what Jesus is all about and contradict all that we say about unconditional love. We should be embracing him, not establishing distance from him in his loneliness and time of need.

"Second, the only difference between Jim Bakker and the rest of us is that they haven't found out about the rest of us yet. There is enough garbage in each of our lives that if all that was true about us was flashed up on a screen in the middle of a Sunday morning service, almost all of us would have to resign and run away and hide ourselves. Almost all of us have secrets, but we haven't been exposed, so it does not befit any of us to condemn someone else who actually has been exposed." There was a shock that went through that gathering of ministers, but none of them protested.

SHANE: A good role model for honesty and transparency was my friend Rich Mullins, the late singer. He owned up to his struggles and contradictions and hypocrisy. I remember one story where he and his buddy were on a train. The two of them were pouring out their struggles and confessing their sins to each other, really having a heart to heart, diving into their own darkness. After many hours, the train arrived at their station and they started gathering their things. As they got up to leave, the woman sitting in the seat behind them said, "Excuse me. I don't mean to interrupt, but are you Rich Mullins?" Rich said at that moment he thought of all the things this woman might have overheard and had to decide if he was Rich Mullins! Of course, he looked her square in the eye and said, "Yes, ma'am, I am Rich Mullins."

The good news is that Jesus didn't come for folks who have it all together, but for folks who are willing to admit they are falling apart (Matthew 9:13). Hopefully, that can also give us some grace with a church full of messed-up people. And with ourselves.

TONY: Christ prayed in John 17 that we might be one. Christians living individualistic lives apart from connectedness to the body of believers is not the will of God. Paul makes it clear in 1 Corinthians that every Christian needs to be part of the church—that no member can exist apart from the body. Each member, Paul points out, needs all the other members of the body. Paul writes that the eye cannot say to the hand, "I don't need you," or the head to the feet, "I don't need you" (12:21).

It's in community that we discover our individuality. I believe Christ called us to be in fellowship with one another so that each of us could discover that unique ministry into which each of us is called, and that we are to celebrate certain rituals such as holy Communion and weddings that will, in fact, renew our faith commitments. These rituals remind us from whence we've come and where we're going, our connectedness with other Christians. And it's within our local churches that we find this.

Dialogue on Liturgy

*Jesus took bread, gave thanks, and
broke it, and gave it to his disciples,
saying, "Take it; this is my body."*

MARK 14:22

TONY: The church invites us to participate in a liturgical ceremony that reaffirms our faith and connects us with a historical corporate body of Christians that reaches back over the centuries to Christ himself.

I have a friend who left the Anglican Church because he "got saved," as he put it. He went on to say that he had attended church for thirty years and never heard the gospel. I had to tell him that was not true. He may not have *heard* the gospel, but it wasn't because the gospel wasn't spoken at every worship service. You can't go through the liturgy of the Anglican Church without reciting the Apostles' Creed and saying the gospel truths that it contains. You can't go through holy Communion without hearing the story of Christ and what his death on the cross accomplished for us. Granted, liturgy can lose its meaning through vain repetition. In fact, Jesus condemns vain repetition in prayers in the Sermon on the Mount (Matthew 6:7), but liturgy need not be that way. It can be a sacred embodying of the truths of the gospel, and it can nurture our souls.

Shane, you cowrote a book on liturgy.[1] What do you say to people who may not be familiar with this faith tradition?

SHANE: Funny how God works. Twenty years ago, I didn't even know what the word *liturgy* meant! In fact, our liturgy book begins by saying, "If you love liturgy, this book is for you. And if you don't know what liturgy is, this book is also for you." Basically, liturgy is the patterns and rhythms of prayer that have been practiced by Christians for nearly two-thousand years. Rituals and traditions and holy habits like taking Communion, baptism, and orienting our lives around the story and calendar of the church, and remembering holy days like Easter and Christmas—not just national holidays like the Fourth of July. Liturgy includes our public worship and reading of Scripture. When Jesus opened the scroll and read from Isaiah in Luke, Jesus was reading from the liturgy. He was celebrating Passover and going to temple. So many of the things he does are a part of the Jewish tradition. Some he would challenge. And to some he would bring new life.

There are seasons and rhythms to prayer just as there are to creation. The sun comes up and the sun goes down, so having a way to pray in rhythm is a part of what creates a healthy community life and a healthy church. We move a little closer to being one just as God is one, as Jesus prayed in John 17:11. For when we learn each other's songs, prayers, heroes, and history, our vision becomes a little more complete as we see through each other's eyes. That's what the Common Prayer liturgy project has been about: learning to pray with the rest of the church, learning to pray with the rest of history.

Now, as Protestants we can only hope that as our Catholic, Orthodox, and Anglican friends see us discovering liturgy, they find it adorable rather than offensive that we're just discovering something they've been doing all along.

I have learned many things about liturgy from Catholics, the greatest of which is the value of embracing the wonderful mystery of what it means to be the body of Christ. Communion is this sense that we are to re-member Christ, to become his hands and feet. In the eucharist, the old saying, "You are what you eat" comes to life. As we perform this ritual—which, incidentally, first-century non-Christians found totally bizarre and led them to accuse the Christians of being cannibals and cultish for drinking blood—we digest Christ and pray that his blood and love and life flow through us. We pray that we are the ones who get digested into his body.

I have seen the mystery of the Communion happen as we have had the Lord's Supper with homeless families out of donated bagels and apple juice. One of my most powerful Communion services was in Australia when I was served the Eucharist by the aboriginal Christians who used their customary damper (homemade flatbread) and Billy tea (red tea) as the elements. But after all, *eucharist* means "mystery." So perhaps we can just enjoy it.

TONY: How is prayer part of the liturgy? And what can we as Red Letter Christians learn from it?

SHANE: I've learned that prayer is not just about trying to get God to do what we want God to do but about getting ourselves to do what God wants us to do. Training ourselves to be the kind of people God wants us to be.

A lot of times, we use prayer as a way of excusing ourselves from action. You know, when you share a deep dilemma you face and someone says, "I'll pray for you," often they are really sincere and don't know what else they can do. And we do need to pray for each other. But sometimes when someone says, "I'll pray about that," it is code for "I'm not going to do anything else for you." So we have to be careful that prayer and action go together. If we hear someone asking for prayer over and over because they need work done on their leaky roof, we should keep praying, but we might also get off our butts and get some people together to fix the roof! When we ask God to move a mountain, God may give us a shovel.

Prayer and action, Jesus and justice, those who believe in miracles and those who haven't seen a miracle in a long time—all need to be working together. What turned into the Common Prayer project started with the desire to see these come together—to bring the ancient liturgy into the contemporary world, and to read the Bible in one hand and the newspaper in the other.

TONY: What do you say to those who say that liturgy replaces a personal relationship with Jesus? What has been your experience?

SHANE: I often hear this criticism said of Catholics, but it's absurd! Sure, there are many valid critiques as liturgy and group prayer can be good places to hide and there are Catholics who don't have a very close relationship with Christ. But there are also Protestants and mainliners and even evangelicals who don't have a really intimate relationship with Jesus either. The fact is that some of my Catholic friends have had the most incredible, deep, some would say mystical and almost romantic relationships with Jesus. Sister Margaret, our Catholic nun in Philly, always calls Jesus her spouse, and it's why many nuns wear rings on their wedding fingers.

At one point, there was a reporter who asked Mother Teresa if she was married. That's a strange question to ask a nun, but maybe the whole nun thing was new to him. But her response was brilliant. She smiled and said, "I am certainly in love. And sometimes my spouse can be so demanding."

It doesn't get much better than that, or much more personal. There's a winsomeness in the kind of intimacy that so many of the mystics write about. When I spent time in India with Mother Teresa, we began and ended every day kneeling before the cross in adoration of Jesus, staring at the cross and soaking in his love.

Prayer is not a formulaic thing but a love life, a romance with God. It's not about the words we speak but about being with God—sort of like marriage. Sometimes you go on spontaneous outings and random adventures, sometimes you just cuddle, and sometimes you go on a formal date. The liturgical prayers are sort of like the date to the opera or symphony.

TONY: Sociologist Émile Durkheim understood the role of liturgy in creating solidarity for a group and enhancing the beliefs and commitments of people who practice rituals. Members of churches that have high levels of liturgy often have high levels of loyalty to their churches. Thus Protestants are not as loyal about going to church as Catholics are. Durkheim explained that liturgy has a binding effect on people.[2]

Liturgy, according to Durkeim, has the function of teaching and also of bringing to mind what must never be forgotten. This is why groups that don't have holy Communion regularly tend to lose the centrality of the cross, and may even lose the centrality of Christ in the lives of their members. Whatever criticisms Protestants may have of Catholicism, there is no question that Catholics never forget the cross or what Christ did there. They hold firm to the belief that his body was broken and his blood was shed to bring about our salvation. That's because every Sunday (and for some, every day) at mass, the good Catholic remembers that sins are forgiven because Christ's body was broken and his blood was shed. I believe that celebrating Communion weekly would help keep us Protestants focused on the basis of our salvation.

In more cases than are recognized, young people who are won to Christ so effectively by groups like Young Life, Campus Crusade, and Youth for Christ are not integrated into lifetime commitments to churches, and are prone to drift away from the faith as they grow older. The fact that such groups lack any kind of liturgy makes it difficult for those who receive the gospel through their ministries to remain faithful Christians, especially when the hectic demands of everyday life can so easily preoccupy them.

Our ministry, the Evangelical Association for the Promotion of Education, once took about seventy university students from across the country to work in a summer ministry with children and teenagers of Camden, New Jersey. As we were looking for places for them to stay, the bishop of the Camden diocese phoned us and said, "We have a large convent with only three old nuns left living there. It has scores of rooms, and I can make the convent available for some of your young people."

This offer turned out to be a bonanza for those young people. They became the envy of all the other university students working in our program that summer, because those three nuns lovingly cared for them and cooked their dinner each evening. As the nuns and volunteers ate together, the young people told stories about the problems and troubles so evident in the lives of the boys and girls with whom they were dealing. It wasn't long before our workers discovered that the nuns were going down to the little chapel in the convent at five o'clock each morning to pray for the children whom they were trying to reach for Christ. These university students told me that it became pretty obvious to them that the prayers of the nuns were having an impact. They saw positive changes in the lives of the boys and girls, and they believed these changes were a direct result of the two solid hours of early-morning prayer, during which the three nuns prayed for each and every one of the children by name.

We had working with us that summer some Seventh Day Adventist Christians who had come to us believing that the pope was the Antichrist and that Catholics belonged to an unchristian religion. When they encountered these nuns, they didn't quite know how to handle it. I asked one of them what she thought about the three nuns, and she said, "You know, for the past two weeks, when they got up at 5:00 a.m. to pray, we would get up, too, and go down to the chapel to kneel and pray with them, because we saw what their prayer was doing for the children." That summer, a lot of attitudes toward Catholics changed.

SHANE: Just like a good carpenter, we need a good toolbox for prayer. Some things have been handed down as really helpful tools we can carry with us. *Lectio Divina* is Latin for "divine reading." It is a way of prayerfully reading Scripture that lets it sink into our souls. The way it works is this: You take a passage from the Bible, and it doesn't need to be a long one, and you read it once slowly. The first time you just listen. Then you read it again and, if you are in a group, share a word or phrase that jumps out at you—and nothing more, just the word or phrase. Then you read it a third time, and each person shares why that word or phrase strikes him or her. Finally, it is read one last time, slowly. Monastic folks around the world practice something like this every day. Some of them have said it is a way of feasting on Scripture, allowing it to digest and leave a taste in our mouths.

It also sort of flies in the face of what I often call "spiritual bulimia," where we gorge ourselves on books and readings, conferences and sermons, and then vomit it back up before truth gets digested. We end up overchurched and malnourished. We don't listen to what the Spirit might say just through the simple text itself. *Lectio Divina* is a good tool to correct us and help us to really learn, study, and feast with God.

TONY: John Engle and Kent Annan, both Red Letter Christians, employ *Lectio Divina* in their missionary work in Haiti.[3] The Canadian Bible Society gives them ten thousand Bibles every year, and John and Kent give out these Bibles to poor Haitians who use them as textbooks in their literacy training. Haitians gather together in small circles of maybe ten or fifteen, and in each of these circles every person is asked to read three or four verses of Scripture, sounding out the words phonetically. Then the leader of the group says, "Stop! For the next fifteen minutes, bow your heads, close your eyes, and ask God, 'What do you want to teach me through the verses I just read?'" The people reflect on the verses they just read, and then, going around the circle a second time, each one shares what he or she believes the Lord told them during the time of reflection.

Without us sending an evangelist, they are being evangelized. The Holy Spirit is doing the evangelizing in the context of *Lectio Divina*. Sometimes we don't take seriously the words of Jesus, who said essentially, "If I leave you, I will not leave you alone. I will send to you the Holy Spirit, and He will teach you all things" (John 14:18–26, paraphrased). Through *Lectio Divina*, the Haitians in this literacy program are being taught by the ultimate Teacher. Commentaries and scholarship are important, but we have to leave room for quiet and stillness following the reading of Scripture to give the Holy Spirit a chance to teach us things we need to know.

SHANE: Another kind of meditation that has been meaningful to Christians for hundreds of years is the Jesus Prayer. It's a really simple prayer that you can pray through the day—"Lord Jesus Christ, Son of God, have mercy on me, a sinner." One can breathe that in and out. It's an easy prayer to memorize and pray through the day, or when you get really frustrated.

I pray the rosary or with beads (I like making my own prayer beads). Many different religions use beads as a tool for prayer, and Catholics have a rosary. Creating a chain of beads can help you have a physical tool as you pray throughout the day. Prayer beads aren't magic, but they can cure some minor cases of ADD. For instance, I have a chain of some different-sized beads (or different colored or textured beads) for various prayers. You might have a large bead for the Lord's Prayer. You might have seven rough beads for praying against the seven deadly sins—pride, envy, lust, anger, gluttony, greed, and sloth—and you might have nine little ones for the fruit of the Spirit listed in Galatians 5, so that you can rest on each one and pray that it would take root and grow like a seed inside of you—love, joy, peace, patience, kindness, goodness, gentleness, faithfulness, and self-control.

On my recent trip to Calcutta, one of the most wonderful things was seeing nuns in a very active life. I mean, pouring themselves out in some of the hardest work I've ever seen. And yet as they walk from the orphanage to the home for the dying, they carry prayer beads and pray as they walk. So beads can be some important tools to keep with us as we try to figure out ways we can pray and concentrate in a world with so much frenzy and noise.

TONY: Another tool is the Prayer of Examen, a practice that is nearly five hundred years old, from the Jesuit tradition, whose forefather was Ignatius of Loyola. Saint Ignatius said that whatever other prayers we miss out on during the day, doing the Prayer of Examen is an absolute must.

Ignatius suggested that the Prayer of Examen is best done as you get ready for bed. It has two parts. The first part requires that you reflect on the day you have just lived, and think of all the good things you did throughout the course of that day. You should name every blessing you may have brought into the lives of others, citing the ways that you lived out the will of God and the instances in which you helped other people. The apostle Paul says, "Finally, beloved, whatever is true, whatever is honorable, whatever is just, whatever is pure, whatever is pleasing, whatever is commendable, if there is any excellence and if there is anything worthy of praise, think about these things" (Philippians 4:8 NRSV). Then Paul says, in the next verse, to keep on doing these things.

After you've reviewed all the good things you've done during the day, Ignatius suggests that you are then ready to go on to the second part of the Prayer of Examen, which requires us to do the unpleasant task of reflecting on the sins and failures of the day. He cautions, however, that you dare not look at the sins and the failures of your day until you have first affirmed yourself. In other words, he is saying that you should not do to yourself what you know you should not do to a child. If you are going to point out the shortcomings of a child or correct that child, you have to do so in the context of affirmation, lest the child become emotionally crushed (Ephesians 6:4). Affirm yourself. Only after affirming yourself should you go through the day a second time and remind yourself of your sins and failures. Name them one by one and confess them to God. Then ask God not only to forgive you but also to cleanse you of your sins. The apostle John says, "If we confess our sins, he who is faithful and just will cleanse us from all unrighteousness" (1 John 1:9 NRSV).

SHANE: The Prayer of Examen is a great way of being conscious of God's presence in our lives. Lots of folks end the day with it, or stop in the middle of the day to pause and be mindful of God's presence.

One of the other tools we use at the Simple Way is called "Prouds and Sorries." We gather in a circle and each person shares a "proud" and a "sorry"—something we are proud of that we or someone else did that day, and something we are sorry about that we could have done better. It is a way of safely opening up a space to celebrate each other and to confess things we have done wrong. And the idea is that everyone should have something to be proud of and something to be sorry about.

TONY: The kinds of spiritual disciplines we've been talking about are essential if we are to do the work of God in the world. Each time Martin Luther King organized a march for social justice for African Americans, he would call would-be participants to come together at least two days in advance to spiritually prepare themselves for the march. People don't always get the whole picture when they think about Dr. King's activism, but he wanted all the people who marched with him to first spend time in prayer. He knew that out on the street, people might mock them, policemen might beat them, and dogs might be ordered to bite them. They had to be spiritually prepared to love their enemies and to do good to those who would hurt them, as Jesus had told them to do. Otherwise, they would be emotionally and spiritually crippled by the hostilities they would encounter.

Our mutual friend Mary Albert Darling, a professor of communications at Spring Arbor University in Michigan, cowrote a book with me called *The God of Intimacy and Action: Reconnecting Ancient Spiritual Practices, Evangelism and Justice.* The book is about connecting these practices with Christian activism, and it makes the case that if we try to do evangelism or work for social justice without first having taken time each day to be spiritually empowered, we will burn out. Jesus very carefully called upon his disciples to recognize that they needed the power of the Holy Spirit to do the ministry he had given them to do. He let it be known that without his Spirit in us, we could do nothing (John 15:5).

Spiritual disciplines, which include liturgical practices, are requirements for those who are committed to living out the red letters of the Bible. Such disciplines keep us focused on Christ and facilitate our surrendering to an infilling of Christ's spirit. Without that infilling, we will fail in our aspirations to live out his commandments. He said, "Without me ye can do nothing" (John 15:5 KJV).

Dialogue on Saints

Truly I tell you, among those born of women there has not risen anyone greater than John the Baptist; yet whoever is least in the kingdom of heaven is greater than he.

MATTHEW 11:11

TONY: As we try to understand what the Bible is saying to us in our own day and age, it is important for all of us to know how Christians, down through the ages, have interpreted Scripture. The writer of Hebrews tells us to be sensitive and aware that we are encompassed with a "great crowd of witnesses" (Hebrews 12:1). I have come to realize that the witnesses of saints who have gone before us can help us in our efforts to interpret Scripture. We Protestants did not invent Christianity, but sometimes we read the Bible thinking that we have the right to interpret it as though there have not been saints around for two thousand years interpreting Scripture. We need to seriously consider what they had to say.

Shane, you frequently reference Saint Francis of Assisi. How has this thirteenth-century saint impacted your life?

SHANE: The life and witness of Francis is as relevant to the world we live in today as it was seven hundred years ago. He was one of the first critics of capitalism, one of the earliest Christian environmentalists, a sassy reformer of the church, and one of the classic conscientious objectors to war.

Francis was the son of a wealthy cloth merchant, born into a society where the gap between the rich and the poor was increasingly unacceptable. It was an age of religious crusades, where Christians and Muslims were killing each other in the name of God. Sound familiar?

Francis did something simple and wonderful. He read the Gospels where Jesus says, "Sell your possessions and give the money to the poor," "Consider the lilies and the sparrows and do not worry about tomorrow," "Love your enemies," and he decided to live as if Jesus meant the stuff he said. Francis turned his back on the materialism and militarism of his world, and said yes to Jesus.

One of the quotes attributed to Francis is a simple and poignant critique of our world, just as it was to his: "The more stuff we have, the more clubs we need to protect it." It does make you wonder if he'd have been on Wall Street protesting in our time.

With a childlike innocence, Francis literally stripped naked and walked out of Assisi to live like the lilies and the sparrows. He lived close to the earth and, like Jesus, became a friend of the birds and creatures, whom he fondly called brother and sister. In light of that, many Christians brought their pets to my church yesterday for a special all-pets-allowed service, an annual tribute to Francis. And many a birdbath wears his iconic image. But it's easy to turn our best movements into monuments. His life was a powerful critique of the demons of his day, which are very similar to the demons of our day.

One of my favorite stories about Francis was when he decided to meet with the Muslim sultan during the Fifth Crusade. It was a tumultuous time. War had become a necessity and a habit, and was sanctioned by much of the church. Francis was sent off as a soldier, but he could not reconcile the violence of war with the grace of Christ . . . and so he got off his warhorse and put down his sword. He pleaded with the military commander, Cardinal-Legate Pelagius, to end the fighting. Pelagius refused. Instead, Pelagius broke off all diplomatic relations with the sultan of Egypt, al-Kamil. The sultan in turn decreed that anyone who brought him the head of a Christian would be rewarded with a Byzantine gold piece. Francis, however, pursued his vision in steadfast faith, surmounting all dangers in a journey to see the sultan. He traveled through fierce fighting in Syria and inevitably was met by soldiers of the sultan's army, who beat him savagely and put him in chains, dragging him before the sultan himself. Francis spoke to the sultan of God's love and grace. The sultan listened intensely and was so moved that he offered Francis gifts and money. Francis, of course, had no desire for the money, but he gladly accepted one gift, an ivory horn used in the Muslim call to prayer. He took it back with him and used it to summon his own community for prayer. Both Francis and the sultan were transformed by that encounter.

In an age of religious extremists, Francis offers us an alternative. We have seen religious extremists of all stripes— Jewish, Muslim, Christian—distort the best that our faiths have to offer and hijack the headlines with stories of hatred. We've seen Christian extremists burn the Koran, blow up abortion clinics, bless bombs, baptize Wall Street, and hold signs that say "God Hates Fags." But Francis invites us to become extremists for grace, extremists for love.

Although the church is prone to forget his witness or to make a monument of his movement, we can still celebrate his critique of an economy that left masses of people in poverty, so that a handful of people can live as they wish. We still rejoice in his love for the earth as we work to end the ravaging of our world. We remember his witness that there is a better way to bring peace than with a sword. And we remember the whisper he heard from God, *Repair my church which is in ruins.*[1]

These are the words of the famous prayer attributed to Francis. May they inspire us to become better people and to build a better world.

> *Lord:*
> *Make me an instrument of your peace.*
> *Where there is hatred, let me sow love.*
> *Where there is injury, pardon,*
> *Where there is discord, union,*
> *Where there is doubt, faith,*
> *Where there is error, truth,*
> *Where there is despair, hope,*
> *Where there is sadness, joy,*
> *Where there is darkness, light.*
> *O Divine Master,*
> *Grant that I may not so much seek to be consoled as to*
> *console;*
> *to be understood as to understand;*
> *to be loved, as to love;*
> *for it is in giving that we receive,*
> *it is in pardoning that we are pardoned,*
> *And it is in dying that we are born to eternal life. Amen.*[2]

TONY: What about Saint Clare of Assisi?

SHANE: And of course Clare. She shone. She kept living with the folks on the street. When Francis went to the mountains and his cave up on Mount Subasio, she would pull him back to the people. In fact, it's important to note that though many of us know Francis, he was not a lone ranger. There was an entire youth movement in Assisi.

They believed that Christianity had gotten sick. What sparked that movement around eight hundred years ago were these young people who read the Gospels, sold everything, and gave up fighting in the war.

If you look at his early rule of life for the community, it's almost entirely Jesus' words. It's all taken from the Gospels. Of course, over the years, things got much more complicated and the rule got thicker and thicker. But it started as a youthful prophetic critique of the Christianity that had stopped taking Christ seriously. They started with what they could change, which was themselves—the logs in their own eyes. It wasn't a pretentious thing, but it was a genuine desire to really try to be the church that they dreamed of, and to live the things that Jesus talked about.

Clare started her own order of women, the Poor Clares, who are still around. At first her family was totally upset and thought she was abandoning the church and disrespecting her family and everything else. But what is fantastic is that, by the end of Clare's and Francis' lives, they had wooed so many people, including members of their own families, back to Jesus. Eventually, Clare's own sister joined her order. They had brought the church back to Jesus and back to the poor. And they were teenagers when all this was happening! These were kids. And they changed church history forever.

One of my favorite Franciscans was Brother Juniper. Francis was famous for saying, "I wish I had a whole forest of junipers like him!"[3] But Brother Juniper also got in a lot of trouble. At one point he was left in charge of the cathedral and some folks came in need of money, so he gave them all the treasures from the altar of the cathedral (and it didn't go over well with the church!). At one point he had given his clothing away so many times, he got scolded by his superior and ordered not to give his garments away anymore. Immediately after his little rebuke by the superior, he was walking down the street, and a half-naked beggar approached him in need of clothing. Juniper thought for a moment and said something like, "My dear brother, you have caught me at a bad time. I have been forbidden by my superior to give my clothing away; however, if you tried to take it from me, I sure won't stop you."

Part of what was exciting about that movement was that they didn't hate the church. They actually loved the church, and they loved it enough to try to change the things that were wrong. I think that's why it was so dangerous. Francis was one of the most quickly sainted folks in history—only two years after his death. I think the church knew they needed his witness and movement.

TONY: Francis also was a poet. One of his poems is the prayer in which he talks about Brother Sun and Sister Moon, giving us insight into the spiritual connection he had with all of nature. That poem is a classic, and many literary experts say that it was the beginning of modern poetry.[4] Then, of course, there's that wonderful line of the prayer that begins, "Lord, make me an instrument of thy peace, where there is hatred, let me sow love . . ."

Given what Francis represents, you can understand why so many young people who are turned off to religion are turned on to Francis, and why, other than the Bible, more books have been printed about Francis during the last twenty years than on any other subject. Lord Chesterton once said, "Francis may have been the last true Christian."[5]

SHANE: Lord Chesterton may be a little dramatic; neverthe- less, we look at Francis and Juniper and so many other holy fools, and we see that they unveil our contradictions with humility and humor. They make our hypocrisy so apparent that we want to change our lives—not because of guilt but because we want to be alive, we want to be more like Jesus. They move us in that direction. Frederick Buechner said saints leave us the scent of God, the aroma of Christ. In God's flirting with humanity, God occasionally drops a handkerchief—and these handkerchiefs are called saints.

Dialogue on Hell

*Enter through the narrow gate. For wide is
the gate and broad is the road that leads to
destruction, and many enter through it.*

MATTHEW 7:13

TONY: I am not a universalist. I believe there are people who, as it says in the book of Hebrews, chapter 3, have been so hardened that they would reject Christ even if they were staring at him face-to-face. There are those who are so entrenched in sin and have done so much evil that they have become resistant to all appeals for their salvation.

Justice requires that I not be a universalist, but I am not the one to decide who is in and who is out. Judgment belongs to God, as it says in Deuteronomy 1:17. I believe that Christ is the only way of salvation, but I am open to the possibility that there are those outside what I believe to be true Christianity who might have an indwelling presence of the will of God, and who could be saved even though they do not say yes to *my* doctrinal beliefs and commitments (Romans 2:14–16).

SHANE: I believe in hell. I just don't know who's going there. And the good news is that it's not for me to know. Mother Teresa once said, "When we get to heaven, it may be full of surprises." Jesus affirms it himself in Matthew 25.

I know the way to heaven, so that's what I share about. I

figure if you know the cure to cancer, you shouldn't go around talking about cancer all the time. You should tell people the cure.

I'm not sure when we got so hell-obsessed. Jesus talks about it some, but not nearly as much as he talks about the kingdom of God. But his accounts of hell are interesting to begin with. His big hell sermons are about a rich man who doesn't care for the beggar outside his gate (Luke 16), and the other is about how God will separate the sheep and the goats according to how we care for the least among us here on earth (Matthew 25). Jesus' harshest hellfire sermon is in Matthew 23. And it is targeted not at gay folks or drunkards, but at the religious elite. His harshest words were reserved for the teachers of the law, who thought they were the moral gatekeepers of society. In Matthew 23:33 he says, "You snakes! You brood of vipers! How will you escape being condemned to hell?" Those words were for the self-righteous religious folks. And his most aggressive act, where he flips over tables and clears house, is not on the Boardwalk during Mardi Gras, but in the temple itself. Interesting.

But I think there is a reason the gospel means "good news." Perhaps the Bible verse that has been the cornerstone for evangelicalism is due for a fresh visit—John 3:16. It goes like this: "For God so loved the world that he gave his one and only Son." And here's the next verse, John 3:17: "For God did not send his Son into the world to condemn the world, but to save the world through him." That actually sounds like good news.

I remember when I was a kid in East Tennessee, I got involved in a charismatic church. I loved it. But I will never forget one thing we did each year called "Heaven's Gates and Hell's Flames." It was something to see. We did these terrible skits, like one where a bunch of kids are riding in a bus and it crashes. All the kids are killed in the crash, and the demons come and drag all the kids who don't know Jesus to hell, as they are shouting to their friends, "Why didn't you tell me?"

My friend's dad was the devil—and he was really good. So then we'd give an altar call and pretty much everybody got saved, even the pastor. It scared the hell out of you, literally.

The strange thing is that we didn't even hear much about Jesus; we just heard about hell. There's something wrong with that gospel; it's really out of proportion. It's like when someone who has had a radical conversion shares his or her "testimony," only, as you listen to them share, they spend 90 percent of their time talking about their life before Jesus and end by saying, "Then I gave my life to the Lord." And you wonder why they didn't talk more about Jesus. After all, they left such an interesting life to follow him, so he must be pretty special.

I have a friend who was going to a music festival, one of those huge gatherings with tons of bands and thousands of people. My buddy is a Christian, but he was going to the festival with another friend who isn't a Christian, who, in fact, is pretty unfamiliar with Christianity. As they were entering the festival grounds, there were a bunch of fire-and-brimstone folks lining the street with signs that said, "Bob Marley is in Hell," "Janis Joplin is Burning in Hell." The non-Christian fellow looked over to my friend and said, "I don't know much about hell, but it sounds like they've got some good music down there." I'm not sure that was the message they were shooting for.

For me, I did not choose Jesus because I was scared to death of hell. Nor did I choose Jesus because I wanted mansions in heaven and streets of gold. I chose Jesus because he's wonderful, absolutely wonderful. We can live without fear. After all, nothing can separate us from the love of God (Romans 8:38–39). Nothing.

TONY: What happens on the Day of Judgment is important to me, but if there wasn't any heaven, and if there wasn't any hell, I would still be, as I am today, committed to evangelizing. Most days, I am out on the road, preaching to people and asking them to come forward and accept Christ as their personal Savior. I do that not only because it guarantees them a ticket to heaven but also for two other reasons. Number one is that we, who have allied ourselves with Christ and the work of his kingdom, want to recruit others to join us in the task of changing the world into what God wants it to be. Evangelism, as I view it, is recruiting agents for God's work in this world. Second, I believe that by calling people to Christ and asking them to participate in his work in the world, I am offering them a calling that will give ultimate meaning to their lives. Viktor Frankl, the psychologist who developed what is called "logotherapy," has said that the greatest problem of troubled human beings is the absence of meaning in their lives.[1]

The question, What is the meaning of my life? is of ultimate importance. My answer is, "You are here in this world because God wants you to partner with him in bringing love and justice into the world." It sounds like the first of the Four Spiritual Laws,[2] but that's because God really *does* have a wonderful plan for every person's life. That plan is for each of us to be an agent for the evangelization and transformation of this world into a world of justice and well-being for God's children. That's God's plan, and God is calling each of us to participate in a great revolutionary movement for renewing the world, rescuing the perishing, and saving the lost.

Calling people to give themselves to Christ is what you captured so well in your important book, *The Irresistible Revolution*, Shane.[3] You shared with your readers the wonderful reality that in committing themselves to Christ, people are committing themselves to a lifestyle prescribed by Jesus, which promises joyful fulfillment. It's about living life to the fullest. This is not a promise for superficial happiness but a promise of a deep sense of actualizing all the glorious potentialities that God intended for each and every person. God's promise is, "You will have an abundant life. You will have meaning in your life. You will be lifted up and be living on higher ground" (John 10:10, paraphrased).

When I consider the joyful fulfillment and the meaningful existence one can have in Christ, I have a strong compulsion to call people to surrender their lives to him and to be filled with his Spirit. For me, that's one very important motivation to do the work of an evangelist, in addition to introducing the Christ who saves from sin and gives eternal life.

SHANE: There is a growing number of young people who have grown up in a pluralistic sort of world, thinking, *We need to be more inclusive of everyone.* There is a beautiful side to that, but I think it can cheapen the things that make us different when we ask, "Why can't we all just get along?" There's just something a little bit politically incorrect and exclusive in saying that Jesus is the only way to God. And yet, that's one of the things at the heart of my faith that I am not able to compromise. There are all kinds of other questions that arise, like if Christianity is the only way to Christ. Karl Barth was asked at Princeton, "Are you saying that Christianity is the only way to God?" And his answer was, "No, no religion is the way to God. I'm saying that Jesus is the way to God."[4] I know this: Jesus is the way. And there are many who say that they have rejected Jesus, but the more I talk with them I discover they actually are quite fond of Jesus. They just aren't crazy about the Christians they've met.

TONY: I agree with you that the red letters of the Bible send a clear message. In John 14:6, Jesus says, "I am the way and the truth and the life. No one comes to the Father except through me." That's pretty strong language. And those who hold to an exclusive point of view would say, "See! See what Jesus says. Are you going to take those red letters seriously?"

My answer is, "Very seriously." The place where I broaden my perspective is that, while I know that Jesus is the only way to salvation, I am not sure that the grace of God we experience through Jesus and his death on the cross is *only* available to those who are inside the church. If I am asked if there are people outside the church who might be saved by Jesus, I can only reply that I don't make judgments about who is in and who is out. I believe the message of the Bible is not that salvation is through the group to which you belong, or the name you apply to yourself, but that Jesus is the only way to eternal life. People are saved by what Jesus did for them on the cross.

I contend that on Judgment Day, as it says in the book of Matthew, there will be many people who weren't in the Christian church who will discover that they did have a relationship with Christ (Matthew 25:41–46). There is reason to believe that there will be some who, on the day of judgment, are not aware that they had a relationship with Christ, when, in reality, they hadn't rejected Jesus at all. What they had not accepted was a distorted presentation of Jesus, even one that we Christians may have given them. We have to ask ourselves if it is Jesus whom someone has rejected or only a misinterpretation of him. The Bible *does* say that there's no other *name* under heaven whereby anyone can be saved, and there's no way to avoid that (Acts 4:12).

As I remember, Billy Graham, at the 1987 Urbana missions conference, told about going to a monastery in China to talk to some Buddhists. When he got there, he saw one particular monk in deep meditation, and felt led by the Spirit to go and talk to the man about Jesus. With his translator, Dr. Graham opened the Scripture and explained the way of salvation, giving the details about what Jesus had done on the cross and how giving one's life over to Christ would give a person eternal life.

Dr. Graham could sense that this Buddhist monk was taking all of this in, and was so moved by it that there were tears in his eyes. He said to the monk, "Are you willing to invite Jesus into your life right here and right now as we pray together?"

The monk looked back at him in dismay and said, "Accept him into my life? I would accept him, but you must understand that he is already in me. He has been in me for a long time. I didn't know all the things about him that you have just told me, but this Jesus that you have been telling me about is within me, and as you spoke, his Spirit within me was confirming everything that you said. I believe in what you said because his Spirit has convinced me that these things are true. I would accept him, except that he is already within me."

That story left open this question: was Christ alive in that monk before Billy Graham ever got there? And, if Billy Graham had not gotten there, would that Christ, insofar as that monk claimed to know him as an indwelling presence, been enough for his salvation? I'm not about to answer those questions. Instead I go along with what Billy Graham once said, "My task is to bear witness. It's the Holy Spirit's task to convict. And it's God the Father's task to judge."[5]

Picking up on that same theme, in the book of Romans, Paul seems to suggest that God will have to make an exception for those who never got the law of God but who, nevertheless, had something written in their hearts that made them try to do what God expected of them (Romans 2:13–15).

My wife, Peggy, loves to tell this wonderful story when she speaks. She says that in heaven Peter is in charge of checking people in at the gate. Paul, on the other hand, still the great administrator he had proven himself to be here on earth, is in charge of keeping track of the people in heaven. It disturbed him that he always found more people in heaven than Peter was admitting. This discrepancy greatly annoyed them both. Then one day, Paul came running to Peter and said, "I found out what's been happening! *It's Jesus! He keeps sneaking people over the wall!*"

Peggy loves that story because she believes it is saying that even though the church sometimes thinks it can determine who can and cannot get into heaven, Jesus may be at work outside the church, loving people and lifting them into his kingdom.

Dialogue on Islam

No one comes to the Father except through me.

JOHN 14:6

TONY: There's a lot of debate over religion right now and a lot of hostility between religions. I find it interesting that the question of whether or not Christians and Muslims worship the same God has become such a hot topic. Christian media has picked it up; radio shows, television shows, books, and magazine articles are dealing with that question.

Before we try to answer *that* question, we have to ask another question: do any two of us worship the same God? Stop to think about it for a minute. Is your concept of God the same as mine? Most sociologists and psychologists say that the image a person has of his or her *earthly* father has a great deal to do with that person's concept of his or her *heavenly* Father. Add to that the differing social situations in which we grow up. We are raised in different churches, which give us differing images of God. Also, our concepts of God are highly influenced by the collective values of the dominant culture in which we are raised. For example, many Americans make God into an American. All of these forces help to mold each person's image of God. Given these social and psychological factors, do any of us end up with the same concept of God?

Author Anne Lamott says, "You can safely assume you've created God in your own image when it turns out that God hates all the same people you do."[1] How often do we create an image of God that serves the interest of our own ethnocentric values and prejudices? Before we begin to ask whether Christians and Muslims worship the same God, we have to ask if it is possible for any *two* of us have the same image of the same God.

Ultimately what I know about God is what I find in Jesus. The Bible says that Jesus is "the fullness of God" revealed (Colossians 1:19 ESV), and what we know about Jesus comes from the Bible. Red Letter Christianity is about critiquing our socially generated concepts of God with the revelation of Jesus in Scripture, such as that put forth in Hebrews 2.

Before we pass judgment on the Muslim concept of God, we must consider that there are many Muslims who take Jesus very seriously, and whose ideas of God are highly influenced by what they find in Jesus and his teachings. As you know, the Koran has a great deal to say about Jesus, including that he was born of a virgin, sinless, and that he is coming again. The Koran says that Jesus performed miracles and that Mohammed never performed miracles. There are even some Muslims who pray to Jesus for healing because they view him as a miracle worker. The founder of the Sufi sect of Islam was so in love with Jesus that other Muslims said, "If you love Jesus so much, we'll put you to death on a cross so that you can die like he died." And they did! The fact is that the Koran attests to some orthodox things about Jesus that some Christians do not accept such as his virgin birth and that he performed miracles.

From churches and theologians, I get conflicting images of God. It's only when I view Jesus in the red letters of the Bible that I am able to say, "Ah, here's a clear image of God. God is like Jesus! Jesus *is* God!" What I know about God is what I find in Jesus, and anything that deviates from the revelation of God found in Jesus' words is not part of what I believe to be the true image of God. I am constantly comparing the images of God that have been conjured up in my own imagination with what I find in the Bible. I regularly go back to the

Jesus I find in Scripture, and time and time again I ask myself, *In what way does my thinking about God conform to what I find in Jesus?* The writer of Colossians tells us that in him the fullness of God is revealed (2:9).

SHANE: God is fully revealed in Jesus. If we want to see God, then we look at Jesus.

One of my all-time favorite theological stunts in the Scripture is when the veil of the temple is ripped open. As Jesus is dying on the cross, the veil of the temple (which folks said was as thick as your hand, as big as a basketball court, and took dozens of priests to move) is ripped open. It is as if to say, God cannot be held hostage. God is bigger than our images, icons, and temples. God doesn't need mediators and isn't confined to the Holy of Holies. God is alive in the world and is in the streets. God can heal people with dirt and spit. God can fry fish. God is with us. No longer do we have to go to temples to find God. God has come and found us—in Jesus.

Jesus affirms people whenever they do something redemptive, whether they have all the right beliefs or not. Think about the scandalous parable of the good Samaritan. Jesus says something like, "I've got a story for you. So this guy gets beat up on the road to Jericho. Then a priest comes along and passes right by on his way to worship. Next, a Levite, a really religious guy, also passes right by and doesn't do anything because he was late for a board meeting. And then comes a Samaritan. [You can almost hear the crowd snicker since Jews didn't even walk through Samaria, much less talk to or touch a Samaritan.] But the Samaritan takes care of the guy in the ditch."

The story is all about challenging who's in and who's out. The religion of the first two guys did nothing to move them to compassion; but the Samaritan, who didn't believe all the right stuff according to the Jews, shows compassion and is hailed as the hero of the story.

I'm sure some of the listeners were ticked. According to the religious elite, Samaritans did not keep the right rules, and they did not have sound doctrine. But Jesus shows that true faith has to work itself out in a way that is good news to the most bruised and broken person lying in the ditch. The point is clear: God may indeed be evident in a priest, but God is just as likely to be at work through a Samaritan. It is exactly this challenge we see over and over in Jesus. He says to the religious folks: "The tax collectors and prostitutes are entering the kingdom of God ahead of you" (Matthew 21:31).

Scripture is full of God using folks like a lying brothel owner named Rahab and an adulterous king named David. At one point God even speaks to a guy named Balaam through his donkey. So if God should choose to use us, then we should be grateful but not think too highly of ourselves. And if we meet someone we think God could never use, we should think again. These Bible stories are an assault to our notions of who is right or wrong, and invites us to celebrate whenever anyone does God's work—whether they know God the same way we do or not.

Don't get me wrong: there are things I believe very strongly and want others to believe as well, like Jesus was God's Son, died on a cross, and rose from the grave to conquer all sin and shame. But that's not a prerequisite for working together or for friendship. In fact, it's the opposite. As Christians, we should be the best collaborators in the world. We should be quick to find unlikely allies and subversive friends, like Jesus did.

There's that beautiful text in the Gospels where the disciples say, "Master . . . we saw a man driving out demons in your name and we tried to stop him, because he is not one of us." Jesus then lets them know that they're looking at it all wrong: "Do not stop him . . . for whoever is not against you is for you" (Luke 9:49–50).

TONY: Then there is the time when Peter is about to preach a sermon, and he "opened his mouth, and said, Of a truth I perceive that God is no respecter of persons: But in every nation he that feareth him and worketh righteousness, is accepted with him" (Acts 10:34–35 KJV). That's pretty all-encompassing! And John writes in his epistle, "Love comes from God. Everyone who loves has been born of God and knows God . . . No one has ever seen God; but if we love one another, God lives in us" (1 John 4:7, 12). That's whoever loves—even if they're a Samaritan or someone we wouldn't expect.

Jitsuo Morikawa, one time head of the Department of Evangelicalism for American Baptist Churches USA, tells about being incarcerated in a "detainee camp" in Arizona during World War II. His mother, who was a Buddhist, taught him to love those who had imprisoned them for no other "crime" than having been born Japanese. She told him to forgive those who had done great evil to the family. He said that though his mother never became a Christian, he was sure that the spirit of Jesus was within her. There are many evangelicals who would question this, but for him, there was never any doubt.[2]

Shane, you have your own experience with unexpected people showing kindness to you.

SHANE: One of the most powerful experiences of my life was in Iraq in March 2003: a modern remix of the good Samaritan story. As we were leaving Baghdad, my friends and I had a terrible car accident on the desert road to Amman, Jordan—and the Iraqis saved our lives. I've written and told that story hundreds of times.[3]

But this year I got to go back to Rutba, Iraq, with the friends who had been in that accident, to visit the people who saved our lives. When we were there, we heard them talk about the rescue not as anything heroic but just as a gesture of love. One of the doctors said, "When we saw you bleeding, we did not see you as an American or as a Christian or Muslim; we saw you as our own flesh and blood, as our own brothers and sisters."

Then I said, "This is what Jesus teaches. You all are doing what good Christians should do." And one of them said, "We are doing what good Muslims should do too."

At one point we got to talk with the sheikh, the head Muslim leader for the town. We talked for hours and hours, and then it became time for Muslim prayer. We said to him, "It's okay if you need to leave for prayer." And the sheikh said, "This is prayer. I am happy to stay and talk."

While we were there, we visited a school to speak to the students about our friendships with folks in Iraq and about our faith. Afterward, the principal said, "The kids have never been this quiet. They have had soldiers come and bring toys, Frisbees, footballs, and things. But when they started speaking, the kids talk and throw things at them and are very disrespectful. They listened to you, every word." Then one of the kids came up, talking rapidly. "What is he saying?" I asked. The principal said, "He is saying that he has never heard this kind of Christianity before."

What occurred to me is how extremists have distorted the best of our faiths. Jewish, Muslim, Christian extremists blow up things, burn holy books. But sometimes the extremist version is the only version of Christianity some people have ever seen. So as we travel and meet with folks in Iraq, what is really at stake is not just the reputation of America but the reputation of our faith and of Christ—and Christ's words, heart, and message.

Our hosts in Rutba gave us a copy of the Koran. From their perspective it was the greatest gift they could possibly give us. Can you imagine if we refused to take it?

I later heard of all the risks that they were taking to show us hospitality and build friendships with us. At one point we were invited to tea at the home of one of the town elders. We were excited to go, but our Iraqi guide refused. Later he told us that we would have been fine, but it was likely that after we left, the generous old man would have been killed. But then my Iraqi friend said, "But you should be grateful. He knew the price of his invitation and was willing to risk death to extend hospitality to you."

They made sure that we understood that the Iraqi people were wonderful folks, but that there were a few who might want to kill us. So they said, "Don't worry; we will protect you." And they slept by our beds with AK-47s. This didn't fit into my theology, but I appreciated their hospitality!

Of all people, we Christians should be building friendships and protecting the dignity of human beings, even those of other faiths. I loved seeing Christians in Iraq stand guard as peacekeepers outside the mosques while Muslims gathered for prayer, and Muslims doing the same for Christians.

Even though that was in Iraq, we have similar challenges in the United States where our country is increasingly hostile to Muslims. I see hope, though. In fact, one of the first people to invite me to speak about my trip to Iraq was a Muslim, Eboo Patel. I have also had Muslims tell me that they are doing a study of my book in their mosque. What a compliment! I really don't know why we are scared of dialogue and friendship, since it doesn't mean we have to be any less zealous about our love for Jesus or our hope for others to experience that love.[4]

TONY: You're good friends with a few of your Muslim neighbors in Philly, right?

SHANE: Yes, one even tried to convert me! One night we were having dinner together with a good friend. This time, however,

I noticed he had a little bit of an agenda, and had even brought along a few friends. We had a great conversation, and he said, "Do you understand? We love what you do and that's why we want Allah to get all the glory, and not Jesus, because it's Allah's work."

This opened up a door for a really great conversation, but what I had to keep in mind was that this was a friend I was having a conversation with—a friend who loves and admires what we were doing in the neighborhood. Let's start there. And what an idiot I would be if I didn't come out of that conversation with a renewed zeal to continue the friendship, to work together in the neighborhood to stop the violence and feed hungry folks and visit the elderly.

We may not see God in the same way, but we have many common passions. We want to keep kids from killing each other and help folks get off drugs. So let's be quick to find the things we have in common.

TONY: When it comes to who is embraced by God, and who is rejected, we have no alternative but to leave judgment in the hands of God.

SHANE: I find it very interesting that Jesus uses his harshest judgment on his inner crowd. After all, the only person Jesus calls "Satan" is the soon-to-be rock of the church, Peter. Jesus was continually scolding and sharpening his disciples. He was calling out their lack of faith and their judgmentalism. And he was pulling out the best in others, applauding the faith of folks like the centurion, the Syrophoenecian woman, Samaritans, and tax collectors.[5] Jesus does exactly the opposite of what most of us do. Most of us find the best in ourselves and the worst in others. Jesus invites us to find the worst in ourselves and look for the best in others.

So it's not surprising that Jesus told the disciples: "If you are not for us, you are against us" (Luke 11:23). And just a few chapters earlier he said of those who were doing the work of God but not followers of his, "Whoever is not against us is for us" (Luke 9:50).

Certainly one starts to ask, "Then how do you control who is 'in' and who is 'out'?" And that is precisely the point: that's not our job to do. We are not to try to separate the weeds from the wheat. We let God do that. One of the best illustrations I've heard for how to build community came from a farmer: "You know, there are two ways to keep your cows in. One is by building fences. The other is by having a really good food source. Then you don't need all those fences."

That's what Jesus was doing; he's protecting the food source at the center of the community—and you can see all the crowds that are magnetized by it. He's rigorously disciplined toward his disciples and wildly gracious for folks who are beginning the journey in.

TONY: Right. I know that Jesus is the only way of salvation, but I am not ready to limit the salvation that Jesus offers only to those who are in the evangelical theological camp. I think it's almost a truism that Jesus and his salvation are greater than my theology would define. His love is greater. His love is broader. The love of God encompasses far more people than I am ready to accept.

So often we want to make God our exclusive possession, and so, too, did the ancient Jews. There were times when they wanted to believe that because they were God's chosen people, God only loved them. That's why when God sent Jonah to Nineveh to tell the people in that city to repent of their sins, become part of God's family, and be loved by God, Jonah refused to go. The idea that God would love the Ninevites as much as he loves the Jews was unthinkable to Jonah.

After finally calling the Ninevites to repent, Jonah went and sat in a shelter that he had made for himself, over which God had provided a vine that shaded him. He waited for God to destroy Nineveh, but when the Ninevites repented and turned to God instead, Jonah became furious. He got angry with God because, in his opinion, God was willing to save the wrong people. When the vine that God had provided to shade Jonah died, he got even angrier with God. But God said, "Look! You want me to have mercy and save this vine just so that you can be comfortable, but you don't want me to have mercy on the people of Nineveh?" (Jonah 4:10–11 paraphrased).

SHANE: It's also worth saying that the real world doesn't seem to exist in such carefully constructed categories as "Christian" and "non-Christian." C. S. Lewis does a great job explaining that things are not as cut-and-dried as we would like to make them: "The situation in the actual world is much more complicated than that. The world does not consist of 100 percent Christians and 100 percent non-Christians. There are people (a great many of them) who are slowly ceasing to be Christians but who still call themselves by that name: some of them are clergymen. There are other people who are slowly becoming Christians though they do not yet call themselves so."[6]

TONY: I do believe we have landmark moments in our faith journeys where we may have radical conversion moments as Saul and others did. But much of the salvation story is a gradual conversion so that our lives grow closer and closer to Jesus. As the Scripture says, "continue to work out your salvation with fear and trembling" (Philippians 2:12). We can pray that the Spirit continues to draw us all—Muslim, Jew, Hindu, Atheist, and Christians—closer to God and the things that matter to him.

Dialogue on Economics

*No servant can serve two masters. Either he
will hate the one and love the other, or he will
be devoted to the one and despise the other.
You cannot serve both God and money.*

LUKE 16:13–14

SHANE: The entire world economy is being questioned right now. The recession has created a hiccup in business-as-usual. Folks are beginning to reconsider the current patterns, where CEOs make four hundred times what their workers make.

Without trivializing how difficult the recession could be for many people—without a doubt the poor will always suffer the brunt of hard times—it could also be a time where our imagination comes back to life. We may be forced to relearn how to live: how to grow food, how to store food and can veggies, how to live locally and use less oil, how to make things again. One of my older friends said this is exactly what happened in the Great Depression. It is alarming that many of these skills are endangered. A generation or two ago, folks knew how to survive off the land. We have become dependent on technology, artificial stuff, gas, and things like that, and many don't even really know how to cook for themselves, much less know how to sew.

A friend who has studied periods of economic recession

and periods of struggle pointed out an unexpected trend: people come to life during hard times. Community flourishes during times of struggle. Initially, it's sort of like detoxing from drugs; it hits hard and folks feel as though they are going to die. But after the initial detox, they start to breathe again and see that there is life on the other side. In fact, people start to realize what's really important in life, and how temporal the stuff of earth is. As the old hymn goes, "On Christ the solid rock I stand, all other ground is sinking sand."

God's dream for creation is different from Pharaoh's dream or Rome's dream or Wall Street's dream. And at the center of God's economy is the idea of redistribution. One of the first stories in the Hebrew Bible is the Exodus, where God rescues a group of Hebrew slaves from the oppressive rule of Pharaoh. Ironically, they were making bricks for the storehouses of Egypt. They were building banks to store other people's money in, while their own families were struggling to make it. God hears their cry and rescues them.

As they are being led out of Egypt, God establishes some new laws and patterns for these people. God is forming them into a new people, a "holy nation" (Exodus 19:6). *Holy* means "called out" or "set apart." They are God's little counterculture, God's peculiar people called out of the destructive patterns of their world to show the world what a society of love looks like.

As God is forming this holy counterculture, there are new laws put in place. Keeping the Sabbath is one of the Ten Commandments, which includes resting our bodies and land so that we don't work ourselves (or our animals) to death; the work is kept holy and doesn't become meaningless toil. The Hebrews are commanded to practice hospitality to strangers and have special care for immigrants and foreigners. (Maybe some of the politicians in Washington DC talking about immigration would do well to have a little Bible study on Leviticus, eh?) The Hebrews are to enact practices like gleaning, where farmers were to leave the edges of the crops unharvested so that the poor could freely gather them. And of course, there is the Jubilee. Jubilee, or year of emancipation, was God's regular and systemic dismantling of inequality where slaves were set free, property was redistributed, and debts were freely forgiven.

In all of this, it is as if God is saying, "If you do not do these things, then you will end up like you were in Egypt again." God is a God of abundance when we trust, and a God of redistribution when we do not. God's people are not to accumulate stuff for tomorrow but to share indiscriminately with the scandalous and holy confidence that God will provide for tomorrow. Then we need not stockpile stuff in barns or a 401(k), especially when there is someone in need.

As the Hebrew folks wander through the wilderness, they begin to moan and complain about how hungry they are, and they even whine about how much they miss the food in Egypt. Again, God hears their pain and drops manna (which simply means "what is this?"—probably their first response) down from heaven to feed them in the wilderness. God poured out bread from heaven, which is a beautiful vision of a God of abundance. But as the bread fell from heaven, God commands the Hebrews not to take more than their daily bread. They are not to store up bread for tomorrow. God even goes so far as to say, if they try to take more than they need for one day (and they do), it will be consumed with maggots. They are commanded to carry one "omer," one day's ration, with them—an iconic reminder that God will provide "this day our daily bread" and will send maggots to remind us if we lose faith and try to provide for ourselves (Exodus 16:16).

This lesson will be echoed throughout Scripture. It is not only in the Lord's Prayer; Paul also quotes the original Exodus

16 verse word for word as he reminds the early church in Corinth: "At the present time your plenty will supply what they need, so that in turn their plenty will supply what you need. Then there will be equality, as it is written: 'He who gathered much did not have too much, and he who gathered little did not have too little'" (2 Corinthians 8:14–15). God promises that there is enough. As Gandhi said, "There's enough for everyone's need but not enough for everyone's greed."

There is no place that it is more clear than in the life of the early church—that little community Jesus formed to live in that ancient hope that the people of God could show the world what a society of love looks like. In the book of Acts, the Scripture says this: "All the believers were together and had everything in common. Selling their possessions and goods, they gave to anyone as he had need. . . . All the believers were one in heart and mind. No one claimed that any of his possessions was his own, but they shared everything they had. . . . There were no needy persons among them" (2:44–45, 4:32–34).

All the believers were together and shared everything in common. They put their offerings at the feet of the apostles to meet needs. The text even says that there were no needy persons among them—they ended poverty!

One of the first things they had to figure out was the best way to care for their most vulnerable members, the widows and the orphans (James 1:27). If the early church had committees, one of the first was devoted to meeting the needs around them. Throughout the life of the early church, we see how central need-sharing and redistribution is. Bearing one another's burdens was a part of who they were (Galatians 6:2). If one person suffered, they all suffered (1 Corinthians 12:26). The resources of one person were God's instruments of provision for another; all things were held with thankful hearts and open hands.

Consequently, one of the terrible tragedies of the early church occurred, which is told in Acts in the story of Ananias and Sapphira. The story goes that Ananias and Sapphira held back their possessions from the common pool and lied to God about it, and God struck them dead. That's not something we see much of in the New Testament. But the lesson is unmistakable: economic sharing was part of what it means to be Christian.

One of the places we can see this vision of a new humanity and a new economy most clearly is in the Eucharist, or the Lord's Supper. This meal, which Christians still share all over the world every single day, captures part of the mystery of what it means to be Christian. The Communion meal is a vision of the divine banquet where rich and poor come as new creations to the same table. Incidentally the elements of Communion are not bread and water but bread and wine. Bread is a simple, staple food of the poor. Wine is elegant, often seen only as a luxury of the rich. But the two come together in holy Communion. Both bread and wine have some things in common: they are made up of parts that have to be crushed and broken in order to become something new. Grapes are crushed to become wine, and grain is ground down to become bread. The same happens to us when we become part of the body of Christ.

The apostle Paul scolds the early church in Corinth because some of them are coming to the Communion table hungry and others are stuffed full of food. They have desecrated what the meal is really about. "When you come together, it is not the Lord's Supper you eat, for as you eat, each of you goes ahead without waiting for anybody else. One remains hungry, another gets drunk. . . . What shall I say to you? Shall I praise you for this? Certainly not" (1 Corinthians 11: 20–22). We hear echoes of the prophet Amos as he scolds the Hebrew people for worshiping God while ignoring the needs around them, saying the worship is noise and the incense stinks unless justice rolls down like a river for the poor (Amos 5:21–24).

One of the fundamentals of Communion is sharing bread. We break off a pinch and pass it to a brother or sister. No one is to go without. It is a symbol of what is to come. And as one of my Catholic friends says, "As long as a belly is aching in hunger, the Eucharist is incomplete." The banquet is still imperfect, unfinished. And part of the prayer we are taught by Jesus, which so often accompanies the Communion feast, is, "Give us this day our daily bread" (Matthew 6:11 KJV). This is a prayer that the poor know well. It is also a warning to those of us who might pray for tomorrow's bread or those of us who might pray for a steak. We are not to pray for "my" bread but to cry out with the poor for "our" daily bread. We are not to pray for the poor, but to pray *with* them—and to realize that as long as anyone is hungry, all of us are hungry.

TONY: Jesus tells a story about the vineyard workers who are hired at various times of the day (Matthew 20). Some workers start working early in the morning, others a few hours later, and still others later than that. In fact, some are hired so late in the day that they just get started and the workday is over. And then the landowner pays them all the same wage for a whole day's work. There is a clear message: God is not always fair, but he is always just.

Certainly, this contradicts what our present day labor unions would call fair and may even contradict our capitalistic value system by giving to every worker as he or she has need as was the case in the first-century church (Acts 2:45).

SHANE: The world is lopsided when it comes to economics and equality. If life were a baseball game, some people were born on third base and others on first. And some with only one shoe to play with. Jesus has all sorts of stuff to say about how the deck has been stacked, and we have a God of justice who is setting things right again. The mighty are cast from their thrones and the lowly are lifted (Luke 1:52); the hungry are filled with good things and the rich are sent away empty (Luke 1:53); the mountains will be lowered and the valleys raised up (Isaiah 40:4); the last shall be first and the first shall be last (Luke 13:30). This is the upside-down kingdom of our God. The funny thing is that God's justice can look unfair, but it is this justice that corrects the brutal inequities of our world.

One of the most scandalous stories dealing with economics is Jesus' teaching in Luke 16. A manager is about to get fired. The big CEO has reprimanded this man, accusing him of wasting possessions and not gaining the highest profit, so he is about to lose his job. Everyone in town knows his name and has looked at him with some mixture of fear, respect, and angst in the past.

This cubicle-type accountant says, in a white-collar way, "I can't dig and I'm ashamed to beg." Folks probably laughed when they heard that, especially Judaean peasants who knew the caricature. So then the manager calls in all those who owe debts. It is important to note that some of them owe as much as seven or eight years' worth of wages. These are huge amounts of money.

The manager uses the position he is in to recklessly release people from debt and to even up the tables. In some cases, he forgives up to half of what they owe, a unilateral debt reduction. It makes the US stimulus bill look tame. As the manager is doing it, the Scripture says he reasons like this, "When I lose my job, people will welcome me into their houses." He is certainly still thinking with some self-interest, but he is also willing to stay in the homes of the workers. It's like one of the head accountants for General Motors hoping to stay with one of the assembly-line workers when he or she gets laid off.

There is something beautiful here that Jesus wants us to see: the manager wins the hearts and minds of the workers. There is probably partying all over town like in the year of Jubilee. Then the big boss comes in, and you can almost imagine the scene. Word had probably spread far and wide about how compassionate the manager had been on the workers. People are probably yelling out the windows, thanking him for his generosity, or even coming into the streets and putting him on their shoulders singing, "For he's a jolly good fellow!" So when the big cheese strolls into town, he finds himself in an awkward position. He can fire the beloved manager and tell everyone they still owe him all their debts—and ignite a riot or a strike. Or he can act as though he actually is a good boss and embrace the rapport he now has with his workers, maybe even sincerely.

The story ends with the master commending the shrewd manager. It says the people of this world are shrewder in dealing with their own kind than are the people of the light. Jesus is inviting us to use our money to make friends with the poor so that we will be welcomed into "eternal dwellings" (Luke 16:9). We are to be people of Jubilee, to release debt and set folks free who are captive to poverty!

The next verse after the story says, "The Pharisees, who loved money, heard all this and were sneering at Jesus." Jesus responds: "What is highly valued among men is detestable in God's sight" (Luke 16:15). This has to be one of the most scandalous passages in Scripture when it comes to money. If a white-collar criminal is smart enough to pull off this sort of stunt, imagine what the children of God can do! It is an invitation to holy mischief.

TONY: Hungry people often came to the early Christians in need, and if there was not enough food for everyone to eat, then no one would eat. They would fast until there was enough food for all to share. That is a radical economic vision, rooted in love of God and neighbor. It is with this freedom that we can still laugh, even in a recession. For we declare that God is good, no matter what is happening on Wall Street. Our hope is not built on America, or militaries, or the Dow Jones. Our "hope is built on nothing less than Jesus' blood and righteousness ... all other ground is sinking sand."[1]

We trust in the God who led the Hebrew slaves into the wilderness and provided for them. We trust in the God who sent the apostles out with no money, spare clothes, or food, and provided for them. And we trust in the God who cares for the lilies and the sparrows, and invites us to live like them. They don't own much, but they seem to be pretty content with life—and God takes care of them just fine without a 401(k) or savings account. They are free.

In my classes here at Eastern University, I tell my students that the Bible neither advocates capitalism or socialism. As any book on capitalism will tell you, the motivation for production is profit, and Red Letter Christians are never primarily governed by the motive of profit. Rather, we are motivated by love to meet people's needs. There's nothing wrong with profit; in fact, those who don't make profits are not likely to stay in business long enough to meet anyone's needs. But it is love, not profit, that motivates the Christian.

On the other hand, God's economy is not socialistic either. When God placed Adam and Eve in the Garden of Eden, God gave them the freedom to make the decisions that would determine their destiny—and that includes their economic destiny. With socialism, the political state determines people's economic destiny.

God, in giving humanity freedom, lends credence to a free enterprise system in which the primary purpose of production is to bless people by producing goods and services that meet their needs. This is what loving our neighbors as ourselves is all about (Matthew 22:37–40). In doing so, those around us "may see our good works, and glorify our Father which is in heaven" (Matthew 5:16 author's paraphrase).

PART II

RED LETTER
LIVING

Dialogue on Family

*Then Jesus' mother and brothers arrived. Standing
outside, they sent someone in to call him. A crowd was
sitting around him, and they told him, "Your mother
and brothers are outside looking for you." "Who are
my mother and my brothers?" he asked. Then he
looked at those seated in a circle around him and said,
"Here are my mother and my brothers! Whoever does
God's will is my brother and sister and mother."*

MARK 3:31–35

TONY: We Red Letter Christians find a good example in Jesus as
to how to live in community, but what exactly does that look like?
And what does it do to traditional notions of family? Shane, you've
lived in an intentional community, the Simple Way, for fifteen years,
but you've recently gotten married and moved two doors down from
where the rest of your community lives.

Perhaps community is something we should urge every young
person to get into during an early stage in life, and then later on,
move out of that community to live a more traditional life while
still staying connected, in one way or another, with that same community. After all, with marriage, things change. In 1 Corinthians 7,
Paul makes it clear that when a Christian gets married, life is not as
simple as it was before. You're going to have to make some accom-
modations to please your partner, while trying at the same time to

live completely sacrificially for God (7:32–34). Do you feel you left something behind when you moved out? As you are going through this transition into married life, do you have any reflections on all this?

SHANE: I'm sure I'll learn all sorts of things I didn't learn as a single person now that I'm married. Both singleness and marriage can be selfish and selfless, and both can teach us discipline and teach us about God. The person who finds commitment impossible should beware of being alone. And the person who is scared of being alone should beware of attaching to someone too quickly. So I was single as long as Jesus was (you never know what would have happened at thirty-four!), but I'm excited about this wonderful chapter of my life with the lovely Katie Jo. I guess I'm just a part-time monk now.

But let's discuss what living in community actually looks like. I don't think community is something we do because we *have* to; it's something we *get* to do. It's a wonderful way to live. The entire story of the Bible is about community. When the first human was made, it wasn't "very good" until there was another one there and they were helping each other. In fact, humans are made in the image of a God who *is* community— this Trinity, this plurality of oneness—Father, Son, Spirit. God's been living in intentional community for a long time. And so we have that hunger within us to be one as God is one.

In the Gospels, Jesus lives and models community, sends the disciples out in pairs, and promises that whenever two or three of us gather in God's name, God will be with us (Matthew 18:20); it is all about community. No doubt, there are many ways we can find community, many different forms it can take—and building a family is one.

That said, we begin to miss things when, instead of everyone being called to community, we assume everyone should have a family or everyone will get married. This is a mistake because it discredits the entire gift of singleness. Singleness, whether for a season or for a lifetime, is a gift. It is a gift to the church and to the kingdom. Can you imagine looking at Mother Teresa and saying, "Poor thing. If only she had met her husband." There are tons of great singles throughout church history, starting, of course, with Jesus.

Our deepest longing is for community—to love and to be loved. And raising a family is one way to do that. But what about the others? Jesus challenges our notions of detached nuclear family. "Who is my family? Who are my mother and brothers?" He answers with "Those who hear God's word and put it into practice" (Luke 8:20–21). He has a new definition of family that runs deeper than biology or ethnicity or nationality.

A few celibate nuns and monks have taught me that our deepest longing is for love, for community. It's not for sex. There are folks who have all sorts of sex and don't find love. And there are others, like my celibate friends, who never have sex their entire lives but experience love and intimacy deeply. So we pursue whatever allows us to seek first the kingdom of God with the most singlemindedness.

TONY: So you don't necessarily think we should urge young people to live communally, but perhaps encourage them to look for the community around them?

SHANE: I don't think that communal living is just a season of life for young radicals. When I hear folks say that radical living is a phase, I tell them they need to meet Sister Margaret, my eighty-year-old Catholic nun friend. She's been in the "phase" for more than fifty years and gets wilder every year. She lives with about fifty folks who are recovering from drug addictions.

She has never married, but she is one of the most content people I've ever met. She has a family and community.

In our intentional community at the Simple Way, we have had married and single folks living together from the beginning. We try to create a support network for singles and couples and families.

For many of my other friends who are married or have kids, they think about family with a big umbrella, with eyes of the kingdom. They are continually opening their homes to people, fostering kids, rescuing people from domestic violence, helping those coming out of prison to reenter society. In fact, it's hard for me to think of many friends who live only with their biological family.

A few years ago, two of my friends, a married couple, were living on their own. The wife, who is a social worker, was helping to pack the possessions of one of her clients; they were going to move this woman who had Alzheimer's into an old-folks' home. As they were boxing stuff up, she found a note that said, "Dear God, let me never end up in an old-folks' home." So the couple talked about it and decided to adopt her into their family. She went from "client" to "live-in Grandma." Everywhere my friends traveled, they had her with them. They sometimes joked that when they invited her in, they had no idea how long she was going to live. But it was a wonderful thing to see all of them around her, loving her up until the moment she died eight years later.

TONY: What a beautiful story! I love that she became part of their family. Can you imagine Jesus referring to someone as a "client"? A client is an object that needs to be worked on, rather than a person to be loved. Social workers sometimes are trained to treat those they try to help as clients, but the people they work with are not so removed; they are people who come as though they were Jesus, waiting to be loved.

SHANE: I always think Jesus would have failed some social-work classes because of that whole professional distance thing. He doesn't treat people as clients or consumers but as friends. He's not the best with boundaries; he's constantly being interrupted, someone pulling on his shirt. But that is where life happens—in the interruptions and surprises. Social activist Dorothy Day once said, "If every Christian just welcomed one stranger into their home, we'd end homelessness overnight."

There are so many different ways to do community, and it doesn't have to be a single house in the inner city where everyone lives together. There are communities in California that call themselves Cul-de-sac Communities, where they share washers and dryers, lawn equipment, and cars, and do community gardens together in the suburbs.

The good news is that we're not alone, and that we get to live outside of this illusion of independence. Independence may be an American value, but it is not a value taught in the Gospels. The Gospels teach us *interdependence*. It's a good thing to need other people and to need God. That's how we are made.

TONY: Over the past seven years, my son, Bart, who lives in Cincinnati, has put together what he calls the Walnut Hills Fellowship. There are now six families living almost next door to each other. They have a couple of cars that they share between them. They share lawnmowers, tools, and other things, just like you described. My son and his wife have two children of their own; a son in his late teens and a daughter who just turned twenty-one. Now they have taken in a young man my grandson's age to be a foster son. Bart, his wife, and their two children are expanding their familial community and saying, "We've got a loving intact family here, but we want to share it with a kid who may not have that kind of family."

My wife and I did the same sort of thing when our kids were still quite young. There was a family in our church that fell apart and left a young woman who, at the age of fifteen, evidently belonged to nobody. We said, "We'll take her in and make her part of our family." You can expand your biological family by reaching out to someone who needs love and a sense of belonging, and, in a way, create community.

SHANE: Exactly! If we are truly Christians, if we are born again, then we have new eyes with which to see family. That's exactly what Jesus did when he was dying on the cross and said to John basically, "This is your mom now" (John 19:26). He had a broad vision of what family looks like.

TONY: When Jesus asked, "Who are my mother and my brothers?" (Mark 3:33), you know that his answer to those questions involved far more than those who were blood relatives.

There is so much about Jesus that is upsetting when it comes to the traditional family. Sometimes people get the impression that when you bring Jesus into your life, your family is just going to be splendid and beautiful and lovely and harmonious. That's not always the case. Jesus said, "Do not suppose that I have come to bring peace to the earth. I did not come to bring peace, but a sword. For I have come to turn 'a man against his father, a daughter against her mother, a daughter-in-law against her mother-in-law'" (Matthew 10:34–35). When a wife becomes a Christian, but the husband is not, commitment to Christ on the part of the wife can be divisive for the marriage. If children become committed Christians and their parents are not, there can be conflict in the family.

In 1987, I spoke at the Urbana missions conference, and when I gave the invitation for commitment to missionary service there was a huge response. I would say somewhere around nine thousand young people committed themselves to missionary service that evening. Peter Hammond, who was one of the other speakers at the conference, was very excited when he heard the report, and he later told me,

"That's wonderful! Out of a response like that we may get as many as nine hundred people onto the mission field for Christ."

I said, "Wait a minute. There were many more than that who stood up to indicate their commitment to missionary service."

He said, "Oh, yes, but you know what's going to happen. They're going to get home and their parents are going to say, 'Calm down, now. Let's not get carried away with this thing. It's important that you take Jesus seriously, but not that seriously.'"

Peter Hammond was right! It's a sad thing to say, but when young people take Christ seriously, it often can have a rupturing effect on what goes on in the family. We must be careful to not paint in glorious colors what will happen to family life when some members become Red Letter Christians. Even the relationship between a husband and a wife can be strained if one of them becomes a committed follower of Christ and the other one doesn't.

SHANE: Some of the hardest words Jesus says are against the family. He's protecting something bigger—his kingdom, which is the divine, beautiful Family with a big *F*. Jesus is clear that one of the biggest barriers to the kingdom can be the people closest to us (Luke 14:26).

We tend to make justifications and compromises in the name of our family that we would never make for ourselves. We begin to lose some of that edge if we don't have a bigger vision than our immediate family, our tribe, or even our nation. I'm all about loving those nearest to us, but Jesus doesn't draw a line in the sand. He invites us to love other people's kids with the same passion with which we love our own.

TONY: Several years ago, I was part of a panel on family life along with a priest, a rabbi, and a minister. The rabbi started with, "I don't know why you [pointing at the Protestant minister] and you [pointing at the Catholic priest] are even here. If you take the New Testament seriously, you won't have much to say that would promote traditional family values. You are the followers of a Messiah who asked, 'Who is my mother, and my father, my sister, and my brother,' thus disparaging what we Jews respect as a family. What's even worse is that Jesus never even got married. Also, the apostle Paul, one of your founding theologians, said that it's better to remain single, and to marry only if you burn with lust. The more I think about it, the more I realize that your religion just might be antifamily.

"For instance, if a Jewish person were to walk into your office [pointing at the Protestant minister] and say, 'I want to become a Christian,' you would lay out your way of salvation and make sure that he said yes to an invitation to accept Jesus as Savior. On the other hand, if a Christian came into my office and said, 'I want to become a Jew,' I would be obligated to discourage him. Jews know that if he converted, it could alienate him from his Christian family and destroy the oneness that to me is more important than winning another convert to our faith."

That rabbi was right! As Christians, we have a fellowship that transcends biological and cultural ties, and there are times when living with the demands of that fellowship just might set us at odds with the obligations of our families.

Certainly, missionaries who serve on foreign fields have witnessed the problems that conversion to Christianity can create for families. There are cases in which someone is converted to Christ, and the new Christian becomes alienated from the entire tribal family to which he or she previously belonged. We always deem such a convert heroic, but sometimes there is a hard price to be paid if a person is going to follow Christ. Christians might have to experience the pain of estrangement from literal families, but we receive an eternal family in exchange. The church has to step up and become the new family when new Christians find themselves estranged or at odds with their old ones.

Dialogue on Being Pro-Life

I have come that they may have life, and have it to the full.

JOHN 10:10

SHANE: One of the most important issues of our day is the need for a consistent pro-life ethic. Catholics and evangelicals and all sorts of folks have begun to resonate with this idea— not just in the sense it is talked about in abortion debates.

Jesus talks about life a lot. Life to the fullest (John 10:10). The narrow way that leads to life (Matthew 7:14). He is the way, the truth, the life (John 14:6). His message and his life are an interruption of death. He constantly interrupts whatever is destroying the life and dignity of other people—and invites us to do the same. As a young Christian, I was confused about the inconsistency with which we address issues of life. No group or party seemed to be seamless. Some folks were against abortion and euthanasia, but were pro–death penalty and pro-military. I found myself at odds with some of the positions that had come to characterize traditional evangelicalism, but I sure didn't fit into a progressive or liberal camp either.

As Red Letter Christians, we need to be pro-life from the womb to the tomb. Abortion and euthanasia, the death penalty and war, poverty and health care—all of these are issues of life and death. And they are issues Jesus cares about because they affect real people.

The death penalty has been a huge deal in the news this past year, with some high profile cases like Troy Davis in Atlanta.[1] I think we are at a crossroads on this issue, and it is possible that we could see it come to an end in our lifetime. We are one of very few nations in the world that still kills its own people.[2] What is even more wicked is how we make theatrics of death as we execute. Though lethal injection is the most common form, there are still states in the US that allow government-sanctioned executions to happen by hanging, firing squad, gas chamber, and electrocution.[3]

When presidential candidate Rick Perry celebrated his 234 executions as Texas governor during the September 7, 2011, GOP presidential debate, the audience, who were mainly members of the Christian Coalition, roared in applause. As a Christian, I found that deeply disturbing.

There are many facets to the issue. On the one hand, there are folks who are against the death penalty in principle, like many Christians. The pope has spoken out poignantly against the death penalty on behalf of the Catholic Church. There are others who believe in capital punishment in principle but have become deeply concerned that we often do not simply end up killing guilty folks as much as we end up killing poor folks, people of color, and those who can't afford good lawyers and don't know all the ins and outs of the legal process.

In 2000, George Ryan, Republican governor of Illinois, called for a moratorium on the death penalty. Persuaded by the work of law students exposing race and class discrimination, he called for a halt on executions. The 2000 moratorium fueled the fire of many Christians and other abolitionists who are working for restorative justice and for an end to the death penalty.

Jesus was confronted with this issue in John 8, when crowds were preparing to stone a woman for adultery. But when they questioned him about it, the first thing he did was peculiar—he bent down and wrote in the dirt. We asked the kids in our neighborhood what they thought he was writing, and one of them said, "If this doesn't work, run, woman!"

We don't know what he wrote, but we do know what happened next. He addressed all the men who were ready to kill: "If any one of you is without sin, let him be the first to throw a stone at her." And of course, Jesus has already taught that if we call our neighbor a fool, we are murderers. If we look at someone with lust in our eyes, we are adulterers (Matthew 5:22, 28). I can hear the stones start to drop as the men walked away, and soon the only one who was left with any right to throw a stone was Jesus. And he has no inclination to do so. We can see that the closer we are to God, the less we want to throw stones at other people.

This dual conviction that no one is above reproach and that no one is beyond redemption lies at the heart of our faith. Undoubtedly, it's why the early Christians were characterized by nonviolence, even in the face of brutal evil, torture, and execution. Of all people, we who follow the executed and risen Christ should be people who are pro-life, pro-grace, anti-death.

TONY: We should be that way, but that's not always the case in our American society. For instance, the Sermon on the Mount raises questions among those people for whom the death penalty is readily accepted. What's particularly troubling is that studies made by sociologists indicate that evangelical Christians are more in favor of the death penalty than are secularists, in spite of the fact that Jesus made it clear that for his followers the "eye-for-an-eye-and-a-tooth-for-a-tooth" morality (Exodus 21:24) should be transcended.[4] Many evangelicals are prone to say, "If a man takes a life, he should have to pay with his life"—namely, the very eye-for-an-eye standard that Jesus rejected. If we take seriously what Jesus said in the Sermon on the Mount, we have to be against capital punishment because Jesus said, "Blessed are the merciful, for they will be shown mercy." He went on to say essentially, "If you want mercy from God, you have to start showing mercy yourself" (Matthew 5:7). He impinges on some of the practices and values that too many American evangelicals embrace enthusiastically.

SHANE: Apart from Jesus' example, the other thing that has really been powerful for me is getting to know folks who are living in prison, some of whom are on death row. I exchange letters regularly with many of them.

A friend of mine is spending life in prison for committing a terrible crime, which he says he has regretted every day of his life since then. But when he went to trial, the victim's family happened to be Christians, so they argued against the death penalty. They knew that there is something wrong with killing someone to show that killing is wrong. They said, "God may not be done with this guy. It's not going to bring our kid back, so we want him to think about what he did." Because of their witness in court, he was not given the death penalty. He said, "So then I had a lot of time to think about grace." While he was behind bars, he kept hearing their words, that he was not beyond redemption. He started reading the Bible and ended up having a powerful conversion. Now he sees the point of his whole life and his vocation behind those bars as trying to continue to speak that grace to other imprisoned men and women.

TONY: In the library here at Eastern University, there is a plaque in memory of In Ho Ho, a student who came from Korea to study. He was a brilliant student, graduated near the top of his class, and went on to attend the University of Pennsylvania medical school. His desire was to go back and serve the poor in Korea. But one night, while he was on his way to mail a letter home to his parents, a gang of young thugs accosted him, stole the $3.52 he had in his wallet, and then beat him to death.

At the trial, not just the mother and father but the entire extended family of In Ho Ho, traveled all the way from Korea to beg the judge not to give the death penalty to those evil young men. These bereaved people took seriously the beatitude in which Jesus says, "Blessed are the merciful, for they will be shown mercy." They lived it out in that courtroom. The judge acceded to their request.

SHANE: I know too many victims of violent crime, and the ones who have healed the best are ones who have been able to forgive. One family member of a murder victim told me she works against the death penalty because the more she met other victims, the more she realized the unhealthiest ones were those who were punitive and vengeful.

Restorative justice is some of the most redemptive and the most Christ-like work happening in the justice system. Much of it was started by Quakers who did not believe in punitive justice, but rather restorative justice. That's the idea that God's justice is not just about getting what we deserve but about restoring what has been broken—about healing and forgiveness. That's what makes biblical justice different from other justice. The word *penitentiary* shares the same root as *repentance*, and the original intention was not to create a dead-end trap for criminals or a business of incarceration but to give people the space to repent, to rethink their lives, and ultimately to be restored to society. One of the oldest prisons in the United States is here in Philly, and it was started by Quakers for that very purpose.

Bible scholars often point out that the words *justice* and *righteousness* are the same word in Hebrew (*tsedeq*) and Greek (*dikaios*) for both the Old and the New Testaments. One friend of mine said the phrase that best captures the original meaning of the Greek is "restorative justice." That's what Jesus is talking about in the Beatitudes: "Blessed are those who hunger and thirst for [restorative justice]" (Matthew 5:6).

Our musician friend Derek Webb says, "Murdering to show that killing is wrong is like trying to teach holiness through fornication." And there is a theological element to it too: if anyone deserved the death penalty, it's me. And Jesus spared me the sentence of death I deserved. Many evangelicals believe that Jesus' own death on the cross was an interruption of the natural consequence of our sin, which is death (Romans 6:23). According to conventional evangelical wisdom, our sin would warrant us all the death penalty were it not for Jesus. How then can we who have been spared death so quickly become people who are so eager to dish it out?

TONY: The writer of the book of Hebrews tells us that when we sin, we crucify Jesus anew (6:4–6). We are constantly crucifying him every time we sin. There is no passage of time with God. Like the speed of light, all of time for God is compressed into a simultaneous moment, which is why Jesus could say, "Before Abraham, I am." He wasn't using poor grammar; he was declaring that what happened thousands of years earlier was present tense for him. Thus when we sin, in his eternal now, the Christ on the cross absorbs our sin into his own body and experiences the same agony as he did two thousand years ago. For those of us who realize that our sin is responsible for murdering Christ, supporting capital punishment for other murderers becomes impossible.

SHANE: The other thing that I find really troubling about Christian acceptance of the death penalty is that our Bible is filled with murderers who were redeemed and given a second chance, like David.

We remember David as a man after God's own heart (1 Samuel 13:14). And he was, on some days. But on other days, he was breaking commandments. In two chapters of the Bible, he breaks every one of the Big 10—he lusts, lies, covets, commits adultery, and has the woman's husband literally killed. He's a murderer. Yet, he has a firm rebuke from a prophet and goes on to write much of the biggest book of the Bible—Psalms. He was not beyond the grip of grace.

Then a genealogy appears in the first chapter of Matthew, which at first might be a little bit boring, but then it gets to David and says, "David was the father of Solomon, whose mother had been Uriah's wife" (Matthew 1:6). There's a little Gospel humor here, as Uriah was the man David had killed. Clearly that was a sin, but God is bigger than the sin.

TONY: Whenever somebody says to me, "My sin is so great that God could never forgive me," that person is really saying that his or her sin is greater than God. Talking that way, in a sense, may be the greatest sin of all.

SHANE: Same thing with thinking that someone else's sin is so great that God can't forgive them. Shouldn't we try to be as gracious as God, as merciful as Jesus? We should be the hardest people in the world to convince that someone is worthy of death.

This is the good news: mercy triumphs over judgment (James 2:13). Death has been interrupted by grace. No one is beyond redemption—no one.

TONY: It's not enough to only save the lives of "the born" as we try to do in our endeavors to abolish the death penalty. We must also do all we can to protect the unborn. We have to raise serious questions about abortion, which has become all too common in our society. When we talk about being pro-life, we have to be, as Ron Sider says in his book *Completely Pro-Life*, consistently pro-life. You said it well: we have to be pro-life from the womb to the tomb.

Barney Frank, a liberal Democratic congressman, in a personal conversation, made the challenging statement that the problem with evangelicals is that they think that life begins at conception and ends at birth. He was basically saying that we're willing to protect life from the moment of conception until the moment of birth, but once that baby is born, we don't want to do what is needed to take care of the baby. As evangelicals, with our pro-life politics, we seldom want to put the necessary money into health services, day care, and education.

The late Cardinal Bernardin of Chicago talked about the seamless robe. If you are going to talk about being pro-life, he said, it has to be a seamless statement of life that reaches all the way from abortion to war to caring for the poor.[5]

When I served on the platform committee of the Democratic party for the 2008 election, my evangelical friends asked how I could possibly do that. I answered them by saying that I thought there needed to be a pro-life voice when the party platform was developed. While I wasn't able to get a plank in the platform document that called for the abolition of abortion, I was able to support efforts that would cut the number of abortions performed each year.

Almost 70 percent of all abortions performed in America are economically driven, according to the Guttmacher Institute.[6] Many women have abortions because they lack the economic means to take care of a baby. Consider a woman who works at a Walmart for minimum wage, has no hospital coverage, and is pregnant out of wedlock. She knows she can't support a child. She's having a hard time supporting herself, so she has an abortion. She's one of those people whom we call "the working poor," and she lives in a society that tells her, "We're not going to provide for you if you have your baby. We're not going to cover your hospital bills, and we're not going to cover the cost of daycare so you can work. We're not going to provide any prenatal care for you, and we're not going to raise the minimum salary so that you can earn enough to support yourself as well as your child." Society is telling her that it absolves itself of all responsibility once her baby is born.

To be pro-life is not only to be committed to protecting the unborn but also to protecting the child after birth. Being pro-life goes much further than criminalizing abortions.

When I'm asked if the zygote becomes a human being at the moment of conception, I say, "I don't know, and since I don't know exactly when the unborn becomes human, I have chosen to be pro-life." If I err, I'd rather err on the side of life, lest I support murdering an unborn child. The Roman Catholics have consistency. They say essentially, "We don't know when the 'ensoulment' begins, so we're not only against abortion, we're also against contraception."

SHANE: When I was speaking out in Michigan, one of the guys who came up to talk to me afterward said he had always been pro-life and he still was passionately pro-life. But he said, "I began to realize I was pro-life but I wasn't proactive. I wasn't really doing anything other than protesting."

Then he went on to share with me that he had started a counseling service for young women and an open adoption agency to help find homes for new babies who need families.

TONY: Both Jerry Falwell and Mother Teresa didn't just *say* they were pro-life, but each took care of troubled pregnant women who didn't want abortions. Mother Teresa would say to such women that if they were pregnant and thinking of getting rid of the child, they shouldn't do it. She pleaded for them to give those babies to her, and she would see that they were cared for and nurtured.[7]

Jerry Falwell, on the religious Right, did exactly the same thing. Not only did he preach against abortion but he provided women with problem pregnancies with housing, financial assistance including medical expenses, and loving support, even arranging adoptions for those who chose not to keep their babies. Dr. Falwell's commitment to care gave integrity to his pro-life preaching.

My own ministry, the Evangelical Association for the Promotion of Education, is affiliated with Aquila Way, a ministry in the northeast of England that, along with caring for homeless women with children and battered women, takes care of pregnant women. Those who minister there work with about thirty women at any given time. It's easy to say you are pro-life, but if you are not doing anything to help take care of pregnant women in need, you are really saying, "You got pregnant. Having the baby is your responsibility."

SHANE: When I was in India, there were two street kids I got really close to. They must have been about seven and ten years old, and totally on the streets, orphans. So I called my mom and said, "Do you think we could find anybody to take these kids in?" She did a little research and found one of her friends who said she would actually love to do it. So after going through the ranks in India, I ended up talking to the person right under Mother Teresa, and she said, "Actually, I will go and talk to Mother Teresa for you." She came back and said, "It's been our definitive position and continues to be Mother's conviction that we shouldn't have kids come from India to the US until you change your abortion laws because that's a more urgent issue right now."

When I was in India, I learned that folks there did not call Mother Teresa "Mother Teresa"; they just called her "Mother." The reason was that she *was* a mother. Over and over I met kids she had raised. She earned that title, and her credibility as a champion for life, not because she went around picketing abortion clinics with signs saying "Abortion is Murder." She was a champion for life because she accompanied women and kids in tough situations—integrity you can't argue with.

Our ideologies come with responsibility. In my neighborhood, to be against abortion means we have to figure out what to do when a fourteen-year-old girl gets pregnant. If we are really pro-life, we had better have some foster kids and teen moms living with us to prove it. I don't want to just be anti-abortion or anti-death. I want to be pro-life. For far too long, we Christians have been known more by what we are against than by what we are for. I am ready for a Christianity that is consistently committed to life and all about interrupting death everywhere it shows its ugly face.[8] We are Resurrection people. When Jesus rose from the dead he declared essentially, "Death, thou art dead." I am ready to see Christians make that same declaration. Death, thou art dead.

Dialogue on Environmentalism

See how the flowers of the field grow. They do not labor or spin. Yet I tell you that not even Solomon in all his splendor was dressed like one of these.

MATTHEW 6:28–29

TONY: Most Red Letter Christians are waking up to the importance of rescuing the environment. We talk a lot about how we're polluting the oceans and the air we breathe, and about the fact that global warming is being caused by carbon dioxide collecting in the upper levels of the atmosphere because of our use of fossil fuels. Not much is being said about environmentalism being a pro-life issue, but the two are related.

SHANE: Yeah, this really is another pro-life issue. I heard a lot of theology growing up that was about how this world is not our home, so how we live in it doesn't really matter. I've come to see the terrible repercussions of that theology. I love some of the old songs like "I'll Fly Away," but there is a danger if our sense that "this world is not my home" affects how we respect the earth and how we leave it for our kids.

When we disregard the creation, it must sadden the

Creator who made it all and happily pronounced it "good" (Genesis 1:31).

Creation care has everything to do with loving our neighbor. Poor folks carry the heaviest burden, as we can see in my neighborhood or in places like Camden, New Jersey, that have been devastated by what we call environmental racism. By this we mean that some of our poorer neighborhoods have more superfund sites (which get their names from the fact that they are so polluted it would take "superfunds" to clean them up). In fact, they have more of these sites in them than some states have in their entire state. These are not natural catastrophes; they're human made. That's what happens when you take sewage from our biggest cities and dump it into a few miles of geography. You can literally smell the pollution in the air in Camden. The waterfront, which is why folks moved there decades ago, is so polluted there are signs that say "Don't Fish, Don't Swim, Do Not Enter"—the very stuff you are supposed to do in water.

And it is not just the cities. Take for instance areas like Columbia, Mississippi, where fifty-five-gallon drums of toxic waste were buried in the ground of their community. They began to leak so much that you could light the dirt on fire.

People talk about how they feel close to God in nature, and we see how Jesus went up to the mountains to pray and how God met people in the wilderness. The flip side is also true: When we lose touch with creation, we can lose touch with God. When everything we look at is ugly, it's hard to believe there is a beautiful Creator. So part of our mission at the Simple Way is what farmer and theologian Wendell Berry calls "practicing resurrection."[1]

One of the most beautiful things we get to do here at the Simple Way is plant gardens in the concrete jungle of North Philadelphia—and see kids discover the miracle of life and fall in love with the Creator of life. Gardens have a special place in the human story. After all, God first planted humanity in a garden in Eden, the most redemptive act in history began in a garden in Gethsemane, and the story ends in Revelation with the image of the garden taking over the City of God, with the river of life flowing through the city center and the tree of life piercing the urban concrete.

Now, as we approach fifteen years of community at the Simple Way, we have half a dozen lots that we are gardening on. And we are seeing a neighborhood come back to life. We see kids discover the miracle of life. We plant all sorts of community gardens and are starting to do some urban farming.

Kids get so excited when they see tomatoes grow for the first time. When we harvest the first cucumber of the season, the kids cut it into slices and hand it out like communion. Hunting potatoes is like digging for treasure. I will never forget when one of the kids picked a carrot out of the ground for the first time. With wide eyes and an ear-to-ear smile, he lifted it out of the dirt and said, "It's magic!" And we get to say, "It's not magic. It's God. And the God who made that carrot made you, and loves you." The more they see things that are alive, the more filled with wonder they become at the God who made all this wild and wonderful stuff like fireflies and butterflies, hummingbirds, and earthworms—and you and me.

When you look at concrete, buildings, trash, tires, all the stuff of humans, sometimes you can wonder if there is a God. When you see nature, life, beauty, you can't help but know there is a God.

One of the other dimensions of this, especially when it comes to gardening and healthy food, is what many folks like Michelle Obama have started calling the "food deserts."

Studies have shown that there is a disturbing correlation between the density of populations and the number of healthy food stores. What studies found over and over is the complete opposite of what you'd expect and hope: the areas with the highest populations of people have the fewest healthy food stores and the areas with the fewest people have the highest number of healthy food stores.[2]

There is an epidemic of obesity, diabetes, hyperactivity, and malnutrition in poor neighborhoods. Kids drink soda and eat junk food and TV dinners because they can't get to good food or because healthy food can't compete economically with McDonald's. I will never forget the haunting words of a neighborhood kid who once said years ago, "It's easier to get a gun in our neighborhood than it is to get a salad." His words broke my heart. And they have continued to fan a flame all these years to try to change that reality.

As Christians, we've got to look at the environmental issue for so many reasons. Jesus sure talks about a God who cares about the lilies and the sparrows, so God must care about the polar bears and penguins as their ice melts. And we should care all the more because issues of the environment and nutrition and pollution affect people. And we *know* God's crazy about people.[3]

Stephen Bouma-Prediger, in his book *For the Beauty of the Earth*, dissects some of the bad theology that has led to Christians abusing the planet. One of the things he looks at are the images of the earth being consumed by fire, which appear in places like Peter's epistle (2 Peter 3:10). These verses often say the world will be "destroyed" by fire. But Stephen points out that these words and images are used in Scripture as a "refiner's fire," one that restores life.[4] How we think theologically can make a big difference in how we live. Whether we think God's end plan is to restore creation or to burn everything up affects how we walk on the earth.

TONY: Paul, in 1 Corinthians, wrote about "fire" that would burn away hay, wood, and stubble, leaving only gold, silver, and precious stones (3:12–13).

A real problem with the evangelical community is that it has allowed the New Age movement to kidnap the environmentalist movement. The minute we start talking about the environment, some of our evangelical brothers and sisters label us "New Agers." The truth is that being concerned about the environment is a biblical mandate and should be *our* concern as Red Letter Christians.[5]

SHANE: And creation is simply amazing! This past year we had fireflies in our neighborhood. I hadn't seen one of those in the past twelve years I've lived here. The kids were so amazed they ran in circles. "Why does it glow?" one of them asked. I said, "I think God was just feeling really creative that day—'Hey how about a bug whose butt glows in the dark?'"

TONY: Nature, in all its splendor, exists for the glory of God (Psalm 19:1). The Bible says that the stars, the planets, and the galaxies were all created to worship God; and the psalmist calls upon the "leviathans of the deep" (the whales) to sing their songs of praise to God (Psalm 148).

When people sing the words of the Doxology, "Praise God from whom all blessings flow, Praise him *all creatures* here below," I wonder if they ever think about the words. There is more to nature than can be discerned through empirical and nonmystical observations. There is something very spiritual about nature.

In the book of Romans, the sons and daughters of God are called upon to rescue nature: "All of nature groans and is in travail waiting for the sons and the daughters of God to come and rescue it from its suffering" (Romans 8:21–22, paraphrased).

SHANE: Shortly after the verses about creation groaning comes Romans 12:2, which says, "Do not conform any longer to the pattern of this world, but be transformed by the renewing of your mind." We are to have a new imagination. The prophets invite us to imagine a world where we beat our swords into plowshares and our spears into pruning hooks (Isaiah 2:4). We turn the tools of death into tools of life. I recently learned to weld from a buddy of mine. We literally took an AK-47, dismantled it, and then turned the barrel of it into a shovel and the gun itself into a pitchfork. Now we just need to learn how to turn a tank into a tractor.

But we really need that imagination when it comes to the environment. The current patterns are terribly unsustainable. In the United States, 5 percent of the world's population is consuming nearly half of the world's resources. If the whole world were to pursue the American dream, we'd need four more planets. The world can't afford the American dream. The good news is that God has another dream, and he is inviting us to be a part of bringing it to pass.

Corporations have been wickedly shrewd in devising ways to get us to buy stuff we don't need. There are engineers who use their imaginations for the opposite of life—to engineer seeds so the plants they grow don't reproduce, making it necessary for folks to buy new ones every year. We've seen imaginations used for death and for destruction in things like the atomic bomb and the capacity to drill holes underwater for oil.

I am excited to be alive today. I see imaginations being used for life, for redemption, for the kingdom of God. A group of engineers has designed merry-go-rounds that pump water as kids play on them. So they create a playground for kids in Africa while pumping water for the village.

I visited a college that had created an eco-village. The toilets flushed using dirty sink water. The laundry machines were powered by stationary bikes. We've got a group of elderly folks who rescue plastic shopping bags from the trash and crochet them into mats that we give homeless people to sleep on for padding. Another group of folks in retirement take scrap materials and make sleeping bags for people on the street, which they deliver to us by the truckload. And they use neckties for the shoulder strap to make it easy to carry. Gotta find a use for neckties these days. Imagination.

One really neat project in Philly is a "Greasel Station," where a recovery community makes biodiesel out of waste veggie oil they gather up. It's all being done by folks recovering from drug and alcohol addictions, many of whom have been unemployed. In our neighborhood, drugs are one of the biggest industries, and they wanted to change that. Now they have this biodiesel station. The philosophy behind their business is about how the things we discard still have value. Some of the people have even been treated as waste. So when they take waste veggie oil and make it fuel cars, they are driven by a theology of resurrection. Dead things can be brought back to life.

Another urban farm called Growing Power, in Milwaukee, was started by those in the neighborhood who insisted that nutritious food shouldn't be a privilege available only to those who can afford it. They now have vertical farms that feed two thousand families off two acres of land. And in Brazil, my friend Claudio has chickens, rabbits, and goats on a little urban lot. He even makes soap out of veggie oil waste and creates soil out of McDonald's coffee waste.[6]

Detroit is experimenting with some similar urban farms on the thousands of vacant lots that belonged to factories that used to provide jobs. Vacant lots are being reclaimed as farmland. Our latest experiment in resurrection has been a new greenhouse, which we completed this past week. We built it on the fire-scorched land where our houses burned down almost exactly five years ago. Now our park flaunts a solar-powered greenhouse with an eighteen-hundred-gallon fish pond that can hold more than a thousand fish that will fertilize the water where plants grow on raised beds above the tank.[7] This aquaponics project is an integrated system of fish-farming and hydroponics that mimics what nature does naturally. Building on some of the most creative techniques in urban farming, we are now cultivating life in these post-industrial ruins, where we see the dark side of the global economy every day. Each morning we wake up on the wrong side of capitalism. But we see hope. We are building a new world in the shell of the old one. We see grass piercing concrete. We see a neighborhood coming back to life, rising from the dead. We now have a little oasis in the "food desert" of North Philadelphia. And we'll have fish tacos for everybody!

It reminds me of the new Jerusalem we see in the book of Revelation, where God's holy city is a garden city, an urban garden gone wild. The best of the garden and the best of our cities meet. That's our vision of what the restoration of things will look like.

TONY: When the prophet Isaiah says that the lion and the lamb will lie down together (Isaiah 11:6), he means that nature will once again have peaceable harmony restored. I believe that when sin entered the world, as described in Genesis, it not only affected human beings but all of nature. We live in the context of what theologians call "a fallen creation." I believe that's why there is so much violence in the animal kingdom. Isaiah goes on to say, "They shall not hurt nor destroy in all my holy mountain: for the earth shall be full of the knowledge of the Lord, as the waters cover the sea" (11:9 KJV). That's a good line. It's telling us that when God's will is done on earth as it is in heaven, earth shall be delivered from all the damage we've done to it. Harmony will again be restored to God's creation.

Jesus said that this peaceable kingdom is already breaking loose in our midst. He said, "The kingdom of God is among you" (Luke

17:21 ɪsᴠ). I see signs of that kingdom here and now, and I believe that his kingdom is increasing before our eyes. To be a kingdom people is to join God in what he's doing, and to participate with God in rescuing nature from the mess we've made of it.

SHANE: The transformation does not begin with kings and presidents. It begins with people. Isaiah 2:4 says, "[My people] will beat their swords into plowshares and their spears into pruning hooks. Nation will not take up sword against nation, nor will they train for war anymore." It begins with the people of God who start turning the things of death into things of life. And the kings and presidents and nations will follow.

TONY: In the minds of skeptics, small, incremental efforts such as gardening hardly do anything to change the world and make for global harmony. But Jesus said the kingdom of God is like a mustard seed. Mustard seeds are small, insignificant things in the eyes of most of us. They are so small that we hardly notice them; but Jesus said that they grow and grow until they become large enough for the birds of the air to make their nests in them (Mark 4:31–32). Jesus makes it clear that it is from such little things that great results come.

SHANE: Most of the images Jesus offers for the kingdom of God are small and subtle. Seeds. Light. Yeast. Things you can't even see but they spread like crazy. And I love the mustard-seed metaphor for the kingdom. Mustard grew like a wild and invasive weed. Jews had laws against growing mustard in their gardens, because it would take over the whole garden, leaving them only with mustard.

Mustard is a humble plant though. It didn't grow huge like the cedars of Lebanon or the giant redwoods in California. Mature mustard only stands eight to ten feet high, a modest little bush. What a beautiful garden image of how the kingdom of God takes over the world—a small, subtle, humble invasion of goodness and grace.

TONY: In small projects and programs we see potential for important changes. However, as important as the small things are, we still have to deal with the big picture and address environmental concerns on the macro level.

Not too long ago I traveled to Buenos Aires for a speaking engagement. I flew there during the night, and as my plane flew over Brazil, I was 35,000 feet high. To my surprise, as far as my eyes could see, I saw fires burning all over the Amazon. People were burning down the rainforest for two reasons. One was to make it easier to dig out the minerals buried in the ground. Just as important, however, was to remove trees to create more grazing land for cattle. The earth has become a beef-eating world, and more and more land is needed to raise the cattle to supply that beef.

This raises questions about how much red meat we are consuming. Are our dietary habits related to the destruction of the planet? Most scientists would say that Americans are eating too much and that what we are eating is the wrong food. We're eating ourselves to death while so many in the world are at death's door because of a lack of protein in their diets. Scientists point out that if the grains that produce protein were eaten by people directly rather than being eaten by the cattle, which we then eat, the amount of protein available for the poor people of the world would increase by 90 percent.[8]

Everything is linked together, and when we mess with one part of God's creation, the ramifications reverberate all through the planet, having an impact on people around the world.

SHANE: Even small changes mean sacrifice. To have any integrity as an abolitionist in Europe in the 1800s meant that you didn't have sugar in your tea because the sugar industry was built on the backs of slaves. In the same way, we must ask ourselves, what is the cost of our way of life? Whose pain sustains our lifestyle? We may need to give up some things. It may be meat, oil, or chocolate. We may not want to patronize any company we are not proud of. We may want to grow our own food or run our cars on waste veggie oil. We get to live with a new imagination and not conform to the patterns of death.

Some of the most joyful and alive people I know live close to the earth, spend time in nature. Jesus certainly did and invites us to do the same. In fact, the culture of the early Christians probably more closely resembled the Bedouins we met over in the Holy Land than the 'burbs. Christians born in indigenous culture around the world connect their faith to the care for creation, and they have so much to teach us.

There are good questions we should raise about progress: How much happier people are we? We are busier, but are we more alive? Studies keep showing that the richest corners of the earth have some of the highest rates of loneliness, depression, and suicide. With all our technologies and virtual stuff, studies keep showing that the more virtual friends we have, the lonelier people we become. Maybe it's time to look back at the garden. I'm not saying we should all wear fig leaves, but perhaps we can move a little closer to what God had in mind for this world.

The early Christians said that the cross puts the whole world back together. The vertical dimension of the cross is about reconciling people to God. The horizontal dimension of the cross is about reconciling people to one another. And the fact that the cross is anchored in the ground reminds us that God is restoring all of creation.

Dialogue on Women

*Jesus said to them, "Why are you bothering this
woman? She has done a beautiful thing to me."*

MATTHEW 26:10

TONY: One of the most divisive issues among evangelicals, Anglicans, and Roman Catholics has to do with the roles that woman can play in church life. Red Letter Christians are well aware that Jesus affirmed women. He invited Mary, the sister of Lazarus, to sit with his male disciples and study the Torah (Luke 10:38–42). He broke societal expectations when he sat alone with a Samaritan woman and conversed with her on religious issues (John 4:4–26). He broke rabbinical law when a woman who was menstruating touched him (Matthew 9:20–22). The author of Galatians makes it clear that "in Christ" the religious hierarchy differentiating men and women has been abolished (3:28). Nevertheless, there are many Christians who, citing 1 Timothy 2:11 to 15, claim that women ought not to be priests or ministers.

Shane, what do you say to those who deny women the right to be preachers and teachers in the church? Isn't such denial another form of diminishing dignity and thus dehumanizing women?

SHANE: Why would we want to miss out on half the wonderful gifts God is offering to us? The Scripture is brim full of powerful women—prophets, leaders, disciples. There are volumes of books written on them, so why would we view women as sharp enough to trust as doctors, scientists, pilots, and social workers but not as pastors? We'll trust the sisters to shoot an M16 but not with the sword of the Spirit? There's something wrong with that.

Women are in the center of the Gospels. They are some of the first evangelists to proclaim the resurrection and are some of the most significant disciples (Luke 8:1–3). They were the ones who remained at the cross when all the guys left.

What's also clear is that women quickly rose to key leadership in the early church. Just as the original twelve male disciples mirror the twelve tribes of Israel, we see the community of God continue to be fulfilled as Gentile outsiders become insiders and as women begin to serve in key positions.

Romans 16 gives a glimpse of a husband and wife pastoral team, Andronicus and Junia.[1] We see in Acts 18, Priscilla and Aquila, who taught the evangelist Apollos. Women share in the speaking and prayer during worship in 1 Corinthians 11. And in Romans, we see that women were deacons. Paul and the other apostles appointed women to leadership such as Euodia and Syntyche in Philippi (Philippians 4:2–3).

Undoubtedly, there are verses that can be misused to hold women hostage, just as there were biblical verses used to justify slavery. And it's not our purpose here to take on all those. There are fantastic folks like our friends at Christians for Biblical Equality who have written tons of great articles, many of which you can find on their website.[2]

Ministry is a matter of call and gifting, not gender, and it would be a great disgrace if we lost half our gifted leaders in the church because we misread a few texts. It shouldn't even be necessary to say "men and women are equal," but it is. Hopefully in another ten years, we will end gender inequality. Until then, may we all live in discomfort amid a booming choir of men, while the church is pregnant with women who are ready to lead and write and preach but still get funny looks or cold shoulders.

We give women some of the most vital roles—such as working to raise up future leaders, teaching the Bible in Sunday school, taking off to the mission field and lead people to Jesus— but often with the backdrop, even almost apologetically, that they cannot be pastors because they don't have male genitalia.

Here's the thing: women are as fully human as men are fully human. When God made the first humans, we were made together in the image of God, male and female (Genesis 1:27). Someone once said to me, "Yeah, but women are made from men's side." I responded with, "And men are made from dirt!" The fact is, we are meant to help one another. I look at creation, and most of creation works much better, in a much more egal- itarian way than the human species. There are species where females are in charge and others where males are in charge. And most of nature is better at supporting one another, work- ing as a team, than we are.

Our brother Ben Witherington has said it well: "It was the original curse, not the original blessing that was pronounced in the following form—'your desire will be for your husband and he will lord it over you.' The effect of the Fall on human rela- tionships is that 'to love and cherish' became 'to desire and to dominate,' which entailed unilateral submission of females to males, something that was never God's original creation plan."[3]

From the very beginning we see courageous women like the Hebrew midwives who saved babies from Pharoah. And we see images of women at the center of the story all the way to Revelation where we are incorporated into the Bride of Christ, ready to join the love of our life for all eternity.

If we want to know what it means to be human, we look at Jesus. He does things we'd culturally consider feminine—like weep—and others our culture would consider masculine—like flip tables in the temple. But really all these things are just human. And since Jesus is God, these characteristics are also divine.

TONY: It's important for us to challenge things that our culture considers feminine or masculine. To be compassionate is not necessarily feminine, but our culture has made it so. Sometimes I hear preachers call men to be "real men." By that they usually mean that men should demonstrate nothing of the gentleness, sensitivity, and sweetness that our culture defines as feminine characteristics. A prominent preacher condemned Mr. Rogers, the star of the PBS children's television show *Mister Rogers' Neighborhood*, because he claimed that Mr. Rogers was teaching boys to be sweet, kind, and gentle, which, in his way of thinking, made them like girls. We Red Letter Christians follow a Jesus who *was* sweet and kind and gentle. He was, however, also strong and assertive. Jesus had the traits that our culture defines as masculine, as well as many of those traits defined as feminine. He brought together in himself *all* the traits that make for a complete human being.

In our cultural value system, we have divided up human traits between the sexes and consequently have denied each sex a part of its humanity. Jesus transcended that culturally defined dichotomy. Your statement that Jesus is the fully actualized human being was right on target. Not only is he the fullest revelation of what God is (Colossians 2:9), he is the *only* revelation of what it means to be completely human.[4] As both men and women grow into becoming like Christ, each sex will recover those human traits that society has repressed in them.

SHANE: So Jesus, the incarnation—God with skin on—is playing with kids, drawing in the dirt, debating the teachers of the law. He lets his beloved friend lay his head on his chest. And God is like a father, so we can say Abba (Daddy) as Jesus did. God is also like a mother caring for her babies (Luke 13:34).

Jesus lives the challenge to our gender stereotypes and prejudices, but he is also wonderfully subversive in the ways he legitimates and empowers women. One of the most scandalous stories is his interaction with the Syrophoenician woman (in Matthew 15 and Mark 7). She had a couple of strikes against her: she was a woman and not Jewish. But this courageous woman boldly approached Jesus and asked him to heal her daughter. Jesus seemed to test her—or more likely, test the men around regarding the limits they might put on God. Jesus says, "First, let the children eat all they want . . . it is not right to take the children's bread and toss it to their dogs" (Mark 7:27). I think he is exposing thick cultural norms, raising issues of insiders and outsiders, equality and the economics of divine blessing. The woman rightly pushes back and says, "But even the dogs under the table eat the children's crumbs" (verse 28). Jesus is impressed and applauds her courage. He heals her daughter, and probably gives her the first-century equivalent of a high five. No doubt there were some frustrated men and religious folks after that incident.

TONY: I agree that women should have the same rights as men in the church, so far as preaching and teaching are concerned. When I read Scripture, I find that in Christ, women are given equal status.

In the ancient temple at Jerusalem, there was a partition that separated the Gentiles and women—who were allowed to worship only in the outer court—from the circumcised Jewish men who were privileged to worship in the inner court where they were, supposedly, closer to God. But Ephesians 2:14 says that this wall of separation has been broken down by Christ. This means that in Christ, women and Gentiles have the same status as Jewish men. The second-class citizenship that women and Gentiles had in the old religious system has been abolished in Christ.

There are other things in Scripture that lend support to the idea of women being leaders in the church. For instance, three of Philip's daughters are acknowledged as being prophetesses, which means, in the original biblical language, that they were preachers (Acts 21:8–9). The two leaders in the church at Philippi, Euodia and Syntyche, were women. Then, in the book of Romans, Paul writes about Andronicus and Junia, a man and a woman, as fellow apostles. Apostles held the highest offices of leadership in the ancient church.

All through Scripture, we see the breaking down of the old stratified system wherein circumcised Jewish men were at the top with women and Gentiles below them. Because of Christ, that system is obliterated.

Furthermore, when the gifts of the Spirit are given out (Ephesians 4:11), there is no indication that only men receive the gifts of teaching and preaching. Paul tells *all* Christians—and that includes women—that not to exercise the gifts that are within them is to negate what God wills (1 Timothy 4:14).

SHANE: Didn't this play out in your own family?

TONY: My mother was the best storyteller I have ever heard. She always wanted to be a preacher but lived at a time when she couldn't do that. I always had the sense that she tried to live out her calling through me. Time and time again she would tell me, "You were brought into this world to preach the gospel, especially to the poor and the oppressed. *Do you understand that?*" She had wanted to name me Samuel, and she told me the Bible story of Samuel over and over again. Etched in my memory is the story of that little boy who hears a voice at night, calling him into God's service. My mother told me, "I'm praying every night that you'll hear the voice of God calling you into his service."

Well, I never did hear the voice of God, but I certainly heard the voice of my mother. I'm not sure where her pleading ended and God's calling began, because they merged in my consciousness. My mother made God and my calling real to me. I find it sad that she had to live out her desire to be a preacher through her son because she was not allowed to live it out herself, and it is partly because of what happened to my mother that I am a strong advocate of women being preachers and teachers in the church.

SHANE: As feminists who happen to be men, we need creativity and courage. A few years ago I was invited to speak at a conference. After I had said yes, I noticed that there were only men in the lineup. So I called the conference organizers and offered to open up my spot to a woman, and I named a dozen or so women I thought would do a great job. They didn't take me up on the offer. I continued to pray about it and talked with some close friends. I decided not to take my speaking time to get on a soapbox, but I did feel compelled to do something. As I prayed, I felt the Spirit sort of moving. I went ahead and preached the sermon exactly as I had prepared it. I just wore a T-shirt that said, "God Loves Women Preachers."

TONY: That's a good start, but sexism runs much deeper. We have an oppressive cultural value system that forces women to think that they are supposed to conform to a society-prescribed weight and have a particular sized bust. Consider that the large majority of women who model clothing and appear in advertisements, along with those who give us the news on television, are not only young but also beautiful in a culturally defined way. Many women have breast implants because they feel that they don't measure up to breast dimensions prescribed by our sexist society. In America, women are conditioned to think that they have to look twenty-three forever. Facelifts and plastic surgery are becoming increasingly common.

The feminist Kate Millett once said, "A forty-year-old man is mature, but a forty-year-old woman is obsolete."[5] She didn't mean that a woman can't be attractive at forty, but that if a woman is attractive at forty, it's because she doesn't look forty. So many women feel they have to work overtime to keep themselves looking young. There's a multibillion-dollar cosmetic industry that caters to women who are insecure about their appearance because of what our sexist society has done to them.

Being socialized into accepting sexist values begins at an early age. It happens for many girls when they play with Barbie dolls. Even though it would be physically impossible to have a body like a Barbie doll, we have girls who are dieting, some even becoming anorexic, because they want to be as slim as Barbie. Barbie has had disastrous psychological effects on more girls than we know.

SHANE: When our community has our toy drive every Christmas season, we say no to toy guns and Barbie dolls. Baby dolls, yes. Squirt guns, yes. But no Barbie dolls or toy guns. There's no place for them in the kingdom.

TONY: There was a time when girls played with baby dolls. When girls changed their dolls' diapers and pretended to rock their dolls to sleep, they identified with becoming mothers. According to sociologist George Herbert Mead, their play with baby dolls socialized little girls into the role that society prescribed for women.[6] I'm by no means supportive of limiting the roles of women to that of caring for babies, but I am disturbed when Barbie dolls provide susceptible girls another image that tells them not only what they must be like but what they must look like and suggest the roles they should aspire to as adults.

Too often the church feeds our society's sexism. There have been times when we have asked a Miss America, or a Miss Universe, if she happened to be a Christian, to give her testimony of how important

God has been in her success. When we put her on the speaking circuit to make sure she gives her testimony in churches and youth gatherings, we glorify the sexism that beauty contests promote.

Playboy magazine is another abomination that nurtures sexism. The centerfold in each magazine tells every woman what she's got to be like to score a "10" in the mind of her husband or boyfriend. This drives many women to play the game of being sexual objects instead of actualized persons. Some women don't see themselves as having any worth unless they conform to the *Playboy* ideal. The church should be standing up against sexism, but so far it has done very little about it. Too many Christian leaders are upset over what *Playboy* magazine does to men's sexual imaginations, but they ignore what it does both to the women depicted in the centerfolds of the magazines and the women who look nothing like them.

When women are made into sex objects, it results in abominations such as sex trafficking. Consider a man who looks at his fifty-five-year-old wife, who no longer has the shape that she had when she was twenty-three, and wants to discard her and sleep with a young woman who does have the shape that our sexist culture deems necessary to be desirable. The prostitute he seeks out to serve his socially generated sexist appetite may well be a woman or girl who has been trafficked.

We aren't going to solve the sexual trafficking problem simply by arresting the men who traffik women or the men who use these women. There will be others to take their places. We have to deal with the ugly reality that our society is indoctrinating men with evil concepts of what should turn them on sexually. These wrongs are part of our culture, and it's the church's responsibility to raise up men who do not conform to the culture (Romans 12:1–2) but instead work to change it.

SHANE: The issues get even more complex globally. In extreme cases, women are mistreated, or even tortured by being forced to undergo female circumcision. We must know that these things matter to God. How women are treated is as important to God as how men are treated.

And while we're at it, we might also say that the wages that women get paid matter to God too. Women do so much of the work and get so little of the money and credit. There's a great article in the *College Times* that articulates gender inequity in a really helpful way.[7] They list simple signs that things are not what they should be, including the fact that four in ten businesses worldwide have no women in senior management and that women earn less than men in 99 percent of all occupations. Statistics don't change the world, but they sure can light a fire in us to change the world. And as Red Letter Christians, we need to figure out how to do so.

Dialogue on Racism

If you are offering your gift at the altar and
there remember that your brother or sister has
something against you, leave your gift there
in front of the altar. First go and be reconciled
to them; then come and offer your gift.

MATTHEW 5:23–24 AUTHOR'S PARAPHRASE

TONY: Neither the church nor society at large has erased the racial divide. Eleven o'clock on Sunday morning is still the most segregated time in the week. We both agree that there is an incongruity to claiming to be Christian and embracing racism at the same time, but how have you witnessed it personally?

SHANE: The difficult thing is that no one really wants to be racist, except for a few really mean folks like KKK members and Neo-Nazis. But if we define racism as a system of advantage based on the color of your skin,[1] many of us are benefactors of racism even if we don't realize it. We inherit it. We internalize it. Often it is subtle, but there are *aha* moments when we start to see it. When I first came to Eastern University, I put my high-school yearbook on the shelf, but it had the Confederate flag on it. Some of my friends were like, "What in the world is that?"

TONY: Because of what the Confederate flag symbolizes to most African American people?

SHANE: Exactly. It sparked some important conversations in the five minutes I had it up! And I am thankful for the graciousness with which my friends talked to me about it. Over and over I said things I didn't realize were ignorant. One of my roommates led a group called Students Organized Against Racism, so I learned from him and began to see with new eyes. We even challenged some of the subtle places we saw segregation at Eastern. I was leading the YACHT Club (Youth Against Complacency and Homelessness Today), and we saw that it was mostly white. So my roommate and I brought both our clubs together and hosted Chris Rice and Spencer Perkins, authors of *More Than Equals: Racial Healing for the Sake of the Gospel* and pioneers in reconciliation (not a bad book, by the way).

We all met together and talked about why going downtown to hang out with homeless folks is something that more white folks seemed to be drawn to than black folks, at least from our group.

TONY: Did you get any insight as to why, even at the present time, when we are rounding up Eastern students to go into Philadelphia to tutor poor inner-city children who are mostly African American, we can't get many of the African American students here on our campus to go?

SHANE: A lot of my African American friends who have grown up seeing racism and injustice are more interested in dealing with the root of the disease rather than the symptoms of it. There are exceptions of course, but a lot of folks who grew up poor want to do more than give someone a sandwich. They want to keep people from needing a handout.

Someone like Bryan Stevenson would be a good example. He's the founder of the Equal Justice Initiative, which fights for the legal rights of poor people. He may be less inclined to go feed folks, and more inclined to try to change the things that make them hungry. But we have to celebrate everyone. Some folks give people fish. Others teach people to fish. Others ask, "Who owns the pond? And why does a fishing license cost so much?"

One of my favorite passages in Scripture on this issue is the book of Philemon where Onesimus, a slave, is sent back to his owner not as a slave but, as Paul instructs Philemon, as a brother. While it's an act of civil disobedience, it affects the way that we think of the gospel too.

While the patterns of the gospel call for a downward mobility for the rich and the powerful, they also show other folks being lifted out of poverty and oppression. The last becoming first, the first becoming last. The mighty cast from their thrones, the lowly lifted up (Mark 10:31). The mountains leveled and the valleys raised.

A good friend from my neighborhood had a heart-to-heart with me a few years ago and pointed out something deep: "When you move into the neighborhood, everybody thinks you're a hero; but when I don't leave the neighborhood, people think I am a total failure."

God is saving some people from the ghettos of poverty and some people from the ghettos of wealth. Then, as one of my African American sisters said, "Sometimes you get pulled up, and you realize you need to go back down into the mess." She grew up in a really difficult place and was able to go to school, and now she feels God calling her back to her neighborhood. We have to realize that God is doing something big in the world—and we are part of it. But not everyone's path is the same as ours. We should teach what we know to be true for us, and be quick to listen to another person's story. Their liberation may look a little different.

TONY: In the inner-city ministries that I've helped develop through the Evangelical Association for the Promotion of Education, there is a conscious effort to urge kids to stay in school and even go on to complete college. But we don't tell them that the purpose of education is primarily to get the credentials that make for socioeconomic success. We tell the Latino and African American students that the purpose of education is to equip them to be more effective as agents of God to help change the world. It's no surprise to me that after college many of them return to their old neighborhoods as teachers, pastors, lawyers, social workers, and entrepreneurs.

SHANE: Racism—a system of advantage based on race— is real. There's a study discussed in the book *Freakonomics* where two identical résumés were sent to a bunch of companies.[2] The only difference was the names on them—one was Greg and the other DeShawn. Over and over Greg got the job instead of DeShawn. We have a problem.

To understand how real racism is, all we need to do is look at the prisons; statistics show that one in three black men is incarcerated at some point in his life.[3] Those are stunning statistics. Scholars point out that we did not fully abolish slavery in America. It has just changed.[4] The Thirteenth Amendment to abolish slavery says, "Neither slavery nor involuntary servitude, except as a punishment for crime whereof the party shall have been duly convicted, shall exist within the United States." We have an entire legacy, a scar, that slavery and racism has left us. Entire populations are prone to crime because of economics, or feel forced to create underground economies (like scrapping metal, selling water on corners, or the darker side of sex trafficking, bootleg DVDs, and drug economy). I heard one African American judge say that she realized the role economics plays in crimes when she presided over a trial for someone who had stolen meat from a grocery store to feed his family. I'll never forget one Christmas years ago, when a young man in our neighborhood ended up going to jail for robbing a store. We later found out it was to make sure his family got presents for Christmas. So class, race, economics all create a poisonous matrix of injustice that leaves many people trapped and paralyzed.

Sophia Kerby wrote a great article that points out what the racial inequities look like. People of color continue to be disproportionately incarcerated, policed, and sentenced to death at significantly higher rates than their white counterparts. Further, racial disparities in the criminal justice system threaten communities of color—disenfranchising thousands by limiting voting rights and denying equal access to employment, housing, public benefits, and education to millions more. In light of these disparities, it is imperative that criminal-justice reform evolves as a premier civil rights issue of the twenty-first century for Red Letter Christians.[5]

Racial disparities have deprived people of color of their most basic civil rights, making criminal-justice reform one of the most urgent civil rights issues of our time. Through mass imprisonment and the overrepresentation of individuals of color within the criminal justice and prison system, people of color have experienced an adverse impact on themselves and on their communities from barriers to reintegrating into society to engaging in the democratic process. Eliminating the racial disparities inherent to our nation's criminal-justice policies and practices must be at the heart of a renewed, refocused, and reenergized movement for racial justice in America.

What is even more troubling is when people make profits from prisons, and hire out prisoners because they don't have to pay them a minimum wage—what many have now come to call the "prison industrial complex." And with that Thirteenth Amendment, we now have an entire population of people who are living in prison who are, in some ways, modern-day slaves. They are working for a dollar a day sometimes.[6] Some of the biggest companies in the world use prison labor to make their products. In fact, the Prison Expo came to Philadelphia and showcased ways to profit from prison labor. One of the most disturbing things I stumbled across showed that prisoners are being used to make weapons for the US military. Prisoners earning twenty-three cents an hour in US federal prisons are making missiles. Prisoners are putting together components for Boeing's F-15 fighters and Bell's Cobra helicopters. Prison labor produces night-vision goggles, camo uniforms, and body armor.[7] There's something deeply troubling in all this.

Over the past fifty years, factories have closed in neighborhoods like mine, and many folks have turned to some sort of crime to survive. It's estimated we've lost nearly 200,000 jobs. We have 700 abandoned factories. Eventually many folks who can't find work end up turning to some sort of illegal activity like the drug economy (heroin is one of the most profitable businesses where I live), and they get arrested and go to jail, over 50 percent for nonviolent offenses. Before long they end up doing factory jobs as a new form of labor, and may only make a dollar or two in a day. One of my friends in prison said they pool the little money they get together to help other inmates who can't work to get the things they need, like toilet paper.

In Philly, you can see the irony: there are three prisons within walking distance of the National Constitution Center, where the Liberty Bell and Constitution are. Literally within a block of these prisons, the Declaration of Independence was drafted declaring that all people are created equal with the right to life, liberty, and the pursuit of happiness. We can see how far we have to go if we are to realize that dream. Good thing there's a line in the Declaration of Independence that says "whenever any Form of Government becomes destructive of these ends, it is the Right of the People to alter or to abolish it." Amen to that.

TONY: We have to recognize some of the ways in which Jesus addressed racism. Consider that wonderful passage in Luke 4, where he tells the congregation in the synagogue in his hometown of Nazareth that the Spirit of the Lord is upon him and that he has come to bring good news to the poor, sight to the blind, deliverance to the captive, and to declare the "year of the Lord's favor," what Leviticus 25:10 referred to as "the year of jubilee."

The hometown people were awed. They thought that Jesus might be God's promised Messiah. They were thrilled with him, and they were proud that it looked as though it was their town that may have produced the Savior of Israel. But Jesus lost their adoration when he added that there were Gentile people in places like Syria and Lebanon who would receive the good news of the gospel before they would. He declared that these people from other ethnic groups would be more likely to accept his message and receive his Messiahship than they would.

The people in that synagogue went ballistic. They dragged Jesus to the edge of town and tried to throw him over a cliff. They had loved the idea of having a hometown boy be the Messiah, but they wanted him to be a Messiah only for Jews. The idea that Jesus suggested, that people in other racial and ethnic groups were going to be part of his kingdom on an equal basis and would be more receptive to his gospel than they were, was more than they could handle.

The African American theologian Howard Thurman wrote extensively about racism and was convinced that it is so ingrown within our psyches that it would take a miracle to weed it out and to cleanse it from our minds.[8] I agree with him, which is why I believe we have to embrace the kind of spirituality that makes us new. Only by surrendering to a mystical invasion of our souls by the Holy Spirit can we ever expect to be cleansed of the racism that has been ingrained in us through socialization. Thurman made it clear that there was no way to get rid of racism without this miraculous work of God.

SHANE: Even the way that we learn to visualize this event needs to be rethought. When we are talking about Jesus sitting by the Samaritan woman, sometimes we still have this white Jesus pop into our heads. We have to stop and remember that Jesus actually had dark skin. Jesus wasn't from Sweden. What's at stake, really, is how it infects our Christianity. In the words of former slave and civil rights hero Frederick Douglass: "Between the Christianity of this land, and the Christianity of Christ, I recognize the widest possible difference—so wide, that to receive the one as good, pure, and holy is of necessity to reject the other as bad, corrupt, and wicked . . . I love the pure, peaceable, and impartial Christianity of Christ; I therefore hate the corrupt, slaveholding, women-whipping, cradle-plundering, partial and hypocritical Christianity of this land. Indeed, I can see no reason, but the most deceitful one, for calling the religion of this land Christianity."[9]

TONY: Those doing missionary work these days are well aware that in times past we often have presented Jesus to people of other races as the embodiment of what it means to be a white American. The Jesus we presented was not the Jesus of Scripture. We certainly did not present him as a Mideast Semite. That's why the African American leader Malcolm X called on black people to give up Christianity. Malcolm X would say to his African American sisters and brothers something like, "You are worshiping the blue-eyed, blond-haired Jesus. You have been handed a picture of Jesus in which he is the embodiment of all that white people are about, and if you worship that Jesus, you will be worshiping an incarnation of your oppressor. That, in the end, will make liberation impossible, because you can't rebel against your oppressor if you have been duped into thinking that your oppressor is God."[10]

Malcolm X forces us to ask whether or not the Jesus presented to African American people is the Jesus who is found in the red letters of the Bible, or was he nothing more than an incarnation of all that white people are about? If the latter were so, then some early missionary work was an instrument of satanic oppression, which led oppressed people to worship an incarnation of their oppressor.

It's important for us to recognize that there is a good reason why Scripture tells us that God doesn't want any graven images of him made, nor any pictures of him painted. We would likely portray him in our own image, and thus turn the worship of Jesus into the worship of ourselves—which would be idolatry.

SHANE: It's important to challenge baseless assumptions drawn from someone's image. One of the kids in my neighborhood is about sixteen years old, African-American, and almost seven feet tall. Everywhere he goes, people ask, "Do you play ball?" The fact is, he's okay at basketball; he's not crazy about it. But he's an incredible poet. So I told him next time somebody asks him if he plays football or basketball he should say, "No, I'm a poet. No time for sports."

TONY: Some time ago, we had a student worker in our office who was big and tall and could play basketball, but he didn't like the game. He was a true intellectual. This young man had to endure a lot of grief from his fellow black students because he didn't want to be defined as an athlete. His intellectual pursuits had them accusing him of acting white.

The fieldworkers who serve in outreach-ministry programs in

urban communities tell me about black teenagers who are afraid to study hard and get good grades because other black students might accuse them of acting white or even attack them. A black high school student I know about, who was into classical music, had her violin case ripped from her arms and her violin smashed to pieces as her fellow black students accused her of acting like an "uppity white girl."

SHANE: One of the responses a lot of folks have to racism is that we should be color-blind. But the truth is that unity doesn't mean uniformity. It means we see color, we see diversity, and we celebrate it. Sameness is boring. I heard one scholar speak on the "neither male nor female" verse in Galatians—"There is neither Jew nor Greek, slave nor free, nor is there male and female, for you are all one in Christ Jesus" (3:28)—and he pointed out that we have mistranslated it. It was not "male" and "female," but a better translation is "there is neither maleness nor femaleness." The categories we have formerly put people in do not work as we gain a new identity in Christ. Even though we still have genitalia and skin color, that doesn't define us. There is an inherent paradox in the "there is neither male nor female" verse; after all, we don't all use the same restroom. But we see that we are more than genitalia, more than color, we are family—a wonderful, diverse family. We are all being made into a new creation in Christ.

There's a pastor in Philly, Manny Ortiz, who says, "The church's task is neither to destroy nor to maintain ethnic identities, but to replace them with a new identity in Christ that is more foundational than earthly identities."

That new identity unites us more than our diversity divides us.[11]

Dialogue on Homosexuality

A new command I give you: Love one another.
As I have loved you, so you must love one
another. By this everyone will know that you
are my disciples, if you love one another.

JOHN 13:34-35

SHANE: Tony, gay marriage is such a divisive topic, but I know you have a clear stance on it. Can you give us a bit of insight behind your thinking?

TONY: While I believe that the government should not legalize marriage for people who are gay, I also believe that it should not legalize marriage for heterosexuals either. In fact, the government should get out of the marriage business completely and instead focus on civil rights for all of its citizens. It should treat both homosexual couples and heterosexual couples the same, guaranteeing both the same rights and privileges. Homosexual couples and heterosexual couples should be able to go down to the city hall and register as couples who want to be legally recognized as belonging to each other, and receive the same civil rights available for all citizens who want to be in committed relationships. Then, if a couple wants to call the relationship a marriage, that couple should go down to a church, and let the church perform the ceremony.

When George W. Bush said, "Marriage is a sacred institution," I agreed with him.[1] But if marriage is a *sacred* institution, then why is the government involved with it? Isn't it the prerogative of the church to perform sacred ceremonies and declare couples married?

SHANE: Don't folks ask about how some churches will marry homosexual couples and others won't?

TONY: They do, and I respond, "That sounds right!" Because I am a Baptist who believes in the autonomy of the local church, I think that each church should have the right to decide for itself its own rules and its own regulations concerning marriage. It should be up to the local church to decide who it's willing to marry.

Consequently, my wife, who believes in gay marriage, goes to a church where they do perform ceremonies to marry gay people, while I go to another church, where they don't. We are both Baptists and belong to the same American Baptist denomination, but we go to two different churches.

Stop to think about it: Would you want the government to decide who could and who could not take holy Communion? Would the church want to turn over the rite of baptism to the state and say, "It's up to the government to decide who can be baptized and who cannot be baptized"? If you believe that marriage is a sacrament, or a holy ordinance, then why would you leave who can enter into the covenant of marriage in the hands of the government?

As Red Letter Christians, we should give a great deal of thought to gay and lesbian issues. While nobody knows what causes a homosexual orientation, we *do* know that people don't choose to be homosexuals. I have met a number of Christian men who are gay, who talk about having walked the floor at night, crying out to God for deliverance, and their sexual orientation has not changed. Many of them have gone through extensive counseling, hoping that this would lead to a heterosexual orientation, but to no avail. Sometimes they act as though God has played a dirty trick on them because they believe that God created them to be gay, and therefore predestined them to damnation.[2]

I'm *not* saying that people are born gay. Nobody knows for sure what causes people to be gay or lesbian or bisexual or want to be transgendered. I do believe, however, that sexual orientation occurs so early in the development of children that they never remember choosing. What's just as important is that change in sexual orientation is extremely rare. Often attempts to change sexual orientation through what is called reparative therapy can do great psychological harm.

The church needs to come to grips with these realities, and I think that's beginning to happen. Many churches are coming to see that we are dealing with hurting people who are in situations that they have not chosen, and they are suffering a great deal, often because of how churches treat them and the misinformation that churches have sometimes spread about them. When I hear some radio preacher say something erroneous like, "Boys become gay because they have weak fathers or absent fathers," I feel like shouting, "That's terribly wrong! And you're creating unnecessary suffering with that kind of talk."

Most parents of gay people, when they find out their children are gay, go through extremely painful self-examination. Even if such parents accept a gay son or a lesbian daughter, they know that their child is in for a difficult time in life. These parents don't need some preacher who doesn't know what he or she is talking about saying to them, "You have to face the fact that your kid is gay because you failed as a parent." To blame the parent, when there is no evidence to substantiate that neo-Freudian claim that it was a weak or absent father who created the homosexual son, is a horrible thing to do. These parents are already enduring pain and shame at the hands of the church, and what they don't need is someone laying guilt on top of that.

SHANE: When I was in India, I worked in Mother Teresa's first home, Home for the Dying. There were dozens of volunteers, some of the most extraordinary people I've ever met. Each day we'd commute back and forth on the buses. One day one of the volunteers shared with me that she was gay. She was wrestling with what to do with that, and how to live a life that honors God as a lesbian. As we were talking, I asked her if she thought about talking to Mother Teresa about it. She said she had been thinking about that.

So a few days later I asked her again if she had talked to Mother Teresa. She said yes. When I asked what her response had been, the woman smiled and said, "She didn't say much." That alone is deep, but I kept probing, "Well, did she say anything?" My friend said, "She mostly just listened. But then after I had poured out my heart to her, she asked me if I would read the Scripture in Mass tomorrow."

How beautiful is that? So often we think it is our job to push people, and it really is a lack of faith that the Spirit is already at work in them, leading them. We think the Spirit can't work without us jumping in to help make sure they know what the Bible says, or this or that.

Too often we mix up our role. Our friend Andrew Marin, the author of *Love Is an Orientation*, which is a great resource for dealing with this issue, said when Billy Graham was asked about the gay issue, this was his response: "It's the Holy Spirit's job to convict, God's job to judge, and my job to love."[3]

When we get those out of order, we get ourselves in a mess. I remember being at Eastern and meeting a kid who became a really good friend of mine. He told me that he was gay and that he had been told his whole life that he was a mistake. With tears running down his face, he told me he wanted to kill himself because "how can God make mistakes?"

I can remember thinking to myself, *If this kid can't find a home in the church, then what have we become? And if he can't find a friend in me, then who have I become?*

TONY: I wonder how many people like him live out their lives in quiet desperation. Some are even driven to suicide. The US Department of Health contends that suicide by young men and women over sexual orientation is the second largest cause of death among teenagers.[4] The only thing that beats it statistically is drunk driving. I don't know what else the church is about, but when dealing with gay, lesbian, bisexual, and transgender people, if it's contributing to driving people to suicide, there is something wrong with the church.

SHANE: Our friends at the Barna Group conducted a study a few years ago where they asked young non-Christians about their perceptions of Christians.[5] They found that the number one answer to the first thing non-Christians thought when they heard *Christian* was "anti-homosexual."[6] It should break our hearts that often we are known more for what we are against than what we are for, for who we have excluded than for who we have embraced. That's not what people thought of when they met Jesus. Folks didn't have an encounter with Jesus and walk away saying, "Man, he sure doesn't like gay folks."

TONY: Nor did they think that way about those who were in the early church. Non-Christians didn't say about those first-century Christians, "Behold how anti-gay Christians are." Instead, they said, "Behold how Christians love one another."

There are passages of Scripture that people use to lay judgments on gay, lesbian, bisexual, and transgender people. There are at least seven passages of Scripture that they commonly refer to, but it's interesting to note that none of the red letters have anything to say about this issue. Jesus never spoke about homosexuality, and it was not that he didn't know about it. He knew, and undoubtedly supported, the teachings on same-gender eroticism as found in Deuteronomy and Leviticus, but he never said anything about them in his recorded sayings. Homosexuals were not on his big-ten hit list of people to condemn. Number one on his list were religious leaders who made it a policy, according to Matthew 23:4, "to lay heavy burdens on people and do nothing to lift those burdens." Sadly, too many in the church often make those burdens borne by lesbian, gay, bisexual, and transgender people heavier and heavier, thinking they are driving these children of God to repentance when, in most instances, they are driving them to despair.

Instead we should err on the side of grace, as a college chaplain I know demonstrated beautifully. A young woman once came into his office crying because she had been outed. The word was around campus that she was a lesbian. She knew that it was only a matter of time before the news would get back to her father who was one of those austere preachers who, with fair regularity, would bash gays and lesbians with his use of Scripture and preach against them from the pulpit. She said, "When my father finds out I'm homosexual, he's going to reject me. I know that. And I've got to tell him because it's going to get back to him, and I'd rather be the one who tells him."

The college chaplain said, "You don't have to tell him. I'll tell him. You sit right there." He picked up the phone, dialed up this preacher and said, "Your daughter's here in my office. Over the last two years, she has proven to be one of the best Christians we have on campus. She leads a Bible study group that I understand is the most faithfully attended and most effective Bible study here at our school. She's also on the worship team that leads the chapel services here at the college. I have to say that she is a living testimony to what Jesus wants a young Christian woman to be."

The father immediately took off with an enthusiastic response. "That's my daughter," he said. "When she's home during the summer months, the youth program really picks up. She gets more teenagers to come to our youth group during the summer than attend during any other time in the year. She visits the elderly and makes hospital calls. People talk nonstop about what a saint she is."

The chaplain interrupted and said, "Then we're agreed. Your daughter is a wonderful Christian woman—and in the next thirty seconds I am going to find out whether *you* are worthy to be called her father."

I think that's the way Jesus might have handled that situation. Perhaps he would have said, "Before you say anything about your daughter, maybe you should take a good look at yourself."

I do know that while Jesus never spoke to the homosexual issue in those red letters, he did speak specifically about divorce and remarriage in the Sermon on the Mount and has strong words on this matter (Matthew 5:31–32). It seems hypocritical to me that this evangelical community, of which we both are part, is quite ready to pounce on couples who are in sexual relationships that Jesus never mentions and, yet, is usually gracious toward divorced and remarried people in the church. Don't get me wrong: I believe that cases can be made for divorce given certain circumstances, but people who are gay often ask, "If you Christians can show grace to them, is there any left over for us?"

SHANE: At one of the places where I was speaking recently, the pastor came up beforehand and mentioned that there were two gay men sitting up front. He said, "I just wanted to make sure you noticed that so you could say something about it if you want to." I said to that pastor, "I'm not sure what you have in mind. I'd like to say that I'm really glad that they felt welcome in your church." That wasn't what he had in mind.

I always tell our community that we should attract the people Jesus attracted and frustrate the people Jesus frustrated. It's certainly never our goal to frustrate, but it is worth noting that the people who were constantly agitated were the self-righteous, religious elite, the rich, and the powerful. But the people who were fascinated by him, by his love and his grace, were folks who were already wounded and ostracized—folks who didn't have much to lose, who already knew full well that they were broken and needed a Savior. And that is part of what being the church is all about. We hear the whisper that indeed we are broken and sinful people, but so is everyone else. And we hear the whisper of grace that we are also beautiful and beloved, created in the image of God— just like everyone else. It's important to reconsider how we think about sin. God hates sin, not because we are breaking random laws. God hates sin because God loves people. And sin hurts people. Sin is falling short of what love requires of us. I'm reminded that the theme verse of evangelicalism, John 3:16–17 says, "For God so loved the world that he gave his one and only Son, that whoever believes in him shall not perish but have eternal life. For God did not send his Son into the world to condemn the world, but to save the world through him." Jesus came not to condemn the world but to save it.

TONY: When discussing sexuality I become aware of how little in the way of a theology of sex has been developed among us Christians. Until we do develop a satisfactory theology, it will be hard for any of us to answer a lot of questions about what is right and what is wrong when evaluating sexual behavior.

I was discussing sexual morality with some of my students at the University of Pennsylvania and realized that these secularists had a clear concept of what it meant to commit sexual sins. Since they didn't believe in God, I asked how they determine what sin is and what things are right and wrong. Their definition of sin deserves serious consideration. They contended that sin is anything that dehumanizes another person.

Does lying dehumanize the other person? Yes!

Does adultery dehumanize people? Yes!

"Sin is not simply the violation of this law, or that law, or some other law," they said. "It's whatever dehumanizes the other person."

You and I know that there are some marriages wherein the wife or the husband is being dehumanized in the relationship. The way one or the other partner is being treated may be so humiliating, so demeaning, and so dehumanizing, that even though they haven't broken any religiously prescribed laws and they haven't committed adultery, there is sin involved in such a relationship.

When it comes to sexuality, the Bible has two words for the sexual act. One is the word *laid*. There are places in the Bible where it says about certain acts of sexual intercourse that "so-and-so *lay* with so-and-so." In today's street language, there are still people who say they are going to go out and get laid. The word *laid* is pretty descriptive, and in today's world there are sexual relationships wherein persons are dehumanized by being treated as things, whose only purpose is to relieve libido urges. In such sexual relationships, people only experience being "laid."

The Bible, however, also has another word for sexual relationships. It's the word *knew*. For instance, we read that Adam *knew* Eve. There is a difference between having a relationship wherein a person gets laid and a relationship wherein a person comes to *know* the other person. Paul so eloquently says this about love: "Then I shall know fully, even as I am fully known" (1 Corinthians 13:12). That kind of intimacy humanizes, whereas getting laid dehumanizes and is sinful. The church should stand against dehumanizing people, whether they be homosexuals or those in heterosexual marriages. To call gay people "abominations," as some religious gay bashers do, is sin, because it dehumanizes them. To pressure persons to stay in dehumanizing marriages is, I believe, also sin.

There are those who challenge me by saying that the book of Leviticus says that such persons are abominations. They're right! It comes right after the verse that says that to touch the skin of a dead pig is an abomination to God . . . which puts the NFL Super Bowl into serious question (Leviticus 11:7–11).

Regardless of the differences that Christians may have on this controversial subject, there should be agreement that gay, lesbian, bisexual, and transgendered people are neighbors who, according to the Red Letters of the Bible, we are to love as we love ourselves (Matthew 22:39).

Dialogue on Immigration

I was a stranger and you invited me in.

MATTHEW 25:35

SHANE: A constant theme in Scripture, from Old Testament to New, is that we are to welcome strangers. At one point Scripture tells us to take care when we welcome the stranger because we may entertain angels unaware (Hebrews 13:2). The Gospel of Matthew tells us that as we welcome the alien, we welcome Christ (Matthew 25:37–40). So when we welcome somebody, we may be taking in Jesus in disguise—or at least an angel. This is a pretty good reason to welcome the immigrant.

I remember hearing about a little community of Christians on the border of the United States and Mexico who were deeply concerned about immigration. They had created an entire network of Christian hospitality houses to welcome people who needed a home. They had lawyers who would help folks get proper documentation if they needed it.

They began a wonderful and prophetic worship service along the border. Christians living in Mexico walked to the wall, where Christians who lived in the United States met them. They sang songs, worshiped Jesus, and then served each other Communion by throwing the bread and bottles of wine over the wall. The wall, which has been created by people, by the governments of this world, is not a barrier to the people of God who are one in the Spirit.

Red Letter Christians must not wait for politicians to tell us how to treat people; the Bible tells us that. We can see the clear command to welcome the alien from Leviticus to James. In fact, James goes so far as to say, "Religion that God our Father accepts as pure and faultless is this: to look after orphans and widows in their distress and to keep oneself from being polluted by the world" (James 1:27). We don't wait for Washington DC to legislate love. We are to be the ones to show the world hospitality and to bear witness of a God whose love does not stop at national borders.

Walls are dangerous things, whether they are picket fences, prison cells, security walls, gated neighborhoods, office cubicles, academic bubbles, or the apartheid in the Holy Land. But our God is a God of reconciliation, who has had some practice tearing down walls.

One of the last images in Revelation is of the New Jerusalem, and Scripture says, "Its gates will never be closed" (Revelation 21:25 NLT).

TONY: The case for receiving aliens as though they were fellow citizens is not only made in the New Testament, as you point out, but is also made in the Hebrew Bible. In what we call the Old Testament, we read that the ancient Jews were reminded constantly that they were to treat the alien with justice and love, remembering that they, themselves, were once aliens in the land of Egypt (Deuteronomy 10:19). God wanted them to remember that when they were aliens, the Jews wished people had been kind and loving to them. God wanted them to treat others as they wished they had been treated.

We have a short view of history. We say to undocumented aliens from Mexico, "You can't come across the border and settle in our land," but we seldom stop to realize that several of the states in the southwest were once *their* land, and former generations of Americans took it from them. I am glad that some Christians are trying to help these aliens on their way to a better life here in the United States by providing them with safe houses that they've established along the border.

The truth is that in one sense, many of us are illegal immigrants, or the children of illegal immigrants. Think about it! Did any of those Europeans who came over here and took land away from the Native Americans have the legal right to do that? Did the American founding fathers and mothers have any right to come across the Atlantic Ocean and take this land away from those who already lived here?

SHANE: That's the story, isn't it? Also, we are all illegals in the kingdom, and Jesus got us in. That should make us want to have more grace, even in this world with issues like immigration. Bob Ekblad, author of *Reading the Bible with the Damned*, wrote an article about how his friends who don't have documentation feel terrible as they are trying to get it.[1] So many feel anything but grace from some Christians who just keep saying it's wrong for them to break the law. Bob talks about Jesus as the Good Coyote ("El Buen Coyote") who is constantly offering grace to outsiders and bringing illegals into the kingdom. (*Coyote* is the name often used for folks who help people illegally cross the border.)

Jesus is the one who got us over the border into the kingdom of God, and he doesn't even charge us a citizenship fee. Jesus always got in trouble for welcoming the "illegals" into the banquet. He's accused of being a glutton and a drunkard for hanging out with the wrong people. But he is constantly challenging and frustrating the Pharisees, who thought that obeying all the rules and keeping all the laws was what got you into heaven.

As the apostle Paul wrote, "[Jesus] came and preached peace to you who were far away and peace to those who were near. For through him we both have access to the Father by one Spirit. Consequently, you are no longer foreigners and aliens, but fellow citizens with God's people and members of God's household" (Ephesians 2:17–19).

The whole Bible is filled with people who are outsiders made insiders by grace. Moses' birth is scandalous, as he is smuggled into this world illegally, an act of civil disobedience. His mother saved him from the sword and floated him down the river, and Pharaoh's daughter took him in and nursed him illegally with a Hebrew midwife (who happened to be his actual mother) (Exodus 2). Ruth, "the Moabitess" (code for "outsider"), is shown hospitality and eventually some fine romance by Boaz, whose cross-cultural marriage is a part of the genealogy that leads up to Jesus (Ruth 2–4). So Jesus had an "illegal" great grandmother. Even Jesus' birth had these dynamics. He was born with no room in the inn. He was born on the move, a refugee. Herod even started killing little babies. There were so many elements that mirror the plight of contemporary immigrants and asylum seekers. You'd think we Christians, whose Savior was born as a homeless baby refugee, would be the most sympathetic and compassionate.

One of the huge debates in the early church was about whether or not Gentiles are welcome into the church or whether it was for Jews only, or Jews first (Acts 11). The answer becomes unmistakably clear. God's grace is huge. And for that, this Gentile is very thankful!

So if we've experienced that kind of hospitality from God, we can't help but extend it to other people, especially to those who are most vulnerable or most marginalized. We have a God who has been making outsiders insiders for thousands of years.

TONY: In a spiritual sense, we Gentile Christians are all aliens. The Bible declares us as such in that we have been grafted (or assimilated) into Israel (Romans 11:17–25). It is by God's grace that we have become citizens of the new Israel (Ephesians 2:14–23).

SHANE: The church has an entire history of "sanctuary," providing refuge for folks in crisis without asking questions. There's a whole new movement of that in Philadelphia called the New Sanctuary Movement, whose mission is to "give voice to injustices faced by immigrants, documented and undocumented alike."[2]

There are lots of other examples of risk-taking hospitality ventures. Recently in my neighborhood a congregation began opening their church building, as many congregations do around the world, to the homeless so they could have a warm, safe place to sleep overnight. The city government got wind of it and began to crack down.

The pastor was told they were not allowed to run a shelter, as they did not have proper permits, nor would they be granted them because the city did not want a shelter there. But you don't mess with Pentecostals.

So the congregation prayed, and the Spirit moved. They came back to the city officials and announced that they would not be running a shelter, but they would have a revival from 8:00 p.m. to 8:00 a.m. every night. It was fantastic watching the news trying to cover the story.

The city did not dare stop that revival—it was brilliant! They began with some great singing, worship, and sharing. After about two hours, the pastor stood up and said, "Well, that concludes the formal service tonight. The next eight hours will be silent meditation. Everyone have a great night." As far as I know, that revival is still going! That's the kind of courage we need.

TONY: Right here in Wayne, Pennsylvania, there's a sanctuary church. They've housed undocumented aliens whom some would call illegal immigrants. Reverend Luis Cortes, who helped found the organization Hispanic Clergy of Philadelphia, does not like the label "illegal immigrants." He says it would be better if we referred to those brothers and sisters as "undocumented immigrants."

Some on the politically conservative side of our society say that we can't just allow all people who want to come across our borders to do so without any controls—and they are right. They say there needs to be what is called "a high wall" to make sure those who want to come here are not criminals or drug pushers or people with contagious diseases. There is merit in what they say. Nobody should be allowed to come into this country who has not had a background check. We ought to know whether or not a potential immigrant has a criminal record or is a drug pusher or a terrorist. We should have some evidence that he or she is going to make a positive contribution to our society. And this can be done. People who want to come here could be vetted at the embassies in their own countries before they cross the border and then, at points of entry, they should have to present documents showing that they are law-abiding people.

On the other hand, if we want to keep people from illegally coming into our country, we have to make it easier for them to enter legally. Presently, if a person wants to come to America and legally get a job, it may take as long as two or three years. Sometimes it requires huge fees for lawyers to get the government-issued green card necessary to be legally employed. Poor immigrants do not have the means to support themselves during that time of waiting, nor do they have the money to pay lawyers to handle the paperwork necessary to get the green cards. It should not come as any surprise, therefore, that so many circumvent the entire legal system and break across the border. The government should issue green cards immediately, once a person has been cleared for admission into our country.

There should be a wide gate for immigrants. We should be ready to welcome these people, not only for their sakes but for the good of our own country. America needs these immigrants. If you don't think so, try talking to farmers in the Southern border states.

SHANE: It's oppressive to feel like you are illegal, especially when you are doing everything, jumping through all the bureaucratic hoops, waiting month after month, trying to have all legal documentation in order.

One of my close friends in Philly is a Korean pastor named Taehoo Lee. He's on our board of directors for the Simple Way and is a hero in North Philadelphia who leads the best summer camps with hundreds of kids. He's an incredible guy who has been pouring himself out in some of the toughest neighborhoods in Philly for more than fifteen years. So this year he has gone through every legal process to stay here and keep doing the wonderful work he does in the city. Yet, he had to wait for months without hearing anything. He had great lawyers working with him. They told him that if he didn't hear something by a certain time, he was in danger of overstaying his visa. If he remained here, he would risk never coming back, for years, maybe ever. So he faced this decision: either stay here and risk it, possibly even get the green light—or cancel all his summer camps and pay thousands of dollars to go back to Korea where he has nothing. Leave his car, house, and all his stuff vacant (in the inner city) indefinitely. It's absurd. Eventually Taehoo was forced to cancel all camps and is now in Korea. He still has not heard when or even if he will be permitted back into the United States. His house was broken into and robbed recently, and he still waits.

This narrative and hundreds of similar ones get repeated every day. We had a Catholic nun from India who worked day after day with recovering drug addicts in Philadelphia who was just sent back home. All Taehoo and Sister Garetti want to do is pour their lives out as missionaries, loving God and neighbors, living off next to nothing and taking care of some of the most vulnerable people here. And both of them are sent away.

TONY: Jim Wallis was in a Presbyterian church in Arizona when he learned that the director of Christian education at the church, who was born in Mexico—brought across the border when she was an infant, grew up here, and went to college and seminary here before becoming a leader in her church—had just been informed that she is an illegal immigrant. She had had no idea she was an illegal immigrant. She is now going through the long process of trying to become a legal resident, and it's questionable whether she's going to be allowed to stay here in the United States.

SHANE: I think stories bring out the humanness of this issue. There are so many of them. I know folks waiting for their papers who are currently living without water and utilities. We know one old Salvadoran family who have lived the most incredible lives—lived deep, seen so much. Now they are treated like criminals.

So often we talk about the issues without the very people we talk about at the table. The problem is not that folks don't care about immigrants; it's that they don't know many immigrants. The more you hear the stories, the more you see that they are not just exceptions. Of course, the great irony is that if we just look back a couple of generations, we see some in our own family. We've developed amnesia, forgetting that most of us come from a lineage of immigrants.

TONY: My father came to this country and, according to the records from Ellis Island, he was vetted there to make sure that he was not a danger to the American people. Immigration officials made sure that he wasn't a criminal and did not have some dreaded disease. My father arrived here with thirty-five dollars in his pocket. The week after he arrived, he had a job and ended up being able to earn enough money to raise a family, buy a house, and share in the American dream. That's not possible anymore. Dad came at a time when the gate was very wide. Now America has made it narrow. When immigrants come, we want them to have sophisticated skills. We make room for someone who's a doctor, an engineer, or a scientist and, consequently, we exercise a brain drain on poor countries. America is no longer saying, "Give us your poor and your huddled masses," as inscribed on the base of the Statue of Liberty. These days, we are saying to disadvantaged countries, "Give us your PhDs, your engineers, your medical doctors, and, yes, we will take just a few of your poor people too."

SHANE: On Second Street in Philly, there's a mural right near the historic area, just a couple of blocks from the Liberty Bell and Constitution Center. The mural is thirty feet high and a hundred feet long, showing snapshots of the struggle for freedom here in the United States—civil rights, Dr. King, women, workers, farmers, and Native Americans. Then prominently under those images is the quote from the inscription on the Statue of Liberty:

> Give me your tired, your poor,
> Your huddled masses yearning to breathe free,
> The wretched refuse of your teeming shore;
> Send these, the homeless, tempest-tost to me,
> I lift my lamp beside the golden door!

There were some homeless folks who started sleeping underneath the mural (it's under an overpass, so it's dry), but it's in the historic district, which means lots of tourism. The city didn't want the huddled masses getting in the way of that, so they put a fence up around the mural to keep them from sleeping there.

TONY: You bring up the important point that there's a lot of horrible stuff being done to poor people, and we are not paying attention to it. It's going on right under our noses. It's going on in New Jersey, and it's going on in Pennsylvania, right around here where we live.

SHANE: I've been privileged to be able to get to know a group of Florida farm workers known as the Coalition of Immokalee Workers. They have been at the forefront of human rights issues, particularly as they relate to modern-day slavery. I've been down to Immokalee to visit them and have marched hundreds of miles by their side.

These workers have put faces on the issue of immigration and the ugly face of modern-day slavery and have won the hearts of so many people. Entire Christian denominations have joined their campaigns and occasional boycotts. In fact, they have had nearly a dozen major retailers join their campaign to end abuse of migrant workers.

The big issue now is that because some of the larger immigration issues have been more visible, the other injustices are hidden. They've seen three cases of modern-day slavery go to trial, and one of those was on behalf of people who were locked in the back of a Penske truck and forced to urinate in the corner of the enclosed vehicle since they were not free to leave. They were locked in at night, brought out in the day to work, and then put back in there. The other was a group of more than one hundred people who were imprisoned on land against their will. These folks were literally fenced in on the land, and it was only exposed when a man joined their group so he could escape and expose it. These cases went to trial, but it's impossible to know how many cases like this exist, in part because people are made to feel and act less than human because they are treated that way.

As Red Letter Christians, we need to ask who the human faces are. Issues like immigration and slavery are not about ideologies; they are about human beings made in the image of God. And sadly, we often have no idea who all the invisible faces are.

Dialogue on Civil Disobedience

Jesus said, "My kingdom is not of this world. If it were,
my servants would fight to prevent my arrest by the
Jews. But now my kingdom is from another place."

JOHN 18:36

TONY: Shane, you get a lot of support from people who say, "We need to speak truth to power," but they get upset when you practice civil disobedience. You're willing to get arrested when you believe that the government is not doing the will of God and needs to be opposed. I know you've been arrested on occasion, such as when you joined with the homeless who were being put in jail for sleeping on Philadelphia's sidewalks. When you slept on the sidewalks with them, you broke the law! How do you reconcile breaking the law and getting arrested with what the apostle Paul said in Romans 13:1–2? He wrote," Everyone must submit himself to the governing authorities, for there is no authority except that which God has established. The authorities that exist have been established by God. Consequently, he who rebels against the authority is rebelling against what God has instituted, and those who do so will bring judgment on themselves."

How do you take that passage of Scripture seriously and still believe that civil disobedience is an acceptable way to speak truth to power?

SHANE: Without a doubt, we need to submit to the authorities, but I think there are two different ways to do so. One is to obey the good laws and the other is to suffer the consequences of disobeying the bad laws.

It is our divine duty not to cooperate with evil. So Paul, who writes in Romans 13 that we are to obey the authorities, is the same Paul who says in Ephesians, "Our struggle is not against flesh and blood, but against the rulers, against the authorities, against the powers of this dark world and against the spiritual forces of evil in the heavenly realms" (Ephesians 6:12). He uses the exact same word—*authorities*. At some point you have to reconcile the fact that Paul, who submitted to the authorities, also got arrested for subverting the authorities.

TONY: I'm always amused by the fact that Paul wrote to tell the church at Rome to be subject to the higher powers while he was in jail—for disobeying the rules of the system.

SHANE: There is a Christian tradition of civil disobedience from the beginning. Moses' survival was an act of civil disobedience: his mama put him in a basket and floated him down the river in the middle of a state-sanctioned killing of babies. The Exodus story is God's Underground Railroad—it's God freeing the slaves from Egypt. There was a collision with power when Shadrach, Meshach, and Abednego disobeyed royal orders and were put in a fiery furnace. Daniel served in the king's court but didn't eat the royal food. Eventually his uncompromising allegiance to God landed him in the lions' den. The prophets were always speaking out as holy agitators. Jeremiah was jailed, John the Baptist got his head cut off, then all the way at the end of the story in Revelation, John got exiled to the island of Patmos. We have an entire history of holy troublemakers, so this issue is inescapable throughout the Scripture.

Jesus is born, similar to Moses, in the middle of what becomes genocide, as Herod kills little babies in the land. The Magi were basically told to go and tell Herod where Jesus was, but they were interrupted by angels in a dream that told them to go a different way. They practiced civil disobedience by not going back to Herod. Paul and Silas were in jail and, literally, angels broke in and set them free. The entire book of Philemon was written to a friend, saying he needed to take back a fugitive slave, not as a slave but as his brother. Philemon is about divine obedience in the face of slavery and injustice.

Then, of course, there's Jesus, who is one of the most spectacular examples of the kind of imagination we need in the face of injustice. Jesus is wonderfully subversive in his interaction with the tax collectors, pulling the taxes out of the mouth of a fish. He is silent before Herod, calling into question Herod's authority. Jesus is accused of subverting the authorities and claiming to be king. I think the reason for that was Jesus actually *was* subverting the authorities and claiming to be king. But he was holy and humble as he did it. Right in line with Ephesians 6, he wrestled the principalities and powers. Jesus nearly promises us that we will get into trouble for the gospel and will be dragged before courts. He basically says, "Don't be surprised when the world hates you; look what they did to me" (John 15:18). So we shouldn't be too surprised if our faithfulness to Jesus leads us to jail. If we look at history, we find ourselves in pretty good company.

When we talk about what the Scripture has to say about civil disobedience, it's important to note that it is never the goal of the people of God to break the law; it's the goal of the people to obey God. It's not just about civil disobedience but about divine obedience. There is a constant thread throughout Scripture, and throughout history, of good folks breaking bad laws.

The first-century Christians had times when they found it

necessary to practice civil disobedience. As you can read in Acts 5:29 (KJV), when the governmental authorities demanded that they stop their gospel preaching, their answer was, "We ought to obey God rather than men." And, as you know, they went right on doing their work of evangelism.

Elaine Pagels, in her book *Revelations*, describes how when Roman emperors tried to extinguish Christianity by making it an illegal religion, the early Christians went right on breaking the law by practicing their faith. She writes that the usually tolerant "philosopher emperor, Marcus Aurelius, who had no tolerance for Christianity, found that the power of the state could not prevent Christians from acts of civil disobedience as they spread the gospel far and wide."[1]

The early Christians were good at practicing divine obedience. As early historian Minucius Felix wrote, "They practice a cult of lust, for they call each other brother and sister indiscriminately and under the cover of these names fornication becomes incest."

Origen, another early historian, said in response to Celsus, "The Christians form among themselves secret societies that exist outside the systems of walls and obscure and mysterious community founded on revolt in the advantage that accrues from it."

As I look at the early church, I have this sense that every time they said, "Jesus is Lord," they were saying, "Caesar is not." It was a radical new definition of who they were; it is a confrontation to the powers, but it's a humble confrontation.

Throughout movements in history, there is a precedent for humble resistance. During the civil rights movement, Dr. King said repeatedly that we need good laws. You know, we need traffic laws, and a red light is a good thing, but when there is a fire raging, the ambulance has to run through the red light in order to put the fire out.

Sometimes urgent crises in our world demand that we go through the red lights in order to save those who are in danger. And we always do that with the humility of Christ.

TONY: Submitting to the authorities does not mean blind obedience. I agree with anyone who says, "An unjust law is no law at all."

Shane, how do you answer people who ask what the church should have been doing in Nazi Germany?

SHANE: Well, we should have been getting in the way of Hitler. Hitler came to power with the Bible in his hand, as much of the church stood by. But did God put Hitler into power? Certainly it is not God's will to have those in power who kill masses of people, but we have to look back to the origins of kingship and worldly power.

The Bible makes it clear that kings weren't God's idea, but ours. From the very beginning, when the first king was put in place, God didn't like the idea. Israel wasn't supposed to have a king, but they demanded one, so they got one. God told them explicitly that a king was going to oppress them, make them slaves, take all their money, and make them serve in his wars (1 Samuel 8). God said, "In my anger I gave you a king" (Hosea 13:11).

So are kings and political leaders ordained by God? Yes, because we demanded it, and so we continue to suffer from it. Just as there were good and bad kings in the Bible, there are good and bad governments today. But we are still called to be a distinct people from that; there are things in government that are always going to be out of line with God's heart.

I think America is a Christian nation only as much as it looks like Jesus. There are some things our nation does that I am proud of, and there are some things that make me deeply embarrassed and saddened as a Christian.

TONY: Exactly. We may live in the best Babylon in the world, but it is still Babylon. And we are called to "come out of her" (Revelation 18:4) and recognize that our ultimate citizenship belongs to another kingdom.

All the world's principalities and powers have a tendency to claim that they are doing the will of God. When they crucified Jesus, the religious establishment and the political leaders who put him there said essentially, "We're doing the will of God." They might have made pious claims, but how could they have been doing the will of God if they crucified his Son? A good look at Calvary is all we need to see that those in positions of power don't always do the will of God. If they did, Jesus would not have been nailed to the cross. That's why Paul wrote in Colossians that the crucifixion of Christ exposed the principalities and powers that nailed him to that old rugged cross as powers that served evil purposes, regardless of their claims to being the upholders of law and order (2:15).

SHANE: So is there a place for civil disobedience in the Christian tradition? Absolutely! Is there a place for wearing a mask and throwing a Molotov cocktail through a window? Absolutely not!

We have a great history of nonviolent resistance, but a peculiar way of fighting evil. We expose injustice by suffering with those who suffer. Dr. King said, "We must expose injustice and make injustice so uncomfortable that it has to be dealt with."

That's what the civil rights movement did: People saw unarmed people getting beaten, attacked by dogs, sprayed with water hoses—and all the evils of racism. Jesus did the same thing on the cross: He suffered nonviolently and experienced hatred and evil—and unmasked it. The apostle Paul says that Jesus made a spectacle of the powers and authorities on the cross (Colossians 2:15).

Mennonite theologian John Howard Yoder called this idea "revolutionary subordination."[2] Through suffering rather than armed conflict, we unmask evil and expose injustice. When my friends and I went to jail in Philadelphia for feeding the homeless and sleeping in the public parks, we raised huge questions about the rightness of the anti-homeless laws the city was passing. We were ultimately found not guilty. The judge even said, "If it weren't for people who broke the bad laws, we wouldn't have the freedom we have. We'd still have slavery. That's the story of this country from the Boston Tea Party to the civil rights movement. These folks are not criminals; they are freedom fighters." In fact, police officers even came to court to argue that the laws were wrong. And it was all because we broke bad laws and we openly and willingly suffered the consequences.

TONY: Similar to what you experienced in Iraq?

SHANE: As we came back from Iraq in 2003, we found that, indeed, we had broken the law. We were breaking US sanctions; our doctors, missionary doctors, took medicine to an enemy country. They said we could face up to twelve years in prison for violating those sanctions.

When we went to court, the first thing the judge said was, "Wow, this is a really difficult case! I think the state's got its challenges to prove this one!" We were willing to suffer for what we did, willing to go to jail for what we did, and it made people crazy. People were saying, "This is insane!" Even the judge said, "This is nuts!"

Instead of jail time, we ended up with a $20,000 fine, which we gladly paid in Iraqi dinar. This money would have been worth about $20,000 US dollars before the war but was worth about $8 US. I think of it as an act of winking at Caesar and of practicing revolutionary subordination. It takes creativity to face the unjust laws and the challenges of today.

We were looking to Martin Luther King Jr. and so many heroes throughout history who struggled for freedom. When it comes to submitting to the punishments of the government, or the "powers" as Paul calls them, nobody in modern times demonstrated this better than Dr. King. When he broke what he believed to be the unjust and unconstitutional laws of Alabama concerning the right to demonstrate against racism, he also presented himself for arrest and went to jail in Birmingham.

As King essentially said, "You can burn down our houses, and we will still love you. You can throw us in jail and squirt us with water hoses, and we will still love you! You can threaten the lives of our children, and we will still love you, but be assured that we will wear you down by our love!"[3] This is the story of our faith. As the early Christians said, "Grace is able to dull even the sharpest sword." That's the kind of movement that I want to be a part of.

TONY: This is also the exact thing Jesus taught in the Sermon on the Mount.

SHANE: Yes! He picked out some familiar scenarios. If someone is doing you wrong and evil, expose the injustice and make a spectacle of it. So if someone is suing you for your outer garment, take off all your clothes. This is a real thing: you could sue someone for the coat off their back. Expose their greed. Take off all your clothes and say, "You can have it all, but you can't take my dignity!" And I think that is what we are called to do. To expose that injustice with revolutionary subordination.

I teach the kids in my neighborhood that you can get in trouble for doing things that are wrong, and you can also get in trouble for doing things that are right. So the question is, are we doing things that honor God? Even if they collide with the kingdoms of this world? There are lots of bad laws that have existed throughout history, so just because it's legal doesn't make it right. It was legal to ban black folks from stores and from sitting in the fronts of buses, but that didn't make it right. It was legal to take people from Africa and make them slaves and treat them like animals, but that didn't make it right. It might have been legal to take this land from the Native Americans, but that didn't make it right. It may be legal to sell assault rifles in North Philadelphia, but that doesn't make it right. It may be legal to create weapons that can kill a hundred thousand people at one time, but that doesn't make it right. It might have been legal to nail our Lover and Savior to a cross, but that doesn't make it right.

TONY: Shane, I saw this revolutionary subordination during the Vietnam War, when I was teaching at the University of Pennsylvania. There were some student protesters who were pretty obscene and destructive in what they did. However, there were others who wanted to oppose the war and resist being drafted in ways that were decent and respectful. I remember three young men coming to me in distress, saying, "Professor, we have a problem. We think this war in Vietnam is immoral. In good conscience we cannot be a part of it, but all three of us have been given our selective service notices and are supposed to report for induction into the army. We are opposed to this war and don't want to support it by becoming soldiers, so we are considering leaving the country and going to Canada."

In response, I said, "If you are really going to be Christian about this, you *won't* go to Canada. You will present yourselves to the selective service office and say, 'Arrest us! We find this war to be immoral, but we are submitting ourselves to the jurisdiction of a government that says that it will punish anybody who violates the legal ruling that we must report for military service.'" I then explained why this was the only recourse for a Christian who believed as they did.

Those students did it! They went to jail because they believed that, according to Romans 13, they were required to submit to "the higher powers" (verse 1 KJV). They only stayed in jail for two days because what the government didn't want was good, upstanding Christian men behind bars, and the word getting out that these fine young people, out of conscience, were opposing the war. The government wanted all the protesters against the war to be seen as hippies throwing rocks through windows, blocking traffic and creating an uproar. They wanted only negative images of protestors, and certainly not any image of a protester standing behind bars and saying, "I am here in the name of Jesus Christ."

There is a place for righteous defiance, especially when the government calls for action that violates Christian values. Those young war resisters were making the point that you don't have to go along with the system. There may come a time when going along with the system is immoral, and the only thing you can do is stand up and say, "No!" That was what Shadrach, Meshach, and Abednego did in that Bible story in which they were told to worship Nebuchadnezzar's golden statue or be thrown into a fiery furnace. They said to the king, "We're going to do what God tells us to do, and when we are told to bow down and worship the king, we're going to say no! And if you throw us into the fire, maybe God will deliver us—or maybe God won't deliver us. But regardless of what God does, we still have to say no!" (Daniel 3:16–18, paraphrased).

SHANE: Or Daniel. There are prophets who are voices in the wilderness such as John the Baptist, and then there are prophets who turn up right in the imperial courts, such as Daniel. Daniel tasted from the king's food. His philosophy was basically, "I'm gonna serve in the king's court but I'm not gonna drink the king's Kool-Aid." He protected his soul. And he got in trouble.

We can have any job as long as we're willing to get fired at any point for not compromising our faith or our conscience. And of course, some jobs make that difficult. Like working at a porn shop.

But what about military service? Or working for a weapons contractor or a company that continually abuses human rights overseas or destroys the environment? What's a Christian to do?

For the early Christians, baptism meant you were a new creation. The old life was dead, drowned, and you arose as a new person. That also meant a new career sometimes, if one was a sculptor of idols, worked in the gladiator games, or served in the military.

We live in a much more liberal society that wants to try to make all things work together, but sometimes they just don't. It's impossible to know exactly what Jesus would do if he lived in the United States rather than first-century Rome. But I can't help but think he'd find a way to creatively critique the priorities of the empire in which we live, just as he critiqued the empire in which he lived. Rome and the United States share some things in common, including that their biggest budget item is military spending. We need only to look at the courage of the early Christian rebels to see what it looks like to be faithful to Christ in the belly of the empire. They refused to bow down to money. They insisted on dying instead of killing. They refused to pledge allegiance to anything except Christ, including Rome and Caeser. And they, like Jesus, were accused of treason and insurrection (Luke 23:2). Their identity in Christ trumped their national identity. Their faithfulness to Christ came before their obedience to Caeser—even if it put them behind bars or cost them their lives. And it often did.[4]

Dialogue on Giving

Take heed that ye do not your alms
before men, to be seen of them.

MATTHEW 6:1 KJV

SHANE: A study I just saw showed that young people are giving less than ever before to the church. But a second finding of the study showed that young people are the most generous generation to ever live.[1] We are outgiving our parents and grandparents, but we don't trust the church with our money. This raises all sorts of good questions.

Because we've grown up with the Internet, we have a pretty clear sense of the desperate economic disparity in our world. The world has shrunk, and now we are able to know what's happening in Sudan and Syria at any given time. Minutes after a catastrophe like a tsunami or earthquake or hurricane, we can survey the damage and start looking for ways to help in places like Haiti and Indonesia.

But that also means we see the disparity between the rich and the poor. We see the contradictions: people are dying in Africa because they don't have three-dollar mosquito nets that would prevent malaria, while church congregations argue about whether or not they need a water heater for the baptismal.

Naturally many young Christians are giving far more to nonprofits and NGOs than they are to the church because they want to make a difference in the world and aren't sure the church is the best steward of their money to achieve that end.

TONY: If Jesus had a choice between spending money on a stained glass window or feeding starving kids in Haiti, which would he choose? The church has been somewhat irresponsible in spending its money, and young people know that. Søren Kierkegaard, as he sat in a cathedral, said, "All this money to build buildings to honor somebody who said, 'I dwell not in temples made with hands.'"

Jim Wallis, founder of *Sojourners*, believes that a budget is a moral document, and when you look at a church budget, you know what that church is about and what it values. In most cases, you will find that church budgets show that churches are self-centered. The reality is, many churches spend little on anybody or anything outside the church. If you look over almost any church budget, you will probably find that the church is paying its bills and taking care of its own needs. It has been said that the church should be the only club in the world that should exist for the benefit of its nonmembers. Few church budgets give evidence of that.

SHANE: There's a good study on church stewardship called the Empty Tomb project. It is an annual report that comes out each year to show how the church is spending money, broken down by denomination. Basically, it lets folks know where their money goes. Nearly every year, more and more money is being spent internally, on things like staff and building maintenance. Across the board, more than 90 percent of the church offerings we give on Sunday mornings stay inside the building (some denominations have as little as 2 percent going toward external, missional needs). This is the antithesis of what the early church was doing. In the book of Acts, it says that the offerings were put at the feet of the apostles and were distributed to folks as there was need (4:35).

TONY: It's no wonder then that young people see what churches spend their money on and say, "I don't think this is what Jesus would spend money on." Then celebrities like Bono come along and call people to respond to the needs of the poor. That really strikes a chord with them.

If I go to a youth conference and ask how many are willing to spend thirty-five dollars a month to support a needy child in a developing country through faith-based organizations like Compassion International or World Vision, I'll get a much better response than if I ask the same of a large group of wealthy adults. Young people want to give their money where it will make a difference for poor people. Unfortunately, it's not the church.

SHANE: A theologian friend, Ray Mayhew, did a study of the biblical tithes and offerings, tracking them from the Hebrew Scriptures to the New Testament. What he discovered is that we have done a terrible disservice to God's original intention, which was to create a system for redistribution of wealth for the care of the poor.[2]

At the Simple Way, our studies of biblical economics have been a catalyst for us, sparking new projects. One of those we call the Relational Tithe, where Christians around the world give a tithe—10 percent of their income—into a fund, and 100 percent of that goes to meet needs of friends and neighbors. Basically, we decided not to pick on the rest of the church but to try to get the log out of our own eye. After all, the best critique of a wrong thing is the practice of something better. It's not perfect, but it's an exciting project that is anchored in good theology, inspired by the early church, and has substance to it. A few weeks ago, my buddy who lives across the street got his tires slashed and his window smashed. I brought the need before the Relational Tithe community I'm part of, and we were able to carry that burden with him and fix his car.

He was so moved by that, he now wants to join. This is just one way we can put flesh on the gospel we proclaim with our mouths and model what the early church was doing—living out a community that fascinated folks by the way they shared and loved people.

Even though studies show the contrary, more and more churches are becoming the exception and creating similar relational tithe funds or common pools that can meet needs as they arise. I know some who have felt compelled by the call to love our neighbors as ourselves in such a way that for every dollar they spend internally, they make sure a dollar goes externally—to dig wells in Africa or repair the local school around the corner. Other congregations have decided to do Jubilee campaigns[3] alongside their capital campaigns, where they can match the money they are raising internally with money they share around the world. I have a lot of hope.

There's a big congregation in Michigan that said, as they started to build a new building, "We're not sure that this is exactly where we should be putting all of our resources," so they declared a Jubilee year. They put the building on hold and gave $400,000 away to alleviate extreme poverty. They still went on to start construction the following year, but I can't help but think God was happy with how they did that. It's not an absolute either/or, but if you're going to have a capital campaign, consider throwing a Jubilee alongside it.

TONY: Oswald Smith, the founder of the People's Church in Toronto, Canada, challenged his people to support missionary work. For every dollar they spent on keeping their church going, they spent a dollar on missionary work, particularly among the poor. That church has earned a great reputation, I think, to a large extent because of its commitment to spending on missions to the poor.

SHANE: Some folks would argue, "Well, how are they going to sustain the institution?" I think that's an interesting question. We have some things to learn from bivocational pastors. It is common for pastors in the inner city and around the world to have other skills that help pay the bills. The pastors in my neighborhood are also electricians and carpenters. In the Bible, Paul was a tentmaker, Peter was a fisherman, and Jesus was a carpenter. We may need to do that out of necessity since so many denominations hemorrhage economically trying to sustain salaries for pastors who may only have a handful of parishioners. There's also something to be said for the way Catholics have lived together in community, taking vows of poverty as clergy and church leaders. That helps make things more sustainable, especially when you add to that a small business like making candles or wine, which monks are also good at.

We could also take some cues from Alcoholics Anonymous, whose organization states, "We will not have paid staff, we will not own buildings. This is a fellowship that's organic and we meet in basements and parks." It's decentralized, unprofessionalized, wonderfully redemptive, and sounds similar to another movement—the early church.

TONY: That's a good point, as churches don't always need buildings. In China, there are few church buildings, and the churches that do have buildings tend to be state-controlled churches that, in terms of winning converts, are the least effective. The most effective churches, on the other hand, are "house churches" where the people share what they have with one another and try to live out their faith with a deep commitment to sacrificial giving. According to the Center for World Missions in Pasadena, California, the result has been that the number of Christians in China has grown from 900,000 in 1945 to almost 80 million today. This explosive growth came because they are vital, living, and giving churches.

Kierkegaard has another story that I think is worth remembering here.

SHANE: We quote him so much we should actually list brother Søren as a coauthor.

TONY: He said, "I went into a church in Copenhagen and sat on a cushioned pew. The velvet-robed minister opened a gilded Bible, marked the place for his reading with a satin marker, and, as the sunlight streamed through the stained glass windows behind him, he read, 'If any man would be my disciple, let him deny himself and take up the cross and follow me.'" Then Kierkegaard said, "I looked around the church and nobody was laughing!" He was emphasizing the ludicrous nature of us talking about a Jesus who calls upon us to sacrifice for the poor and then spending so much money on church edifices.

Whenever we discuss money among Christians, someone questions sacrificing the good life in light of Jesus' quote: "The poor you will always have with you, and you can help them any time you want. But you will not always have me" (Mark 14:7).

SHANE: It's important to remember the context of that verse. Jesus is surrounded by the poor and marginalized. According to at least one of the gospels, Jesus is in the home of Simon the leper when a woman who has been terribly shunned comes in and pours perfume on his feet (Mark 14:3). The poor are literally around him. As the disciples get upset about the value of the perfume, Jesus scolds them (after all, we see what Judas did with money when he sold a brother out for thirty shekels of silver). They are concerned more about money than people, especially the one right before them.

So sometimes, we hear folks say, "The poor will always be with us," as a way of excusing ourselves from action, a way of saying, "We really need to be concerned about saving souls, not about poverty, because Jesus said the poor will always be here." But a better reading of the text would be: "We will always be with the poor." We must ask, "Where then are the poor? Are they among us?" We find ourselves far from the suffering that Jesus was so near to because of bad theology.

Notice also that Jesus is quoting, word for word, Deuteronomy 15, which begins with God saying, "There should be no poor among you" (verse 4). And God gives commandments on how we are to care for the poor and welcome the alien and the stranger. The church should be with the poor, and they should be among us as they were with Jesus.

In fact, the next statement in Deuteronomy after "There will always be poor people in the land" (15:11) is this: "Therefore I command you to be openhanded toward your brothers and toward the poor and needy in your land." Jesus is not excusing us from action; he is calling us to action. Poverty is our responsibility.

Of course, James went so far as to say: "Religion that God our Father accepts as pure and faultless is this: to look after orphans and widows and to keep oneself from being polluted by the world" (James 1:27).

TONY: I also have to pick up what our friend John Perkins had to say about what Jesus said to the rich young ruler in Mark 10: "Go sell everything you have and give to the poor" (verse 21). John believes Jesus was saying that not only because the poor needed help but also because he knew what giving to the poor would do for the rich young ruler. It would change him.

Few things transform us more than giving to the poor, because as we encounter them, we often sense that we are encountering Jesus himself *in* them. When we give to the poor, we are likely to feel that we are giving to Christ much more directly than when we put our money in the offering plate at church. This is not to discount giving to the church. That's important. But not as important as giving to the poor. There's no way to come up with a formula for how a Christian should break down what percentage of his or her giving should be set aside to give to the church and what percentage should be set aside for the poor. Such decisions about giving must be made individually after we scrutinize our church budgets to ascertain how responsibly our churches are spending their financial resources.

The important question you have to ask about giving is this: are you spending your money the way Jesus would want it spent? For instance, do you have an expensive car? Couldn't you buy a second-hand car for a fraction of the cost that would get you around just as well? It may not be as comfortable and it might not be quite the status symbol that a BMW or a Mercedes would be, but you would have all that leftover money to use to meet the needs of others. Consider other lifestyle questions: Do you really need all those rooms in your house? How many dress suits do you really need? How many pairs of shoes do you need? Jesus said, "He that hath two coats, let him impart to him that hath none" (Luke 3:11 KJV). Was he really telling us that it is wrong to have a surplus of such things when others are in need?

SHANE: Surplus not only hurts the poor but also those who are rich. In the Gospels, it's interesting that the rich man starts by asking Jesus about how to find life. If you look at the richest corners of the world, they have the highest rates of loneliness, suicide, and depression. Some of the richest folks in the world end up the saddest. I'm not just talking about celebrities. Ordinary folks around the world are asking, *Where can I find life, love, contentment?* And here's the great paradox: if you want to find your life, you've got to give it away. The way to become free of possessions is to start giving them away. Otherwise they own us. And we find, as Mother Teresa said, "The more we have, the less we can give."[4]

Salvation is often manifested by the release of possessions. It's not a prescription for salvation but a description of salvation. When we are born again, we want to share! We realize we have siblings we didn't know about, and many of them are suffering deeply.

Zacchaeus is another good example of a rich man, a tax collector who meets Jesus and gives half his stuff away to the poor. And Jesus celebrates with him, saying, "Today salvation has come to this house" (Luke 1:9). We don't even know if Zacchaeus said a prayer, but we do know he met Jesus and it transformed his economics. He was set free. And so was his family.

TONY: Jesus tells Zacchaeus essentially, "Let's go to your house and celebrate! Let's have a party!" There's always room for celebration in the context of fulfilling your responsibility to the poor. The message is simple: good stewardship requires that each of us should consider the financial resources that each of us enjoys, spend 10 percent on celebrations, as Deuteronomy tells us to do (14:22–27), and then ask ourselves, "How would Jesus spend this money?" Where we put our treasure is where our hearts are. That will reveal the level of our commitments.

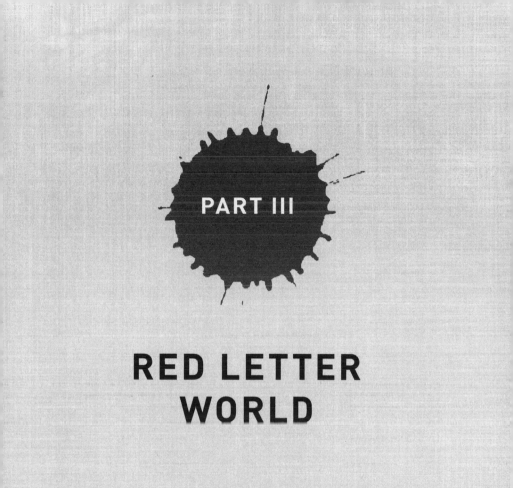

PART III

RED LETTER WORLD

Dialogue on Empire

My kingdom is not of this world.

JOHN 18:36

TONY: Shane, you use the word *empire* a lot when referring to America. What do you mean and why do you use it?

SHANE: I talk about empire because Jesus talked about empire. Nearly every time Jesus opened his mouth, he talked about the "kingdom"—the kingdom of God. But that word *kingdom* was the same word we translate "empire." Jesus pulls much of his language out of the imperial lexicon of his day—he uses images of power and spins them on their heads. Thrones. Banners. Lord. Gospel. Savior. Crowns. These were all images used long before Jesus, but they were used for the Roman Empire and for Caesar. There was already an empire in the land, but Jesus was proclaiming another one. That's the kind of stuff that gets you in trouble.

There are so many things that God's counter-imperial gospel has to say to us in America. We have an arsenal of weapons that is more than that of the rest of the world's combined. We have a small percentage of the world's population, 5 percent, but we use up about half the world's stuff.[1] In many ways, America is the envy of the world, as was Rome. It's not that America is the same empire as Rome or Babylon, but there are many similarities. We don't have statues of Caesar, but we have Mount Rushmore. We don't have the same idols of empires past, but we have new ones. We see patterns of inequality in our empire that look a lot like the injustices that outraged Jesus and the prophets.

So when we see Jesus talk about an alternative empire to Rome, it's wonderful and entirely relevant. We hear Jesus say, "I bring peace, but not the way Rome brings it" (Matthew 10:34). Those words resonate with a world that has grown tired of America's wars. We see Jesus criticize the way the rulers of the world "lord over one another" (Mark 10:42), and we are mystified as we watch him stoop down and wash feet—it's hard to imagine a politician doing that. As he rides a donkey into the Passover celebration, he makes a lampoon of power. Kings didn't ride donkeys. It's like the president riding a unicycle to his inauguration. And, of course, Jesus' crown was made of thorns. His entire life and teaching is full of political satire.

Sometimes folks hear the anti-empire message and mistakenly take it to mean anti-America. I don't think Jesus is anti-Rome or anti-America, but he is pro-world. He is challenging us to a deeper identity. God continually invites us to be "set apart," which is what the word *holy* means (Hebrews 10:10). We are to come out of the empire and become a new kind of nation—a global, transnational, wonderful people, a beloved community whose identity and whose home is in Christ.

One of the final images we have in Scripture is the call to come out of Babylon. We have a new identity—a new "we." "We the people" is bigger than our nation.

There was an entire theology behind the empire in Rome. America has something similar. George W. Bush said this in his 2003 State of the Union speech, "There's power—wonder-working power—in the goodness and idealism and faith of the American people."[2] Putting "the faith of the

American people" in where the old gospel hymn places "the blood of the Lamb" is dangerous theology. And in 2007, Barack Obama said on the David Letterman show: "This country is still the last best hope on earth." This is dangerous theology that sounds very much like that of empires before us.

As Christians, we have a different way of hoping. Our hope does not rest in the markets or on Wall Street. Our hope is not America. No, we have found the light of the world and the true last best hope on earth—and it is Jesus. Interestingly enough, the early Christians were called "atheists" because they had lost their faith in Rome and put it in Christ. But that was misunderstood and many were charged with treason—you dare not lose "faith" in Caesar, as he was the one who folks thought held the world together. All security rested in his armies. But not so with us: we have placed all faith and hope, and all security, in the hands of God. God doesn't need our guns to bring the kingdom.

TONY: The book of Revelation is often used by certain preachers to predict the future. Some of them claim to have figured out what those strange creatures found in that book represent. You know, like the angel with six wings that had eyes covering his entire body. Such preachers relate these images to events in our contemporary society, and their common mantra is, "We're living in the last days! We are living in Laodicea." They see Laodicea, a city spoken about in the book of Revelation, as a symbol of the decadence of our country and the lukewarmness of the church that will be evident just before Jesus returns.

What we read in the book of Revelation deserves another interpretation. The book challenges us to live countercultural, Red Letter Christian lives (Revelation 18–19). Almost all biblical scholars would agree that this book was a help to the early church, which was having a hard time trying to figure out how Christians should live in the context of the Roman Empire—how to remain faithful to Christ in the midst of it.

There is little question among biblical scholars that, when the early Christians used the word *Babylon*, it was a code word for the Roman Empire.[3] When they said Babylon was decadent and going to fall, they meant that the Roman Empire was decadent and about to fall. By using a code name, those early Christians hoped to escape punishment for being disloyal to the Roman Empire. Once we understand this use of the word *Babylon*, Revelation 18 and 19 become incredibly relevant to us in our contemporary societies.

Today, the code word *Babylon* still refers to any dominant society in which any Christian community finds itself. If you are part of the Christian community in France, your Babylon is France. If you are part of the Christian community in Brazil, your Babylon is Brazil. You and I are citizens of the United States of America. Our dominant societal system is the United States of America. Consequently, our Babylon is the United States of America. Don't get me wrong. I love our country. I believe it's the best Babylon on the face of the earth! But it's still Babylon. It's not the kingdom of God. Revelation 18 and 19 are about every Babylon before the Roman Empire and every Babylon since.

First of all, the Scriptures tell us that Babylon is doomed to fall (Revelation 18:2). Sooner or later, every Babylon collapses. You don't have to be Bill Gaither to sing, "Kings and kingdoms shall all pass away."[4] All the kingdoms of this world are going to pass away, including the kingdom we call the United States of America. To say otherwise is to say that our nation is the Reich that will last for a thousand years, and that is to make our nation somehow eternal and immortal, which is idolatry.

When our Babylon does fall, as Revelation says that it will, there will be two consequences to the fall. The first will be that the merchants will weep because everything in which they have invested will be gone (Revelation 18:11–15). When the socioeconomic system to which they had been committed collapses, they will have lost everything that gave meaning to their lives. The Bible explains that the system will fall because "no one buys their cargoes any more" (Revelation 18:11). If our business establishments don't want to believe that people in other countries will no longer buy what is produced in America, then at least they should consider that even we Americans are no longer buying America's cargoes. If people want to argue with that, they just need to check the labels in their shirts. They were not made in the United States. You don't have to be an economist to understand that when America can't sell what it produces, our socioeconomic system will collapse.

The second thing that will happen when Babylon collapses is that it will exhaust nonrenewable resources at an incredible rate. For two verses, Revelation just lists them—wood, ivory, silver, gold, oil, precious wood, brass, iron—and the list goes on and on. This Scripture points out that ultimately such an exhausting consumption destroys any Babylon (Revelation 18:12–13). Christians need to read and take what is written there as a warning. Those nonrenewable resources are not bad things. We need them to live, but we can exhaust them.

After considering what's happening in America these days, it is easy to conclude that like the Babylon described in Revelation 18 and 19, America will also collapse. Does it make any sense to invest our lives in a societal system that is going to collapse, or rather should we disengage from the lifestyle prescribed by this "Babylonian Empire" and invest all that we are and have into God's kingdom, which will never pass away?

SHANE: God calls us out of Babylon and the image of this in Revelation is literally a sexual image of adultery, showing that we are literally commiting adultery against God with the powers and the markets of this world. Babylon is described as the "great whore" or the "great prostitute" (Revelation 19:2). The merchants of the earth have committed adultery with her, and the command is to come out.

One theologian looked at the sexual language and said it transliterates as *coitus interruptus*, "pull yourself out of her."[5] Stop committing adultery with Babylon the seductress.

It's important to note that Babylon does allure us. There is a splendor, a charm, a fascination. America is also mesmerizing and beautiful. But we have to be careful that we do not settle for counterfeit splendor that falls short of God.

At one point, Revelation even says that Babylon offers her cup, which conjures up the Statue of Liberty–type image (16:19). But the cup is filled with the blood of the saints, of the people who have died because of her (Revelation 17:6). It's almost the exact opposite of the Eucharist cup. The blood of the Lamb. The cup Babylon offers is filled with the blood of those killed by her, and the cup of Jesus is filled with his own blood to end all bloodshed.

I love that image! It's as though the grand conclusion of Scripture is being written by John in exile and is riddled with anti-imperial images that provoke our imagination. And they invite us to come out of Babylon and to write the next chapters of God's story. These new chapters won't be in the Bible, but they will be the continuing story of a God who is calling people to be salt and light, to be a different kind of people.

TONY: Our consumption level as Americans is so astronomically high that there obviously are not enough resources to sustain our affluent lifestyles and, at the same time, supply what the rest of the world requires in order to meet its basic needs.

According to the most recent studies, we will reach a crisis point with our access to non-renewable resources by May 7, 2062.[6] When that happens, there will be a fall of our Babylon, and those who have invested in our Babylon will indeed weep.

The good news is that Revelation 19 begins with words of celebration. When Babylon falls, in addition to the weeping merchants, another group of people shout out, "Hallelujah! Hallelujah! The great whore is no more!" (verse 3). These are the people who have lived out the red letters of the Bible.

Babylon is called a whore because the system is so seductive. Whores seduce. No one will question that the American socioeconomic system is overpoweringly seductive. Its merchants, through their ingenious marketing techniques, seduce us to crave their cargoes. Their advertising not only lures those of us who have money; it also seduces those who are poor. The streets of Philadelphia have poor kids robbing and killing because TV ads have convinced them that they must have Nike sneakers and other "must have" things.

SHANE: That's part of it, but there's much more. The system sells us whatever we're not, as if we are incomplete without it. Poor kids want to look rich. And rich kids want to look poor. Kids in the inner city want to look rich, so they've got gold, they've got cell phones, they've got new cars that they've leased. And yet in the suburbs, you can tell who the richest kids are because they look the grungiest. It costs so much to look so poor. You can buy ripped jeans for a hundred bucks. I just saw shirts that have built-in coffee stains—brand-new shirts with coffee spills—that sell for seventy-five dollars. So poor kids are sold riches, and rich kids are sold rags. And so it goes. The myth that we must buy something to be something.

TONY: Given what Babylon had done to its people, it is understandable that the citizens of God's kingdom, along with the angels, sing "Hallelujah!" when Babylon falls. They rejoice because the seductive system with its consumptive lifestyle and its exploitive forms of economics is no more. Such celebration is possible for two reasons. First, Babylon will no longer be able to seduce the world's people into her destructive lifestyles. Second, all they have invested in will have survived this fall of Babylon. They will have laid up their treasures in heaven. They will have spent their lives doing those things that have eternal significance. They will have chosen to invest their lives in that other kingdom—the kingdom of God.

In light of this, we have to ask ourselves, "Of which kingdom am I going to be a citizen? Will I be part of the kingdom that the Bible calls 'Babylon,' or will I commit myself to the new kingdom that Christ is creating?" These questions are especially poignant to students as they graduate and have to decide where they are going to invest their lives. They have to decide whether they will end up weeping with the merchants or singing "Hallelujah!" with the people of God.

SHANE: We still have to remember that Babylon's story doesn't just end with the destruction of everything; it ends with the coming of the New Jerusalem, the City of God.

TONY: One day the kingdoms of this world will be displaced by the kingdom of our God, and he shall reign forever and ever. It's so important to remember that when we're in danger of overemphasizing the power of America and being enamored by American symbolism. So often, when I go into a church, I see a Christian flag on one side of the altar and the American flag on the other side. I like much better the church in South Philadelphia that displays flags for every single nation of the world around the sides of the sanctuary. They do this to recognize that in Christ we are all brought together. They are trying to declare, with this array of flags, the message that Christ makes us one people. Theirs is a house of worship for all nations.

I have concerns about having the flag of any one nation at the front of a church. Isn't church a place where we are to declare our citizenship in a new kingdom that embraces all humanity as one people in Christ? The Bible says that in Christ there is neither Jew nor Greek, bond nor free, Scythian nor Barbarian, male nor female (Galatians 3:28). That oneness in Christ should be evident in each and every church.

Once I was driving to the Atlanta airport when I passed two churches that had wooden crosses on their front lawns, each with American flags draped over them. To me, that's scary. When the American flag replaces Jesus on the cross, something has gone wrong. I love this country, but I give Christ the preeminence. I don't want God and country to be so merged that one does not know where Christianity ends and patriotism begins. We are called by Scripture to be good citizens. There is no question about that. But we are not called to go so far as one of our most noted patriots went when he said, "Our country! In her intercourse with foreign nations may she always be in the right; but right or wrong, our country!"[7] That kind of nationalistic patriotism is idolatry. It would be better to say, "Our country! May she always be right; but when she is wrong I will do my best to make her right."

SHANE: I heard one theologian say that an idol is anything we will die for, kill for, and sacrifice our children for. I'd say, given that definition, any flag can certainly become an idol.

Same with other symbols. For the early Christians, it was Caesar, not God, on their money. We've done just the opposite. We've tried to make America the bride of Christ rather than the church. We've tried to baptize America. There is a whole theological backdrop to the mystique of America, American exceptionalism,[8] manifest destiny—it certainly gets confusing. God's name is on America's money, and America's flag is on God's altar in many churches.

Patriotism is dangerous because it can create tunnel vision, where we act as if our people are more valuable than other people just because of their geographical proximity to us or because of the color of their skin or the language they speak. We protect our families or our nation with an idolatrous fervor. I would also suggest that this is exactly what Jesus is hinting at when he tells the disciples they must forsake their own families in order to follow him (Luke 14:26). We must have a love that is far bigger than the myopic love of biology, tribe, ethnicity, or nation.

It's about identity. And when we come to Christ, we become a new creation. I remember hearing one story when I was in Rwanda. The Hutu militia came into one of the classrooms in a Christian school. They burst in and asked all the kids to line up on opposite walls according to their tribes, undoubt-edly so that they could massacre the Tutsi kids. But one kid stood up and said, "We do not have Hutu and Tutsi; we only have Christian. We are all sisters and brothers." And all the class stood together. The gospel gives us new eyes. Any ethnic or national identity can be dangerous if it trumps our identity as brothers and sisters in Christ.

TONY: That's what happened in Nazi Germany. Every nation has a tendency to make itself sacred, to elevate itself to divine status. Young men and women who would be reluctant to give their lives without reservation to Christ and his kingdom are willing to go to war and literally give their lives for their country. There's nothing wrong with loving your country so much that you are willing to stand up for it, even at the cost of your life; but your commitment to Christ should transcend that. I have seen parents who are proud when their children go off to die for America but who would be furi-ous if their kids wanted to go to Africa or Asia as missionaries.

When Christians say that America is the last great hope for the world, they are contradicting the message of Jesus who offers himself as the hope of the world. We should stand up against that kind of thinking. Too many of our fellow Christians believe we have an obligation to go to other parts of the world to do nation building, which usually means making other nations just like ours. They don't understand that as wonderful as America is, we do not have the right to impose what we are on others. When we use military might to do that, the consequences can be disastrous. As a case in point, many American Christians thought our government was doing the right thing by trying to create democracy in Iraq. Instead, America's intervention there during the Iran-Iraq war of the 1980s ended up creating a totalitarian regime.

Democracy, I've told my students time and time again, is not a society in which the majority rules but a society where it is safe to be in the minority. Americans are inclined to think that a democracy is created when every citizen has the right to vote, and that is an erroneous concept. In 2005, following the execution of Iraq's dictator, Saddam Hussein, there was an open and free election in Iraq. The Shiite majority won and went on to establish an Islamic republic. Now, for the first time in the history of Iraq, Christians are being persecuted and churches in Baghdad are being burned down. Previously, Christian Iraqis lived in peace with other Iraqi citizens and were free to practice their faith and even evangelize. I like to point out that prior to the second Gulf War, I had an invitation from the vice president of Iraq who served under Saddam Hussein and was a Christian, to come and conduct evangelistic services. Back then, there was freedom of religion. But now that the Shiites have won control of the country by means of a free election, that freedom of religion is curtailed and Christians are being persecuted. The rejoicing over the end of Saddam Hussein's oppressive dictatorship has been muted by what has been happening to their Christian brothers and sisters.

Iraq has gone from about 1.5 million Christians down to about 500,000.[9] The number of Christians has been cut by around two thirds. They are fleeing to Jordan and other places outside of Iraq, seeking refuge. Some of these Christian refugees are living on the verge of starvation because Jordan can't feed them. The Jordanians don't have enough jobs for their own people, let alone for the hundreds of thousands of refugees who have fled there. All of this has happened in the name of America's good intention of trying to create a democracy in Iraq.

We've got to stop trying to export who we are to other nations. We must recognize the sovereignty of other nations and not go around believing that we have a messianic calling to make other nations into what we are.

We don't realize what a rich tradition we have here in this country. One of the reasons I love America is because when we have an election and the majority wins, the minority doesn't have to worry that the majority will organize to persecute them. Iraq shows us the results when that is not the case. We may live in the best Babylon in the world, but only because all the other political and economic systems are so much worse.

Dialogue on Politics

Give back to Caesar what is Caesar's,
and to God what is God's.

MATTHEW 22:21

TONY: Shane, I have a question to ask that may make you squirm a little bit. From hearing you talk and reading your books, you often seem to suggest that Christians not participate in the political process, and that political activism is somewhat futile.[1] Have I understood your position correctly?

SHANE: The question for me is not *are* we political, but *how* are we political? We need to be politically engaged, but peculiar in how we engage. Jesus and the early Christians had a marvelous political imagination. They turned all the presumptions and ideas of power and blessing upside down.

The early Christians felt a deep collision with the empire in which they lived, and with politics as usual. They carelessly crossed party lines and built subversive friendships. And we should do that too. To be nonpartisan doesn't mean we're non-political. We should refuse to get sucked into political camps and insist on pulling the best out of all of them. That's what Jesus did—challenge the worst of each camp and pull out the best of each. That's why we see Essenes, Zealots, Herodians,

Pharisees, and Sadducees all following Jesus and even joining his movement. But they had to become new creations. They had to let go of some things. Jesus challenged the tax-collecting system of Rome and the sword of the Zealots.

So to answer the question, I engage with local politics because it affects people I love. And I engage in national politics because it affects people I love.

Governments can do lots of things, but there are a lot of things they cannot do. A government can pass good laws, but no law can change a human heart. Only God can do that. A government can provide good housing, but folks can have a house without having a home. We can keep people breathing with good health care, but they still may not really be alive. The work of community, love, reconciliation, restoration is the work we cannot leave up to politicians. This is the work we are all called to do. We can't wait on politicians to change the world. We can't wait on governments to legislate love. And we don't let policies define how we treat people; how we treat people shapes our policies.

TONY: So you are not calling for noninvolvement in politics. Instead, you are warning Christians not to put their trust totally in political powers. You are calling them to exercise an ongoing involvement with the political process, to constantly speak truth to power in those places where power seems to be asserting itself in ways that are contrary to the will of God.

SHANE: Our goal is to seek first the kingdom of God. What would it look like if Jesus were in charge of my block, of our city, of our country, our world? That's what we get to imagine when we dream dreams of the kingdom on earth. And we get some pretty good glimpses of what that looks like from the Gospels: the poor are blessed and the rich are sent away empty, the mighty are cast from their thrones, the lowly are lifted, the peacemakers and the meek are blessed, and the proud-hearted are scattered (Luke 1:51–53).

And we'll work with anyone who wants to work with us as we try to get to the kingdom—whether that looks like reducing poverty or eliminating abortions, doing something meaningful for the environment, changing bad laws, or trying to make sure the most vulnerable are cared for.

But we do have a peculiar way in which we hope. When I see posters with Barack Obama's name with the word *hope* under it, I cringe. We are setting ourselves up for disappointment if our hope is built on anything less than Jesus.

So when it comes to voting, I look at it not as a place to put our hope but a battle with the principalities and powers of this world. Voting is damage control. We try to decrease the amount of damage being done by those powers. And for the Christian, voting is not something we do every four years. We vote every day. We vote by how we spend money and what causes we support. We vote by how much gas we use and what products we buy. We align ourselves with things all the time. We pledge allegiance every day with our lives. The question is, Do those things line up with the upside-down kingdom of our God—where the poor, the meek, the merciful, the peacemakers are declared "blessed"?

TONY: We have talked about taxes, about funding the empire, and how people often quote to me the verse that gives Jesus' thoughts on whether we should pay. In that passage of Scripture, you recall, Jesus requested a coin and then asked, "Whose portrait is this? And whose inscription?" When the answer given was that it was "Caesar's," he said, "Give to Caesar what is Caesar's and unto God what is God's" (Mark 12:13–17). Tell me how you interpret that in the context of the kingdom of God.

SHANE: There are two occasions when the authorities inter-rogated Jesus regarding taxes. On one occasion, he borrowed a coin. (The fact that he did not have one is significant.) He asked the interrogators whose image was on that coin, and then said, "Give to Caesar what is Caesar's" (Matthew 22:21). On the other occasion, he instructed Peter to go catch a fish, telling him the fish would have a four-drachma coin in its mouth for the tax collectors (Matthew 17:27). (Try that on Tax Day!)

Both of these stories are usually interpreted as proof that Christians must simply submit to the authorities and give Caesar whatever he asks of us (notably with little regard of whether Caesar is a dictator or elected, evil or benevolent). But it seems Jesus has got something more clever up his sleeve.

In both instances, Jesus is asked a straightforward, yes-or-no question: "Do you pay taxes?" In both cases, his response subverts the question, going deeper to challenge its basic assumptions. He doesn't dodge the questions; he transcends them. He forces his listeners, taxpayers and tax collectors, to ponder. To what, exactly, does Caesar have a right? What has Caesar's image, and what has God's image? What is Caesar's, and what is God's?

I am particularly fond of the fish stunt. It is as though Jesus is winking at Caesar, saying, "Oh, Caesar can have his coins . . . I made the fish." Caesar can have his silly metals; after all he can keep making more of them even if they aren't worth a dime. But coins have no life in them. Human life is branded with the image of God, and Caesar does not own that.[2] In a nation where such a high percentage of taxes go to military and hence ultimately to death-dealing pursuits, this teach-ing should give every tax-paying Christian long and troubled pause. Once we've given to God what is God's, there isn't a lot left over for Caesar.

TONY: Jesus seems to be saying that though Caesar's image is on the coin, *you* have to decide whether it belongs to Caesar or whether it belongs to God. Jesus is asking, "Are you going to use your money the way Caesar wants it to be used, or do you want it to be used the way God wants it to be used?" He's throwing the decision back on those religious leaders who are trying to trap him with their questions. Each of them will have to decide whether the money in question ultimately belongs to Caesar or should it be used the way God wants it to be used. When there is conflict between what God requires and the demands of the government, each of us has an important decision to make concerning taxes.

We have talked a little bit about taxes and military spending. Now here is a related question that I am asked regularly: "Where in the Bible can you find any justification for the government taxing us and then using our money to help poor people?" My questioners go on to say, "I agree with you that Jesus calls upon us to respond to the needs of the poor, but isn't this the task of the church? It doesn't tell me in the Bible that it's the task of the government to take care of poor people." Of course, they don't mention the fact that the church isn't doing it. What's more, they don't acknowledge that the needs of the poor are so massive that the church doesn't have the financial resources to meet those needs.

While I can see how the government has, at times, wasted taxpayers' money and I can admit that too often its programs are ineffective, I also can see the good that government does. My task as a citizen is to get the government to do more good and less inefficient and wasteful work. There is no question in my mind that God is bigger than the church and that the church will be used in God's endeavors, but not only the church. In God's work in the world, all principalities, all powers, all dominions, and all thrones will be used (Ephesians 1:19–23).

If you go to the book of Colossians, you will find that all the principalities and powers were created by God and for God's purposes in the world (Colossians 1:16–17). It is the task of government, which is one of those principalities and powers, to do the will of God every bit as much as it is the task of the institutional church to do the will of God. Insofar as the church fails to do the will of God, I am called upon to help it discover and to do the will of God; and I am called upon to help the government to do the same. Not only am I supposed to challenge the government to do God's will but I am to do the same for other powers. Included in these principalities and powers are corporate structures such as labor unions, General Motors, Ford, IBM, Apple, and Walmart. I have to ask all these suprahuman entities if they are functioning in accord with the will of God, because they are imposing themselves on people and influencing their everyday lives.

If a government that is able to deliver massive numbers of people in Africa from poverty fails to do so, then Christians should challenge that government to do the will of God, especially when the government of our own country has taken 40 percent of the world's resources in order to make possible our affluent, middle-class lifestyle, despite the fact that we make up only 5 percent of the world's population.[3]

Consider the AIDS crisis in Africa, which President George W. Bush addressed with a commitment of $19 billion.[4] Our people should lend support to such an effort. This is not a Democratic thing, nor is it a Republican thing. It's the thing that God calls the government to do in order to bring good to all humanity. Governments are created, says Romans 13, to do good for their citizens, and we have the right to resist governments when they don't do what is good for their people. We also have the responsibility to encourage governments when they do act in ways that are good.

In Matthew 25:31–46, we read that God will judge the nations in accord with how each nation cared for the poor, cared for those in prison, and how well they accepted aliens. Please note that God holds nations, not just the church, responsible for caring for the poor. That passage of Scripture should answer those who question whether or not there is a national responsibility to care for those who are needy.

Given the times in which we live and the vast needs of the poor in both America and the world, the good that should be done for those who are impoverished requires that church and state work alongside each other to achieve this. My hope is that Red Letter Christians work together toward that end.

Dialogue on War and Violence

Put your sword back in its place . . . for all
who draw the sword will die by the sword.

MATTHEW 26:52

SHANE: I have a pile of letters from soldiers that say things like, "I feel like I'm trying to serve two masters—my God and my country—and I don't know how to reconcile the cross with a gun. I don't know how to love my enemies and prepare to kill them." Another one said, "I feel like I'm fighting for abstract nouns, like *freedom* and *democracy*, but it doesn't feel like the gospel."

There comes a point where we have to talk about militarism and war, and ask tough questions like, Should Christians serve in the military? In the early church, there was a clear transition, recognized when people were baptized, that their old life was gone and a new life lay ahead. They were bold enough to say that sometimes that meant a career change. If you were a sculptor of idols, worked in the gladiatorial games, ran a brothel, or served in the military, you were to rethink your job. We are much more timid or polite. Sure, we would say that if you own a porn shop, you need to find a new line of work. But we don't as often say that for folks who work for companies that are notorious human rights abusers or companies like Lockheed Martin, who have made a business out of war. So folks end up stuck, trying to serve God and make a living. And especially for Christian soldiers, that can end up in a paralyzing conflict, a crisis of identity. Many men and women who have fought in America's wars are suffering from emotional breakdowns and psychological disorders, substance addiction, and homelessness.

And the suicide rate is alarming, sometimes over twelve suicides a day of veterans and soldiers.[1] There are more soldiers dying from suicide than from combat.[2] We really do see the pattern Jesus warns us about: "Pick up the sword and you will die by the sword." Not only do innocent children suffer as collateral damage, but the one who picks up the sword also suffers. We've learned that lesson all too well. We are not made to kill. So when we do, it kills a part of us. The good news is that God can heal all wounds and forgive all transgressions.

I will never forget one kid who came up to me at a college after I spoke. With tears coming down his face, he told me about how he had dropped bombs in Iraq and couldn't live with what he had seen and done. He was nineteen—not old enough to buy alcohol, but old enough to drop bombs. We prayed together, and you could feel the burden lift off his shoulders. Then he took off his dog tags, gave them to me, and said, "I need to be set free of these chains. They have held me captive too long."

TONY: A lot of young men and women who go over to Afghanistan or Iraq end up saying something like, "What is this all about? I am supposed to be doing this in the name of God and country, but I am not sure that God and country are necessarily together when it comes to this war. It feels like the people who live here don't want me to be here. Is my patriotism such that I fail to ask questions about what I am doing?" The more they ask such questions, the more the inner conflict sets in.

SHANE: With the marriage of God and country, it's not just the reputation of America but the reputation of the Christian witness that's at stake. They are so closely associated in the minds of many people. I remember seeing one woman throw her hands into the air and say, "I am done with God." When I talked with her more, she explained that she had been raised Muslim but had been moving toward Christianity because of the message of grace. But as she watched the war, she had come to give up on a God that blesses bombs and killing. In her words, "My government and your government are both doing the same thing—creating terrible violence and asking God to bless it. I want nothing to do with that God."

TONY: When I was young I pastored a church on the edge of Fort Dix and witnessed the process of getting soldiers ready for the Vietnam War. The first thing they had to do was to get the soldiers to dehumanize the enemy, to not see them as human. The soldiers were taught that when they went to Vietnam, they should call the Viet Cong "geeks" and "gooks." They were conditioned to not see the enemy soldiers as humans because if they did it would hinder their capacity to kill them.

It's not enough to be antiwar. We have to ask some really hard questions, like what to do with evil.

SHANE: Evil is a real thing that we must take seriously, and a lot of activists don't offer real alternatives to what to do about evil.[3] The mission to rid the world of evil is a captivating one. Plenty of movies and presidents have championed it. It's one that taps into our deepest human hunger that good should triumph over evil and the bad guys should lose in the end. People cheered when Osama bin Laden was killed. But Christians have a strange way of reading history and looking at evil. Jesus tells us we are not to try to rid the world of evil and rip up the wheat from the weeds; there is a God who is in charge of judgment and vengeance (Matthew 13:24–30). And God is much more trustworthy than we are with those things.

Jesus shows us how to deal with evil. If we want to see what love looks like when it stares evil in the face, we need only look at the cross. We can see the triumph of love over hatred. But the cross doesn't look very triumphal at first. It is a call to suffer.

That is what Christ invites us to: "Greater love has no one than this, that he lay down his life for his friends" (John 15:13). It is absolutely at the heart of what it means to be Christian. The early Christians said, "For Christ we can die, but we cannot kill." When we start to kill someone in order to protect someone else, it may seem like the right thing. It may be courageous. It may be patriotic. It may be selfless and sacrificial. But when we kill, it diverges from what love is like—at least what love looks like in Jesus.

TONY: Can we read the Sermon on the Mount with all of those crucial red letters and not come away committed to nonviolent resistance to evil? Note I didn't say *pacifism*. I don't think Jesus ever asks us to be passive, but he does call upon us to resist evil in a nonviolent fashion.

SHANE: Author and professor Walter Wink does brilliant work demonstrating what creativity Jesus has in his teaching in the Sermon on the Mount, around the familiar "turn the other cheek" verses. Wink points out that Jesus was not suggesting that we masochistically let people step all over us. Jesus taught enemy-love with imagination. He gave three specific examples of how to interact with our adversaries. In each instance, Jesus was pointing us toward something that disarms others. He taught us to refuse to oppose evil on its own terms. He invited us to transcend passivity and violence by finding a third way.[4] When hit on the cheek, turn and look the person in the eye.[5] Do not cower down and do not punch them back. Make sure they look into your eyes and see your sacred humanity, and it will become increasingly harder for them to hurt you.

Only the poor were subject to such abuse. If a poor person was being sued and had nothing at all, they could be taken to court for their outer garment (Deuteronomy 24:10–13), which was not uncommon to peasants who lost everything to wealthy landlords and tax collectors. So here Jesus was telling impoverished debtors, who had nothing but the clothes on their backs, to strip naked and expose the greed of the repo man. Nakedness was taboo for Jews, but the shame fell less on the naked party and more on the person who looked on or caused the nakedness (Genesis 9:20–27). "You want my coat? You can have it. You can even have my undies, but you cannot have my soul or my dignity."

Here is another instance of dealing with the troubles of everyday life: "If someone forces you to go one mile, go with him two miles" (Matthew 5:41). This may seem like a strange scenario, but for first-century Jews it was a common occurrence to be asked to walk a mile with a soldier. With no Humvees or tanks, soldiers traveled by foot and carried large amounts of gear, so they were dependent on civilians to carry their supplies. I'm sure there were plenty of Zealots listening to Jesus who shook their fists in the air when they were asked to walk with a soldier. Roman law specified that civilians had to walk one mile, but that's all (in fact going a second mile was an infraction of the military code, not to mention that it was simply absurd for a Jew to befriend an occupying soldier and want to walk an extra mile with him). It is a beautiful scene to imagine a soldier asking for his backpack but the person insisting on another mile. Getting to know him, not as an enemy, but as a person. Talking with him and wooing him into the movement with love.

In each of these instances, Jesus is teaching the "third way." It is here that we see a Jesus who abhors both passivity

and violence, who carves out a third way that is neither submission nor assault, neither fight nor flight.[6] But all of this only
makes sense if you realize Jesus is not talking about the best
ways to successfully win the age-old battle to restrain evil. He
redirects this urge by saying, "Do not resist an evil person";
he has an entirely different way of viewing evil (Matthew 5:39).
It is this third way that teaches "evil can be opposed without being mirrored . . . oppressors can be resisted without
being emulated . . . enemies can be neutralized without being
destroyed."[7] This is the prophetic imagination that can interrupt violence and oppression.[8] If the peculiar people of God
were to transform the world through fascination, it seems
these amazing teachings should work at the center of it. Then
we can look into the eyes of a centurion and see not a beast
but a child of God, and then walk with that child a couple of
miles. Look into the eyes of tax collectors as they sue you in
court, see their poverty, and give them your coat. Look into
the eyes of the ones who are hardest for you to like, and see
the One you love. For God actively loves good and bad people.
Even God sends rain to water the fields of both the just and
the unjust (Matthew 5:45). Enemy-love makes a person like
God—perfect.

TONY: We have to find ways to spread Christ's message of nonviolence. One small way in which some Red Letter Christians spread
this message is by giving out bumper stickers that state, "When Jesus
told us to love our enemies, he probably meant we shouldn't kill them."
Even the most militaristic person, seeing that bumper sticker on a car
in a church parking lot, will probably smile. There is the realization
that there is something ludicrous about saying, "Love your enemies,"
and then concluding that it is justifiable to kill your enemies.

I know it's possible to describe all kinds of hypothetical and real
situations in which nonviolence seems unreasonable. For instance,

I am sometimes asked, "If someone broke into your home and was threatening to kill your wife and children, and the only way to stop that would-be murderer was to shoot him, would you do it?" I don't have an easy answer to that question, and to be honest, I probably would shoot that person.

Dietrich Bonhoeffer raised the question as to what to do about the likes of a Hitler. Having to face that question in a real life situation, Bonhoeffer joined a plot to kill Hitler. It's easy to scoff, given Bonhoeffer's pacifist convictions, but we weren't in his shoes. We didn't have to face what he had to face. And you should know that even as Bonhoeffer participated in the plot to kill Hitler, he did so with great ambivalence, admitting that he was demonstrating his lack of faith and his lack of trust in God at a crucial time in the history of Germany. He never attempted to justify what he did.

SHANE: Bonhoeffer is an interesting case because while he plotted to assassinate Hitler, he knew it was sinful. He wasn't asking people to pray for him or bless him; in fact, just the opposite. It was as if he were saying, "I'm getting ready to sin, but I don't know what else to do and I'm willing to face God with this sin on my hands." That's different from how we tend to speak of violence and ask God to bless our wars and bombs. We may not all agree on whether or not there is a place for necessary evil in the world, but perhaps we can agree to always call it evil, even if we deem it necessary.

TONY: When the apostles were asked by the government to do something that was contrary to their convictions, they said essentially, "We must obey God rather than do what you are asking us to do" (Acts 5:29). That kind of response is needed in this day and age when many Americans act as though they should support their nation's foreign policies regardless of what evils those policies might entail.

SHANE: Many of our friends in the military feel they are at an irreconcilable impasse as they try to follow Christ and serve in the military. Many of these Red Letter Christians have created a support network for one another called Centurion's Guild.[9] It's made up of current and former service members trying to walk alongside each other. They're committed to serving God and country . . . in that order.

TONY: They're not the only ones who have ambivalence about all of this. You and I have the freedom to talk and write about our opposition to militarism because countless numbers of brave American men and women fought and died in order to give us that right. While you and I can state our opinions boldly, we have to be conscious of that reality.

SHANE: Ron Sider put it best when he spoke at the Mennonite World Conference in 1984. His words helped give birth to the Christian Peacemaker Teams who are doing some of the most daring and redemptive work around the world for peace: "Unless we are prepared to risk injury and death in nonviolent opposition to the injustice our societies foster, we don't dare even whisper another word about pacifism to our sisters and brothers in those desperate lands. Unless we are ready to die developing new nonviolent attempts to reduce international conflict, we should confess that we never really meant the cross was an alternative to the sword. Unless the majority of our people in nuclear nations are ready as congregations to risk social disapproval and government harassment in a clear call to live without nuclear weapons, we should sadly acknowledge that we have betrayed our peacemaking heritage. Making peace is as costly as waging war. Unless we are prepared to pay the cost of peacemaking, we have no right to claim the label or preach the message."

Dialogue on National Debts

Forgive us our debts, as we also
have forgiven our debtors.

MATTHEW 6:12

TONY: The financial crisis has debt on everyone's mind. Many citizens are scrambling to deal with massive personal debts, while our nation is facing frightening prospects for the future—prospects that are concerning for Red Letter Christians. When dealing with debt on the national level, I listen to the arguments on both sides of the political aisle. The Republicans are saying that there can be no new taxes, even though America has to deal with two expensive foreign wars for which there was no provision for funding. They actually say that there needs to be a reduction in taxes—in spite of the fact that Americans are paying less in taxes today than they were twenty-five years ago. Back then, we were paying an average of 27 percent of our income in taxes. Today, we are paying an average of only 25 percent of our income in taxes.[1] The problem is that without any additional taxes, the only way we are going to get rid of this debt is to cut spending. Neither party appears willing to cut the bloated defense budget, but Republicans are asking to cut "entitlements," which usually include benefits for the poor, the disabled, and the elderly. The Democrats, on the other hand, say they won't tolerate cuts in services to the poor. They are hoping to eliminate the national debt with an increase in taxes for those earning more than $250,000 a year and by eliminating many of the tax loopholes enjoyed by large corporations. Now, it's not rocket science to recognize that in order to cut the national debt, the government will have to take in more money through taxes and, at the same time, spend less.

I am concerned about the American economy because 71 percent of all Americans believe that our country is in rapid economic decline and probably will never recover.[2] This is not some frightening statistic reflecting the rhetoric of a bunch of doomsday sayers. This is the general thinking of the American public. For instance, the majority of young people do not expect to earn as much as their parents earned. Most people think the American dream is ending.

If the American economy collapses, it will affect what the church is able to do. As the resources of the nation are diminished, the resources churches will have to carry out their mission to evangelize and bring help and justice to the poor and oppressed will also be diminished. In the future, we may not be able to support missionary work and relief ministries like World Vision and Compassion International that are now taking care of children in the developing world. So the national debt is a big concern that Christians cannot ignore.

Of course, the debts that we Americans face cannot be compared to the debts the developing nations carry.

SHANE: The International Jubilee 2000 Campaign attracted a lot of people's interest when it was introduced. It brought attention to the terrible reality that some of the poorest countries in the world are paying huge chunks of money to the richest countries in the world because they are paralyzed by debt. Many of them have paid off, multiple times, the original amount they borrowed but now pay the interest over and over. This is the kind of thing the prophets of old were outraged by and, no doubt, is why the Scriptures explicitly forbid charging interest. That's a sin that doesn't get talked about enough. We need to exorcise some demons from the banks.

Over the past fifty years, rich countries like the United States have lent money to many developing countries whose dictators were lining their pockets with it and using it to build up police forces to keep their own people in order. A lot of the borrowed money was wasted on programs and projects that either failed or delivered few benefits to the general populace. America often made such loans in spite of knowing of the abuses of much of our foreign aid because, during the Cold War, we were anxious to make the developing world dependent on us, keeping them out of the Communist bloc, and securing their votes in the United Nations.

TONY: In African nations collectively, approximately 40 percent of all the income derived from taxes is spent servicing the debts that these countries owe.[3] In Latin America, the situation in Ecuador is the worst, with almost 60 percent of their tax money being used to service the country's debts. In reality, the debt owed by Ecuador is equivalent to 21 percent of that nation's gross domestic product of $72 billion.[4] Such indebted developing countries cannot provide health care, build necessary roads, or provide good education for their children. It is impossible for them to create the kind of infrastructure a working economy requires because so much of their tax income is used paying off debts.

That's what inspired the International Jubilee 2000 Campaign you were talking about. In the year 2000, some Christians picked up that biblical theme of jubilee. According to Leviticus 25, it is the will of God that every fifty years all debts be canceled. There were many, led by Christians leaders as diverse as Pat Robertson of the 700 Club and Jim Wallis, the editor of *Sojourners* magazine, who, in accord with the admonition of Leviticus 25, called for the cancellation of third-world debts.

In the United Kingdom, the activism of Christian young people was a key factor in promoting debt cancellation for poor countries.

Clare Short, the British international development secretary in Tony Blair's cabinet, said that were it not for Christian young people, canceling the debts of developing countries never would have gotten underway. When the G8 nations met in Birmingham, England, in 1998, several thousand Christian young people showed up to encourage the heads of state gathered there to do something to eliminate the debts owed by the world's poorest nations. They didn't burn anything. They didn't throw rocks. They didn't yell or scream. They simply held a two-day, nonstop prayer vigil outside the meeting place. They sat up at night with lit candles, praying that those leaders of the most affluent industrialized nations would take the action necessary to cancel the debts owed by developing countries. What those young people did so impressed those world leaders that when Bill Clinton presented the proposal for the cancellation of the debts of poor nations, the leaders of other industrialized nations enthusiastically supported it. Great progress has been made toward freeing developing countries from debts. President George W. Bush continued that legacy of Bill Clinton and continued canceling these debts. How this will continue in the face of the enormous national financial pressure that the worldwide recession has created remains to be seen.

The best example of the good that can come from debt cancellation is what happened in Uganda. When the Ugandan debt was canceled, stipulations were established wherein the money Uganda would have had to pay to service its debts was put into a special fund to be used specifically to address the AIDS crisis in the country. A massive education program was established to teach people how to prevent getting infected with AIDS. Clinics were set up all over the country, and large amounts of money were spent on medicines for people who already had AIDS. Consequently, over a five-year period, deaths from AIDS declined 30 percent and there were fewer new cases of AIDS.[5]

SHANE: Dr. King talked about how we are all interrelated in the "inescapable network of mutuality"[6] and that if we look closely we see that we are all interdependent—we drink coffee from South America in a cup from China, and add a bit of cocoa from Africa, stirred up by a spoon from Sweden. King said before we've finished breakfast, we've depended on half of the world. It's the way God has made us to be interrelated. Rather than exploit, we support each other. Rather than enslave life, we cultivate it.

In that sense, the world has shrunk. More and more people want to know where their food comes from and how the people who made their clothes were treated. As we discussed before, these things matter to God. Great movements have brought attention to these things, and some creative businesses like TOMS Shoes continue to pave the way to missional businesses. (TOMS provides a pair of shoes for folks who need them for every pair they sell.) Businesses like Ten Thousand Villages create fair-trade connections to the real people who make the stuff we buy.

One of my favorite missional businesses is a company called CRED that started in the United Kingdom. A movie called *Blood Diamond* raised much public attention to the terrible things that happen to folks as they mine diamonds in Africa. So these jewelers in the United Kingdom became really disturbed. At first they wondered if they needed to leave the industry, but eventually, they decided to dive into the deep end of it and try to do something about the injustice. So they started visiting villages where people were mining for the gold and the gems, and they basically bought out all the ringleaders who were oppressing folks and started their own business. They have to go visit these places regularly to make sure the relationships are maintained. But now it's a pioneering fair-trade jewelry business.

All over, these types of creative businesses are transforming business as usual. When they creatively lodge their protest, they give a voice to the people who are marginalized.

One of the most powerful protests I've ever been to was about sweatshops. But this one was different. Instead of bringing in activists and speakers, they flew in the kids from the sweatshops to tell their stories. I remember this one kid had a scar all the way down his face, and he said, "This is from my master who beats me almost every day." He said, "One day he beat me so bad my face was bleeding and then he took a lighter and burnt my face back together so I could keep working. And all of this was so I could make stuff for you." That was his last line.

I remember thinking, *Jesus feels the scar down that kid's face, for as we do it to the least of these we do it to Christ.* Who are the masters I give money to and don't even know it?[7]

TONY: When it comes down to caring about what happens to people in the developing countries, we talk about free trade, and it sounds so democratic. Both Democrats and Republicans in Congress support free trade, which makes everyone look good. As you know, free trade means that there will be no taxes levied on goods coming into our country or on the goods we ship to those countries that ship to us. That sounds fine, until you consider how free trade creates poverty in the third world. For instance, American farmers were subsidized to the tune of $285 billion a year in a 2007 farm bill passed by the US Congress.[8] That means that American farmers can sell wheat, cotton, and rice to developing countries at prices much lower than those of the same products produced within poor countries. Because our farmers are subsidized and the poor countries cannot subsidize their farmers, hundreds of farms in places like Haiti and South Africa are driven out of existence every year. That's not fair, and that's why we Red Letter Christians want *fair* trade, not free trade.

People ask if we are suggesting that a country like Haiti should be allowed to tax the goods that we ship in there, while we don't tax the goods they ship into our country. Our answer is yes. It is fair if we are subsidizing the production of our products and they are not able to do that. All we are asking for is fair competition. What could be more capitalistic than that?

It is our Christian duty not simply to address problems on the personal or individualistic level but on the societal level as well. I know that a lot of our readers are going to say we sound like communists. We need to remind them that a bishop in Latin America once said in response to such an accusation, "When I give food to the poor, they call me a saint. When I ask why the people have no food, they call me a communist."[9]

SHANE: I've always liked the saying. "Once we really try to love our neighbor as ourselves, capitalism, as we see it, won't be possible, and communism won't be necessary." After all, most of the world wakes up in the morning on the wrong side of capitalism.

Dialogue on the Middle East

For nation shall rise against nation, and kingdom against kingdom . . . these are the beginnings of sorrows.

MARK 13:8 KJV

TONY: I'm disturbed that some evangelicals in this country are so intensely committed to supporting the state of Israel that they have lost sight of the need to stand up for justice for Palestinians, even for those Palestinians who are their Christian brothers and sisters. Note that I referred to *the state of Israel.* It's one thing to love the Israeli people and want to see their borders secure, their children living without fear that terrorists will bomb their school buses, and to call for an end to the rockets regularly being lobbed into Israeli territory by angry members of Hamas in the Gaza Strip. But it is quite another thing to say we are committed to the *policies of the Israeli government,* no matter what it does to the Palestinian people. I am frustrated when I hear evangelicals say that anyone who criticizes the policies of the Israeli government is opposed to God. Then they usually quote the Bible and say, "Whoever blesses Israel will be blessed of God, and whoever curses Israel will be cursed by God" (Genesis 27:29, paraphrased).

There is little doubt that the unquestioning pro-Israeli government mindset among Evangelical Zionists here in the United States has become a major barrier to peace in the Middle East.

SHANE: While I was in the Holy Land last year, a priest told us sadly that if Jesus had tried to make his walk from Bethany to Jerusalem today, he wouldn't be able to make it through the checkpoints. We lamented together the wall that so terribly divides this Holy Land into what one Israeli leader called "the most sophisticated apartheid system the world has ever seen."

As I walked the footsteps of Jesus through the land, I was reminded of a story Jesus told about a wealthy man who built a wall and locked the poor outside of it, a story often known as "the Rich Man and Lazarus" (Luke 16:19–31). In the story, the rich man has created a gated neighborhood and locked the poor beggar, named Lazarus, outside the gate. He's living it up inside the wall while the poor man suffers on the other side. As the story goes, when they die, Lazarus is rescued by the angels, who carry him to Abraham's side in paradise. The rich man ends up in the flames of hell, pleading with the beggar for a drop of water. But Abraham tells him that he received his good things on this earth while Lazarus suffered, but now Lazarus is comforted while the rich man is in agony. It's a heavy story and one that says a lot about class struggle.

The only character in any of Jesus' parables to be given a name is this beggar. And his name is Lazarus, which means "the one God rescued." The rich man, however, is not named. No doubt the fellow had a name on earth; he probably had a street or a corporation named after him! While we don't know his name, we do know that the rich man was religious. He knows the prophets and refers to Abraham as "father," and yet his religion did nothing to tear down the wall he had built between himself and his poor neighbor.

The rich man comes to see that his gated neighborhood not only separated him from the beggar Lazarus but it separated him from God. To love God is also to love the most vulnerable of God's children. We are made for compassion.

So often we build walls and gates to protect ourselves only to find that we are the ones held hostage. We think we are locking others out, but we are really locking ourselves in. Not only are the poor robbed of community and compassion, but so are the rich. If only the rich man had opened his gates, not only would Lazarus have been set free but so would he.

I heard a rabbi say that the parables are like diamonds. As we look at them in different light, they take on new dimensions. When I was in the Middle East, I saw the story with new eyes. One of the most important things I learned in the Holy Land is that both Israelis and Palestinians are being held hostage; there are walls and gates that separate them. I heard folks on both sides say they didn't care if the solution was one state or two states or no state, as long as all people were treated equally and with dignity.

The great thing is that walls are never too big to fall, and Christ has given us the keys to unlock the gates that hold us hostage. One of Jesus' promises in the Gospels is that the gates of hell will not prevail. There are walls and gates that hold people captive today, and we should be storming the gates of hell to rescue them. We can take courage that God has a record of tearing down walls and setting folks free. As the walls fall down, we will discover that both Lazarus and the rich man are better off. As Red Letter Christians, we need to work to tear down all walls and eliminate this hell on earth.[1]

TONY: To call Israel and Palestine "the Holy Land" is a misnomer when what goes on there is so unholy. Evangelical Christians in this country do not realize that there used to be a large Christian community among the Palestinians that has been dramatically diminished. Many Christians have left Palestine because constraints and difficulties imposed on them by the Israeli government made their lives in Palestine more than they could handle. The Palestinian city of Bethlehem was 80 percent Christian twenty-five years ago. Today it's down to 15 percent Christian.² Thousands and thousands of Palestinian Christians have fled Bethlehem because they could no longer live freely in the city in which they had grown up. For them, Bethlehem became an occupied city. The harassment and the difficulty that goes with getting in and out of Bethlehem through Israeli checkpoints is just one of the things that makes life there unbearable for them.

Resolutions of the United Nations calling for an end to Israeli occupation of Palestinian lands have been regularly ignored by the Israeli government. This is significant because the state of Israel would not exist if the UN had not created the nation of Israel with a resolution in 1947. The government of Israel wants UN resolutions that guarantee the continued existence of the Israeli state, but they question those UN resolutions that call for the just return of occupied territory to the Palestinians. The UN policy is that when any war ends, no nation has the right to keep any land they have occupied during the war as a result of military conquests.

When President Obama said he wanted the borders of Israel and Palestine to be reestablished as they were in 1967 prior to the Six-Day War, he was declaring only what is legal and right according to international law. Nevertheless, the president's proposal caused an uproar across this country. There were protests from the leaders of both political parties. Members of Congress knew that the American Evangelical Zionists, who number in the millions, would be on their backs if there was even a hint of asking Israel to give up any land it had taken from the Palestinians after 1967.

It should be noted that President Obama did not demand that Israel go back to the borders established by the UN in 1947. He was compromising by saying that the borders should be as they were in 1967, but that was not acceptable to Christian Zionists. When the prime minister of Israel, Benjamin Netanyahu, told the US Congress that Israel would never return to the borders of 1967, he was given a standing ovation. Those politicians knew right well what Evangelical Zionists, as well as a significant number of Christians in mainline denominations, were expecting of them. Therefore, in spite of what they knew were Israel's violations of rulings from the World Court and the UN, they affirmed the Israeli prime minister. The Israeli government has established scores of illegal settlements on Palestinian land, yet because of the political pressure exerted by Christian Zionists, most of those in Congress are unwilling to raise their voices in opposition. More than 300,000 Israelis now live in settlements in the West Bank and the Gaza Strip.[3]

SHANE: With three bodyguards for every Israeli settler.

TONY: In addition to that, Israelis have built roads from Israel proper to each of these settlements. Israelis have constructed fences and walls along these roads so that Palestinian people cannot travel freely, even to visit relatives who live as little as a hundred yards away on the other side of the road, without going through a checkpoint into Israel proper and coming back on the other side of these walled and fenced roads.

Not long ago I spoke at a conference at the Bethlehem Bible College and had the opportunity to talk with Palestinian Christians whose homes had been leveled by Israeli bulldozers in order to make room for these illegal settlements. In several cases, these houses were on land that had been in their families for generations. This is, quite simply, the robbery of land and the illegal destruction of private property, yet the painful reality is that American Christians seldom ask what kind of justice this is.

SHANE: While in Palestine, the team I was traveling with visited a settlement to hear their perspective. Essentially, one of the settlers said, "God gave us this land. Anyone who has a problem with that needs to take it up with God." He was kind enough to take questions, so I asked him what it said about the character of God if God seems to care more about folks on one side of the wall than folks on the other.

I told him that the God that I know is a God that heard the cry of the Israelites in their captivity, when they were slaves, and continues to hear the cry of the suffering. And I started to mention Jesus, but he stopped me and said, "I'm not a Christian." But the golden rule to "love your neighbors as your-self" is not just a New Testament rule (Leviticus 19:18). It's a rule of the Torah too. And when our theology gets in the way of loving our neighbors, it is time to rethink our theology.

TONY: What's interesting about this theology is that many evangelical Christians point to Genesis 12 and 18 and say, "See, this land was promised to the seed of Abraham." A Muslim Palestinian pointed out to me that while the Jews are the seed of Abraham, the Arabs are also the seed of Abraham. Abraham had a son named Isaac with his wife Sarah and another son named Ishmael whose mother was Hagar. Jews are the descendants of Isaac, and Muslims are the descendants of Ishmael, but both are the seeds of Abraham.

Ishmael is acknowledged as Abraham's son and Ishmael's descendents are cited as descendants of Abraham (Genesis 25:12–17). Both were his seed, as would be their children and all who would be born into their two families for generations to come.

I realize that there are other Scripture passages stating that only the descendants of Israel are entitled to this land. But Scripture makes it clear that Jacob did not fulfill the prophecies of the restoration of Israel without reconciling with his brother Esau. Certainly Jesus declares that if there is a problem of alienation with a brother, reconciliation must take place before there can be any kind of worship of God (Matthew 5:23). In our day, we are given an ongoing ministry of reconciliation (2 Corinthians 5:18), and to that end we must work to bring Jews and Arabs together with justice for both groups.

To many Christians, the future of the Jewish people will be primarily in relationship with Jesus Christ; Scripture says that all people become one in Jesus Christ (Galatians 3:26). The future of Gentiles and their salvation is in Jesus Christ, and the salvation of the Jews is also in Jesus Christ. Through Christ, we all become part of the same family of faith. God wants for the Jewish people what he wants for the Palestinian people. As Christians we become one with the Jews, and together we become the new Israel (Romans 9:25–29, 10:10–13). We should also recognize that there are other Christians who believe that God does not renege on his promises, that the covenant God made with Israel still stands and, therefore, the Jews need not lose their identity as a people in order to experience salvation. I still think the Jews will have a special place in the "end times," according to God's plans, but I am still trying to figure out what that place will be.[4]

SHANE: Do you have some suggestions of real concrete possibilities? Obviously, as outsiders, it's not our place to prescribe all the answers, but we both know tons of folks on the ground, and you've been actively involved in these negotiations for decades. Any thoughts on a way forward that might help solve the problems of the Jews and the Palestinians?

TONY: There are two dominant issues that keep peace from being established in the Middle East. First, there's the problem of the Palestinian refugees who are living in the Gaza Strip and on the West Bank. They want what they call "the right of return." In the midst of the two wars in 1948 and 1967, many Palestinians fled to the West Bank and to the Gaza Strip when the Israeli army moved in and took over their land. Palestinian villages and their vineyards were taken away from them. One of the Palestinian demands is the right to go back and live on the land that was once theirs and to repossess the homes that they believe were illegally taken from them.

The Israeli government reasonably says, "We can't let the Palestinians return. Not now! Over the last fifty years they have reproduced at such a high birth rate that if they return to that land that is now within the borders of Israel, they would outnumber the Jews and, hence, they could vote the state of Israel out of existence." For the Israelis this is a real and understandable concern.

The second major barrier to peace is that the Palestinians in the Gaza strip and the West bank demand that the illegal Jewish settlements be dismantled and the Israeli settlers be sent back to where they came from. But the present Israeli government is unwilling to give back any of that land. The Israelis are not about to dismantle the extensive housing they have built on that land, nor are they willing to drive the more than 300,000 Jews who live in those houses out of their homes.

SHANE: Just give the Palestinians back the keys to their houses, right? Or maybe the keys to the settlements?

TONY: Here is a proposal that was drawn up by the political science department of Princeton University; it is called the "Condominium Solution."[5]

First, it states that there should be a two-state solution. It is proposed that Israel should have a state with safe and secure borders; and that Palestine should also have a state with safe and secure borders. Additionally, each state should have a fully recognized government. Both of these nations would have capitals in Jerusalem. There is a section of Jerusalem, now referred to as East Jerusalem, which belongs to the Palestinians, and this section of the city should be set aside as the capital for this new Palestinian state. The Israelis would have the rest of Jerusalem for their capital.

Second, all people who are of Jewish descent would be required to be citizens of the state of Israel, regardless of where they live. Whether these Jews live in Israel proper, the West Bank, or the Gaza

Strip, those of Jewish descent would have to be citizens of the state of Israel.

On the other hand, every person of Arab descent would have to become a citizen of the new state of Palestine. That means that the Arabs who live within the legal borders of Israel and who have Israeli citizenship would have to give up their Israeli citizenship and become citizens of the Palestinian state. This would be hard for Arabs who are presently Israeli citizens, since they have enjoyed many benefits by being Israeli citizens.

Third, and most important, both Jews and Arabs could live anywhere they wanted in the Holy Land. It means that the Arabs could return to land in Israel proper and the Jews could continue to live in the settlements. Since Jews and Arabs would be mixed up together living side by side, Hamas would probably have to give up lobbing rockets into Israeli territory because by doing so they would be just as likely to kill their own people as their "enemies." There would be Palestinians living alongside Jews within Israel and Jews in the Gaza Strip and in the West Bank living alongside Arab peoples.

Only Jews would be allowed to vote in Israeli elections, so the Israeli government would not have to worry that Palestinians living within Israel proper could vote the state of Israel out of existence. That would be the case even if Palestinians outnumbered Jews within the borders of Israel. Palestinians would only be able to vote in Palestinian elections, and Jews could only be allowed to vote in Jewish elections no matter where Jews and Palestinians lived.

Of course, the United States would have to put up a lot of money for Palestinians to buy back land and buildings that the Israelis have developed in wonderful ways over the last half century, but that would cost a lot less money than we're now spending to make the Israeli army the fourth strongest in the world and also to underwrite the Palestinian Liberation Organization. Better still, the United Nations ought to carry some of this financial burden since it created the problem in the first place.

When I presented this plan both to officials in the Israeli government and to elected Palestinian officials, I got the sense that they saw the plan as plausible. If we are called to be agents of reconciliation, we cannot simply allow the hardened positions that differing Christian groups have established in relation to the Israeli-Palestinian conflict to remain in place. As Red Letter Christians, we have a calling to come up with proposals that offer both these groups a solution to the conflict that each can view as viable.

SHANE: Another reason the United States is so deeply invested in the Israeli-Palestinian conflict is the biblical issue of the end times. The word *eschatology* means the study of *eschaton*, or the end times. This is the backdrop of much of the conflict in Israel-Palestine. In fact, Israel is the biggest recipient of US foreign aid. It can feel like we are stocking up weapons and preparing for the apocalypse.

It's interesting because in one sense folks are saying, "We love the Jews. God bless Israel." But then if you press them, the same folks will say, "But if you don't become a Christian, then you're going to go to hell."

TONY: I was on a radio show in New Zealand with a Christian Zionist who believes that Christ cannot return until the Jews are in sole possession of the Holy Land. I remember saying, "Wait a minute! Do you realize that the land that was promised to Abraham reaches from the Euphrates to the Nile? That's what you read in the book of Genesis. I mean, we're not talking only about what we now call the state of Israel, or even the land occupied by Palestinians. We're talking about all the land from the Euphrates to the Nile. That includes a good chunk of Jordan, all of Lebanon, a good part of Egypt, and a good chunk of Syria. All of these lands would have to be cleared of non-Jews according to your beliefs, and only Jews would be allowed to live on that land. What do you propose should be done with all the people who live in that land right now?"

He said, "Well, they will have to leave, and if they won't go voluntarily they must be forced to leave. And if they won't leave, they will have to be killed."

Shocked, and disbelieving what I had just heard, I asked, "Are you talking about genocide?"

His response was: "Well, didn't God ordain genocide when the Jews went into the Holy Land the first time? Were the Jews not ordered to kill every man, woman, and child, along with every animal? Were they not called upon to exercise genocide back then? The God who ordered genocide back when Joshua invaded the Holy Land is the same God we have today."

I had to tell this Christian that my understanding of God as revealed in Jesus Christ trumps whatever was thought about God back there in Old Testament days. I do not believe that the God who is revealed in Jesus is a God who wills genocide. "If you and I hold opposite positions on this," I told him, "I am not sure we worship the same God."

When Christian Zionists believe that Christ cannot return until the Jews are in sole possession of the Holy Land, they make Paul into a mistaken man. Paul said that every Christian, at every moment of every day from his time on, should live in the expectancy of the immediate return of Christ (1 Thessalonians 5:1–11). If Paul was right, then let it be said to anyone reading this book that, before you finish this paragraph, a trumpet could sound and Christ could return, whether or not the Jews are sole possessors of the Holy Land. To deny that is to deny what Scripture teaches.

Almost two thousand years ago, Jesus said to his disciples, "This generation will certainly not pass away till all these things are fulfilled" (Matthew 24:34). Was Jesus lying? His words led those in the early church to fix their attention on Saint John. He was the last surviving disciple, so folks figured the second coming of Christ would have to occur before he died. The early Christians lived with the expectation that Christ's return was in the immediate future. There isn't a theologian or a biblical scholar of whom I know who will debate the fact that the early church, following the resurrection of Christ, expected Jesus to return at any moment. Are the Christian Zionists then saying, "Oh, those early Christians were wrong. They were mistaken because it's already been more than two thousand years and Christ hasn't returned"? Are they suggesting that Jesus was misleading his disciples, and that Paul made a mistake when he challenged the church to live in the expectancy of a Christ who could return at any moment? To think that way, I say, is blasphemy.

The Scriptures talk about the *eschaton* (the conclusion of history) when Christ returns. Christians shouldn't talk as though the earth will end by being burnt up by fire. The Bible tells us that there will be a new heaven and a new earth (Isaiah 65:17; Revelation 21:1).

Isaiah 65 describes this world in wonderful terms. It says that when that great day comes, everyone will have a decent house to live in. Isaiah tells us that everyone will have a job and that everyone will get fair pay for his or her labors. That means that there won't be children in Thailand producing sneakers and being paid only a dollar a day, so that we can buy those sneakers at bargain prices at Walmart and Target.

Children no longer will die in infancy, and old people will live out their long lives in health and well-being. That's a vision of the eschaton that is "good news." It is a vision of the future that challenges me to work toward those ends in the here and now.

SHANE: One of the clearest signs of hope I've seen happened in the West Bank this year; I got to visit a family who are new heroes of mine, the Nassar family.[6] They put a name and a face on the conflict. They are Palestinian Christians who have lived simple lives off the land for generations, until recently. Israeli settlements have been built all around them, and the Israeli government tried to take their land. Unlike most families who lived in communal handshake agreements on land deals, they actually have deeds going back over a hundred years that prove they own their land, which made things tricky for the Israeli government.

As the Nassar family continued living on their land, a new strategy evolved—harassment. Olive trees were uprooted. Piles of boulders were dumped on the road leading to their home, so they couldn't get any vehicles in and out. Even though they owned the land, they were refused permits for electricity and water. So they went off the grid and used solar and rain-water collection. When they were refused building structure permits for their home, they started building underground, which is where I got to visit them.

It is one of the most inspirational stories of persistent love and Christ-driven nonviolence I have ever seen. At the front of their property is a sign that reads, "We refuse to be enemies." After their olive trees were uprooted, a Jewish group caught wind of it and came and helped them replant them all. One story after another of reconciliation. One final attempt was made to buy them out, and the Israeli government offered them a blank check, telling them to name the price, however many millions of dollars they want for their land. But the Nassar family said, "No, there is no price." They continue to live there and have gotten to know their neighbors. At one point they invited one of the Israeli settlers to dinner. When she came into their house, she started weeping, and said, "You have no water, and we have swimming pools. Something is wrong." And when asked how they retain hope in the midst of such injustice, they simply say, "Jesus" with a big smile.[7]

Dialogue on the Global Church

On this rock I will build my church.

MATTHEW 16:18

SHANE: Let's talk about the church. I'm not referring to buildings or meetings, but the global family of Christ-followers around the world. The church is not so much an organization as it is an organism. People are saying that the church is in a funk, that folks like Jesus but not the church.[1] Institutions are hemorrhaging in almost every way. We have a mess on our hands. We've already talked some about the dilemma we've had over the past few decades when evangelism comes at the cost of discipleship and formation. There is something inherently incomplete when we set out to make "believers" without forming disciples. But let's talk a minute about the model of growth itself. It's hard to do discipleship with a big group. Jesus had his hands full with twelve.

Over the last few decades, Christians have seemed to be obsessed with church growth—the megachurch. Since the emphasis has been quantity over quality, we've lost community in the crowds. And community is what folks are longing for. Half the curriculum coming out of megachurches is about how to get people into small groups. Small groups in megachurches!

That's a funny concept. It seems that we are on a pendulum swing from megachurch to microchurch. People want to do small groups, house church. Folks want to see the gospel lived out around dinner tables and in living rooms. They want a community they can walk to. And there's something great about that. It's almost the return of the parish, the local meeting of Christians that isn't too flashy or sexy, but is really about a group of folks doing life together with Christ and each other.

TONY: There are far too many Christians who believe that theological conformity is a prerequisite for community. Such Christians want no fellowship with those who disagree with them on such doctrines as the inerrancy of Scripture and their specifics about heaven and hell and who is going where when this life ends. People are evaluating whether or not other people are Christian in terms of whether or not they dot their theological *"i"s* as orthodoxy prescribes. This emphasis on theological exactness comes out of the fact that the Reformation came largely out of Germany. In Germany, the word *spirit* and the word *mind* are exactly the same word: *geist*. Hence, the Reformation created an ethos wherein people who *thought* or *believed* the right things were considered spiritual. That intellectualizing of the gospel has come down to us in this present day.

I think the Pentecostal movement has challenged the idea of reducing Christianity to a head trip. Since the early twentieth century, when a handful of Christians gathered in a prayer meeting in Azusa, California, this Pentecostal movement has grown enormously. There are now approximately 800 million Christians worldwide who call themselves Pentecostal. These Pentecostal Christians say it's not enough to be right about the intellectual truths of the gospel. For them, it's not sufficient to have orthodox propositional statements affirmed in your mind. For Pentecostals, being a Christian requires that a person experience something. There's an emphasis on having an inner feeling or a subjective experience of God's presence.

Then there's what the Roman Catholics bring to the table. It is important to them that Christians believe the right things but also that Christians experience God. Many Catholics put an emphasis on developing the inner spiritual life. They ask, "Are you becoming more holy?" The word *holy* is a big word for Catholics. They want Christians to become inwardly transformed into the holy likeness of Christ. As of late, Protestants are giving growing attention to what the Catholic mystics can teach us about the spiritual disciplines that make for holiness. They turn our attention to the writings of such mystics as Saint John of the Cross, Saint Francis, Catherine of Siena, and especially to Saint Ignatius and his book, *Spiritual Exercises*.

You will find that almost every Protestant seminary now has at least one course on spiritual formation. There are Protestants who go on Catholic silent retreats, where meditation and surrendering to an infilling of God's presence are emphasized. The shift to the experiential and the mystical and away from a simple intellectualizing of the gospel is evident in the spirit of the times.

I personally believe that all of these things are coming together to create a more holistic Christianity. However, as you suggested, we must not neglect the intellectual side. To be a Christian is to be a person of solid doctrine, but it is also to have experiential and spiritual dimensions to our faith. The emphasis on right belief given to us from the traditions of Luther, Zwingli, and Calvin is being balanced by Pentecostalism and Catholic mysticism. All of these streams of Christianity are coming together, and no matter which tradition you started in, hopefully you are coming to realize that there is something you need very much in the other traditions.

SHANE: The mystics show us a side of our faith that is wonder-filled and hard to find words for. Their lives are filled with ecstasy, divine romance. They see things a lot of us are only developing eyes to see—demons, fire, angels, miracles.

They have a deep connection to nature and wild animals, a lot like Jesus and the prophets did. They have much to teach us.

In a different vein, the Mennonites have some things to teach us too. Beyond good theology and a commitment to simplicity and nonviolence, they know how to build barns, make quilts, can stuff. In an age when we have tons of books and conferences and talking, they actually know how to survive, how to live.

It seems to me that when it comes to understanding what it means to be Christian in the twenty-first century, we have as much to learn from the Amish as from the megachurch. Think about it: if megachurch spirituality is a mile long and an inch deep, the Amish are an inch long and a mile deep. There are plenty of things to critique about the Amish, but plenty of things to learn too. And not just how to make good furniture.

I'm pretty sure they will survive the recession. And they aren't too worried about gas prices. Though seemingly irrelevant, the Amish are becoming more and more relevant to the world we live in. They have maintained the countercultural, counterimperial essence that marked early Christianity. They understand what it means to be resident aliens, peculiar, set apart, in the world but not of it. So if the mystics can teach us about prayer and being in touch with God, the Amish can also teach us about how to live, and how to see our faith as a way of life.

TONY: The Amish just may be ahead of the rest of us when it comes to addressing certain questions about the environment. They are saying, "We don't pollute like you outsiders do. You people pollute the atmosphere with the exhausts from your cars, and you use chemical fertilizers that poison the soil instead of natural fertilizers." So, in addition to what Reformers, Pentecostals, and Roman

Catholics have contributed to our broadened vision of what it means to be Red Letter Christians, we need to pay attention to Anabaptist contributions because the Anabaptists can help us toward having a holistic Christianity. Groups like the Mennonites, the Brethren in Christ, and the Amish put a strong emphasis on the simple lifestyle and have a historic commitment to nonviolent resistance, and these emphases are gaining momentum among today's young people.

Many young people from other denominations are joining Mennonite churches these days. They are looking for a church that has not raised nationalism and patriotism to the level of idolatry, and they are finding what they're looking for. They are also looking for a church that is into nonviolent resistance. Martin Luther King and the civil rights movement set them up for this. These young seekers are fascinated by Gandhi, too, and they're asking, "Where can we find churches that incarnate the nonviolent resistance that we find in Dr. King and in Gandhi?"

Youth groups from American churches often go on short-term mission trips to developing countries, visiting places like Haiti and the slums of Mexico City where suffering and poverty staggers their imaginations. They come back and begin to ask questions about the lifestyles that we Americans embrace—especially the people in their own churches. They say, "Our way of life is obscene! We are spending too much money on cars and houses and clothes. We are spending too much money on totally unnecessary luxuries while the people we just visited are in desperate need."

One must embrace simple living to follow the red letters of the Bible and endeavor to faithfully live out the words of Jesus. That's why traditions that embrace it seem so attractive.

SHANE: Mennonites like the microchurch. They often just name their congregation after the street it is located on—nothing flashy. And when a congregation does grow, they tend to keep hiving off, like bees. They don't let it get too big. One congregation I'm connected to here in Philly is growing pretty rapidly, but anytime it gets bigger than two hundred people they spin off a new congregation.

One of the interesting things about Willow Creek Community Church outside of Chicago is that it didn't start as a big place. It started with community. Willow Creek started by folks going door-to-door, selling tomatoes, meeting the neighbors and saying, "Hey, we've been pretty burned by the church. What's your church experience? We're thinking about starting something new here." That's how it started.

Part of the problem is that as people now emulate Willow Creek, they just copy the drums and drama, the stuff that happens on stage, and think that they are going to have the same kind of community. Folks at Willow Creek are some of the biggest critics of this. Imitators don't necessarily go door-to-door selling tomatoes and getting to know neighbors. Instead, they start with the JumboTron. That may draw a crowd, but it's not the same as growing a community.

Willow Creek has done some incredible things to stay true to that original vision they cling to from Acts 2 and 4, and to try to figure out what community can look like. They were some of the first people to give the front-row parking to single mothers and to start an auto ministry where they have volunteer mechanics fix people's cars.

TONY: They not only fix up cars that belong to poor people but they ask church members to give the church the cars that they were going to turn in when they bought new ones. Mechanics make sure these donated cars are in first-rate shape, and then they are given to poor people, many of whom need cars to get to work.

During any given week, Willow Creek has approximately four thousand of their people put in at least ten hours of service among the poor in the Chicago area. That's forty thousand hours a week in ministry to the poor and the needy. Nobody can tell me that Willow Creek Community Church is just a lot of show business, because it's so much more than that. Both Willow Creek and Saddleback are doing kingdom work.

Sometimes we see the Holy Spirit blowing through mega-churches and sometimes we find the Holy Spirit in small country churches and at work in struggling inner-city churches. Size is not the criterion for determining the greatness of a church.

SHANE: It seems as though whether it's a little tiny congregation or a huge one, if you only are existing for the sake of yourselves, you implode. We have to exist for Jesus' vision of the kingdom of God, for the mission outside of the church. If we don't, then our churches become unhealthy and die.

Tony, I know you have been connected to the Crystal Cathedral. The fact that it recently announced its bankruptcy is one of those signs that the times are changing.[2]

TONY: In the case of the Crystal Cathedral, the situation may not be as bleak as it appears. If you go there for one of the regular Sunday morning worship services that are viewed on TV, it's depressing, because the once huge congregation no longer comes anywhere near filling the sanctuary. But what the larger public doesn't know is that each Sunday afternoon, the congregation that is part of the Hispanic ministry there has grown so large that it packs out the Crystal Cathedral with standing room only, even after chairs are set up in the aisles. A second Hispanic service of approximately 3,000 is planned because the Hispanic congregation is expected to double in the next few months. The largest Hispanic congregation in Southern California worships in the Crystal Cathedral, but few people outside of Garden Grove, California, even know it exists because most people are so focused only on what's happening to the Caucasian group they see on television on Sunday mornings.

Things are happening in church growth that we may not perceive in mainstream America. Some fifty thousand new members
are added to churches in Africa every week. Christianity is spreading
like wildfire on that continent. And revival is spreading all over Latin
America in ways that stagger the imagination. I was in a church in
Buenos Aires that was not only packed but starting a new church
with about two hundred members every month.

Reverend David Yonggi Cho's church in Korea has a million
members. There are 700,000 who show up for worship on weekends,
with multiple services starting on Saturday night and continuing
through late Sunday night. Nevertheless, there are some serious
problems associated with these fast-growing churches.

SHANE: It's not always a bad thing to struggle. In fact, if you
want to find the church alive, you look at places of struggle.
Whenever we have triumphed and dominated, we get sick.
Christianity is best when it is humble. If we want to see the
ruins of the church, we need only look to Europe where it dominated only a couple of generations ago. Now many of those
cathedrals are museums and monuments, and some are even
bars and nightclubs.

In some ways, our history in the United States is still so
young. America is still an experiment. The history book is still
being written. There is an opportunity for the church in the
United States to discover what it means to be peculiar again, to
find community again, to be a contrasting society to the dominant one again.

Much of the Christianity we have exported has been sick.
We have been predatory with the prosperity gospel. We have
exploited the longing of poor folks for miracles and for prosperity and blessing, and we have sold them a self-centered,
blessing-obsessed, narcissistic message.

We have capitalized on suffering and pain to a form of the

gospel that actually doesn't look like the red letters; it doesn't look like the things that Jesus is saying. In fact, you don't hear much Jesus in it at all. You hear a lot about *your* life and *your* prosperity and *your* blessing, and very little about Jesus' call to us when he said, "Blessed are the poor . . . blessed are the merciful" (Matthew 5). It becomes confusing to people.

TONY: When, as a social scientist, I try to distinguish between religion and magic, I use an operational definition that magic is an attempt to manipulate supernatural forces to get what you want; whereas true religion is when you surrender to what God wants to do through you. Unfortunately, there are preachers who have turned Christianity into a form of magic by promoting a prosperity theology in which Christianity becomes little more than an attempt to manipulate God into delivering wealth and well-being. Too often poor people in developing countries are promised health and prosperity as a reward for giving a tithe of what little they have to preachers who themselves enjoy lavish lifestyles.

Compare prosperity theology to the words of Jesus, who said, "But woe to you who are rich, for you have already received your comfort. Woe to you who are well fed now, for you will go hungry" (Luke 6:24–25). Jesus told his disciples, "Foxes have holes and the birds of the air have nests, but if you follow me, you may end up without any place to lay your head" (Matthew 8:20, paraphrased). He told his followers, "The servants are not greater than the master. If they persecuted me, they will persecute you" (John 15:20, paraphrased). It seems obvious in the red letters that Jesus is not promising health and wealth for those who follow in his footsteps.

I wonder how the apostle Paul would make out at a service where the prosperity theology was being preached. During testimony time I can imagine him standing up and saying, "It's been a wonderful experience following Jesus. I was shipwrecked three times, beaten almost to the point of death five times, diseased, afflicted, and left for dead" (2 Corinthians 11:24–26). Yet Paul was able to say, "I have learned in whatsoever state I am, therewith to be content" (Philippians 4:11). What a contrast between Paul's Christianity and what is referred to as prosperity theology. If faithfulness and giving money guarantee wealth and well-being, it is hard to explain the suffering, poverty, and martyrs' deaths that befell the original twelve disciples.

Prosperity theology is not the biggest problem for many Christians from the developing world. When the Anglican community held its last Lambeth conference in 2008, the Archbishop of Canterbury, Rowan Williams, was put in a difficult position because the clergy from the Southern Hemisphere wanted nothing to do with women in ministry. Female priests and female bishops, with notable exceptions in Malawi and South Africa, were unacceptable to Anglicans in Africa then, and they continue to be opposed to ordaining women or accepting women as leaders in the church. The Southern Hemisphere church, for the most part, has an archaic view of women, which prescribes for them a role of submission. We need to respect the churches in the Southern Hemisphere when it comes to evangelism and zeal, but they need to listen to us when it comes to the role of women in the church.

Then there are the homophobic problems in several African countries such as Uganda, where Christian leaders who have gained great influence in the Ugandan government have tried to pass laws that would have homosexuals put to death or imprisoned for life. There have even been attempts to pass a law that would send to jail any person who did not give the police the names of anyone he or she knew to be homosexual. What kind of Christianity is that?

I think that not only do we in the Northern Hemisphere churches need to listen to what the Southern Hemisphere churches are saying to us, but the Southern Hemisphere churches need to listen to what we have to say to them—especially about the roles of women in the church and the treatment of gay, lesbian, bisexual,

228 // RED LETTER REVOLUTION

and transgendered people. There needs to be a mutuality in which each can help the other to grow into Christ-like practices. So, as Jesus predicted, we see that the wheat and the tares are growing up together (Matthew 13). Good and evil are simultaneously present in the Southern Hemisphere churches and, I must add, in our Northern Hemisphere churches too.

In the emerging global church, Protestants and Catholics are coming together. The Protestant religion doesn't offer salvation, nor does the Catholic religion. Only a transforming personal relationship with Jesus Christ offers salvation. That makes much of the confusion about which branch of Christianity offers salvation superfluous. The Red Letter Christian movement ignores divisions such as that between Protestants and Catholics, which are so prevalent in the American psyche. We emphasize what Jesus has to say, and whether or not we are willing to follow Jesus.

When speakers and leaders of this Red Letter movement come together, there are Catholics among us, and they are often the ones who radiate the most spirituality and the deepest commitment to Christ. I think you'll agree that the spirit of Christ is more evident in them at times than in many of the Protestants we know. Over the past fifty years, Catholic Christians and Protestant Christians have found commonalities and fellowship with each other, so I think the division between them is gradually coming to belong to another place and another time.

We all have to realize that Christianity was alive and well hundreds of years prior to the Reformation. When the Reformation took place, the reformers corrected a lot of theology that had gotten out of whack and did their best to reemphasize the doctrine of salvation by grace through faith, and not of works lest any man should boast (Ephesians 2:8–9). That was the thrust of the teachings of Luther, Calvin, and Zwingli. Having said that, following the Reformation, we Protestants may have gotten rid not only of some bad theology, but also some biblically based spiritual disciplines of the Catholic saints. These days, new books such as *Common Prayer*, which you helped write, are helping us rediscover the validity of many of those Catholic spiritual disciplines.

SHANE: Sometimes folks will ask, "But don't the Catholics pray to Mary and the saints?" Catholics are not praying *to* the saints; they are praying *with* the saints. I asked one of my Catholic friends years ago, "Why do you ask the saints to pray for you?" He said, "Don't you ask your friends to pray for you?" They believe in resurrection. They believe that time and space and death do not separate us from them. So if we ask our friends to pray for us, what's wrong with asking our friends on the other side of death? They're alive and cheering us on. They are worshiping on the other side of eternity, but that doesn't mean that we're not connected.

Still, there are some differences I have with some Catholic theology, just as there are some differences I have with some Protestant theology. We should be confessing the worst of our own tradition and looking for the best in the others.[3]

But the fact is that a lot of Catholics have been better Red Letter Christians than a lot of Protestants have, especially when it comes to seeing our faith as a way of living, not just a way of believing. Catholics have taught about the social implications of our personal faith for a long time and have put language like a "Consistent Ethic of Life" to the implications of the gospel, while much of our evangelicalism has remained inconsistent with its teaching on things like the death penalty, war, abortion, euthanasia, and poverty. We tend to pick and choose and are sometimes more pro-life on one issue than another.

Without a doubt, the future of the church will be influenced by how much we remember the past. We need to look back in order to move forward. One of the critiques of the Reformation is that we did not look back far enough. So it ended up tracing the fall of the church to the papacy rather than Constantine. Without the vision for the early church in Acts, the Reformation ended up often being marked more by what it was against (hence "*protest*-ant") than a vision of what it was for.

As we look back, we can see God at work in the Reformation and in renewals and reformations throughout the ages. Every generation needs a new reformation. But you cannot deconstruct something that has never been constructed for you, which is one of the dangers of some movements in the postmodern, post-Christian, post-evangelical generation. We want to be the church without the church, and the early Christians were clear that if you want God as Father, you must accept the church as your mother, even if she is a sadly dysfunctional momma at times.[4]

Dialogue on Reconciliation

May they be brought to complete unity to let
the world know that you sent me and have
loved them even as you have loved me.

JOHN 17:23

SHANE: There is something powerful about tearing down the walls and getting to know people face-to-face. And Tony, one of the things that came out of this last trip to Iraq is a new movement that you and I have been involved in launching called Friends Without Borders.

Friends Without Borders is a simple vision to create a web of friendships across the walls of conflict and war. We started with a website: www.friendswithoutborders.net. Some folks have called it eHarmony for reconciliation or Facebook for peace. We have a little friendship agreement folks sign when they join, and then a flag goes up on the site when they register. We have folks literally around the world getting to know one another. Last week I was on an international conference call with people from Gaza to Syria, from Canada to Sudan, just listening to each other's stories. And I am excited to say there are a lot of Christians and a lot of evangelicals who are a part of this, but there are also people of all faiths and no faiths. And that's the idea—we don't need to be scared of one another.

But it's just one tool to try to build bridges rather than walls. The hope is to create virtual on-ramps that can lead to real friendships. And it's happening. It's all pretty informal. We've had delegations to Iraq and Afghanistan like the visits I've been on. Elementary schools have created pen pals between classrooms in the US and in Afghanistan.

We kicked off this past New Year by having a twenty-four-hour Skype-a-thon on the Internet with kids in Afghanistan. The kids in my neighborhood could see kids in Afghanistan, and they could bring in the New Year together. Our kids heard the Afghan youth share about seeing their friends get shot and listened to their dreams of a world with less violence. It was amazing. They found they were much more alike than they could have ever imagined.

I don't think there's anything bad that can come out of genuine friendships, so the thought is, if you want to get to know other Christians in Palestine or Iraq, you can. But you can also get to know a Muslim, or a Hindu, or someone of a different faith, and learn from them. What is there to be scared of?

TONY: The apostle Paul writes clearly that God has given to us a ministry of reconciliation (2 Corinthians 5:18), of bringing diverse people of other ethnic groups and religions together and creating a unified mindset of peace in the world. One need not compromise one's commitment to Jesus Christ as the Savior of the world in order to do this. This reconciliation doesn't diminish loyalty to Christ in any way, but rather is a way of living out the truth—that this Jesus, whom we love, has called us to reach out to all nations and to all people with his love. In the face of growing tensions between Western nations and the Islamic world, such reconciliation is not only sorely needed but crucial to the survival of us all.

The late Samuel Huntington, a professor of political science at Harvard University, suggested in his book, *The Clash of Civilizations and the Remaking of World Order,* that unless something intervenes over the next few decades, we can expect a gigantic religious war between the Islamic world and those of us in the West. If he's right, that means we've got to do all we can to keep that from happening. We can do it by bringing together people of goodwill from both sides of the ideological divide that separates the Western community from the Islamic community. That is why developing Friends Without Borders is so important. It is part of the reconciliation process that the apostle Paul was talking about. If we don't do things like this, the future of humanity is very much in danger.

We can't afford to allow radical fundamentalists in the Muslim community to take control of their nations; nor can we allow radical fundamentalists in the Christian community to push us toward World War III. We can't let those people who want to use militaristic approaches to propagate or defend their own faiths control what happens. We have to be people who connect with other people of goodwill on the other side of the ideological fence. We need to live out in our own lives the words of Jesus: "Whoever is not against us is for us" (Mark 9:40). As "Jesus people," let us affirm the good that we find in those who are too often defined as enemies by our increasingly Islamophobic society.

We offer a missions major here at Eastern University. When I was teaching in that program, one of the things I tried hard to communicate to our students was that the Bible makes it clear in Acts 10 that God has revealed something of himself in every ethnic group and in every nation of the world. Because of that biblical declaration, I taught that the first thing a missionary should do when interacting with another ethnic group or living in another society in a faraway place, is *not* to start off by declaring his or her personal convictions. Rather the missionary should listen to the indigenous people and study the ways in which God already has been revealed to them. "When you connect with people on the mission field," I would tell them, "start at the point where you discern how God is already there.

Then you can talk about Jesus and explain how he is the fulfillment of all that is hoped for in their own religion. The missionary is not taking God to where God is not, but in joining with what God is already doing in their midst."

It is important for my students to know that there are no people on the face of the earth who know nothing of God. Romans 2:12–16 tells us that God will probably have to make room for those who may have never heard of the laws or God or the gospel that we preach. Nevertheless, because of what is "written on their hearts," we are called to look for God in people and in places where we didn't expect to see God.

Another thing I wanted my students to learn is that when we do share the gospel with indigenous people, we must express our message with great sensitivity and endeavor to develop forms of worship that fit their culture. For example, while in New Zealand about a month after the evangelical activist John Perkins had been there on a preaching tour, I was fascinated to learn about what had happened while he was speaking to a group of church leaders in that country. After John had told them that they should be open to the good things that could be found in the Māori culture (the Māori people being the indigenous people of New Zealand), he made the concrete suggestion that Māori art and dance should be utilized for Christian worship and that a theology should be developed that would answer the specific questions that had arisen within the Māori worldview. His idea was to let the Māori people express their faith in their own cultural forms, with their own music, especially utilizing the *haka*, a special dance performed by Māori men. John was enthusiastic about the larger church allowing the Māori people to redeem their own cultural art forms and use them as a means to worship Jesus.

When he had finished making his plea, one of the ministers said, "You don't understand, Dr. Perkins, everything about the Māori culture is permeated with the demonic. We can't embrace anything of their culture or allow Christian Māori people to use in worship any of what's in their culture because it's so demonically influenced."

In response, John said, "You are probably right! But before you look for the expressions of the demonic in *their* culture, maybe you should look for the expressions of the demonic within your own Pākehā culture (the white culture of New Zealand). Then, after you have cast out all the demonic influences within your own culture, you might begin to talk about what demonic influences you see in the Māori culture."

Reports of his response spread all over both islands of New Zealand, and by the time I got there, John Perkins' words had brought about a kind of seismic shift in the thinking of the Pākehā people, and especially in the way the Māori people thought about themselves. Several Māori Christians declared, "We are going to change! We have been singing Pākehā songs, and we have been doing worship in Pākehā ways. We were told that we could not worship in Māori ways without surrendering to the demonic. That's wrong! From now on, we are going to worship Jesus in forms and in ways that express something of what we are about as Māori people."

In the book of Revelation, when the new heaven and the new earth are described, it says, "A great multitude, which no man could number, of all nations, and kindreds, and people, and tongues, stood before the throne" (Revelation 7:9 KJV). The word *nation* in the original language of the Scriptures is the word *ethnos*, which means "ethnic." The Bible is telling us that every ethnic group will be there in heaven, and all will be worshiping God in forms that are indigenous to their respective cultures.

Here in Philadelphia, we have what is called a "Super Sunday" every October. Ours is a city composed of an array of ethnic groups, and on Super Sunday they are all represented in a festival held on Benjamin Franklin Parkway. Polish people, Italian people, German people, Scandinavian people, and Irish people are among the many ethnic people who turn out. Each group sets up its own booth. There's

Swedish food at the one table; Jewish food at the next table; Italian food at the next table; Palestinian food at the next table; Turkish food at the next table; French food . . . all kinds of food from all kinds of ethnic groups. Each group provides its unique music and its young people dance their respective ethnic dances. It's a wonderful day in which the people of Philadelphia can enjoy what the people of each and every culture in their city have to contribute. As I've often said to my students, Super Sunday just may be a foretaste of heaven, with each ethnic group bringing the glorious things about its own cultural tradition to the celebration.

In God's kingdom, what is corrupted in each culture will be cleansed. Each will be purified, and in its purity what is unique to each group will be enjoyed not only by its own people but by all God's people. We will all end up enjoying what each ethnic group has to contribute to the glory of God. That's not a bad view of heaven or of the new world God wants to create here on earth!

The only other earthly vision that I have of heaven in this world is the one I get at the end of the Olympics, when all the athletes from each of the participating nations march into the Olympic stadium dressed in the uniforms of their respective nations, with each team carrying its own national flag. Then there's a point in the closing ceremonies when the athletes break ranks and start singing and dancing and mingling with each other. All of a sudden, there are people with all kinds of dress and all kinds of flags, dancing and hugging each other. It's a beautiful scene wherein everybody becomes one. Yes, they still maintain their individual national identities, but in spite of their peculiar differences, oneness has been created among them.

SHANE: Pentecost, meaning "fifty days," is celebrated seven weeks after Easter (hence the fifty), and marks the birthday of the church, when the Holy Spirit is said to have fallen on the early Christian community like fire from the heavens. For this reason many Christians wear red and decorate in pyro-colors.

It's also where the fiery Pentecostal movement gets its name. What happened at Pentecost runs much deeper than fire, and it wasn't just about speaking in a charismatic "tongues-of-fire" prayer language, as beautiful as both of these may be.

What happened was that a really diverse group of people understood each other as the Spirit of God fell upon them. It was a divine moment of reconciliation among people from many different tribes and nations and languages—a reconciliation moment I would say the world is desperately in need of today.

To understand what happened at Pentecost, we need to look back to the biblical account of the Tower of Babel, as it paints the backdrop. After all, Babel is where we got our more than six thousand spoken languages, according to the Bible. The story begins with the whole earth speaking one language (Genesis 11:1). The young human race seemed quite impressed with itself and its seemingly limitless power, so the people set out to build a tower that would reach heaven. It doesn't seem so terrible in itself, but the Scripture speaks of the tower as an idol of human ingenuity, which they built "to make a name for themselves" (verse 4).

God was not impressed. As the story goes, God toppled the tower and scattered the people . . . humbling them, bringing them back down to earth. And as they were scattered across the earth, God confused them by having them speak many languages. (It's also said that Babel is where we get the word *babble*.) This story becomes a central commentary about power. In fact, the Bible ends with the "fall of Babylon," the quintessential symbol of imperial power and the counterfeit splendor of the world.

But here's why Babel is an important backdrop for what happens at Pentecost. Pentecost is the antithesis of the Babel project. According to the book of Acts, during that original Pentecost some two thousand years ago, there were people from "every nation under heaven" gathered together (2:5). The author even went on to specifically name more than a dozen geographical places, large and small, rural and urban, from which people came. They represented the whole earth.

Then the Spirit came upon them. And even though they all spoke different languages, they understood each other. The text says that the folks doing most of the speaking were "Galileans," but everyone heard what the Galileans said in their "own language," their native tongues (Acts 2:6).

I heard some scholars point out that *Galilean* was shorthand for backwoods folks from the hills. They had strange accents and spoke in a really distinct dialect. As a Tennessee hillbilly, I sort of like that the preachers at that first Pentecost were country folk. Galileans were frowned upon by many and seen as unsophisticated, uneducated, and uncivilized. For this reason, folks were stunned that Jesus came from Galilee, from where people thought nothing good could come (John 1:46).

But regardless of whether the preachers spoke with a country twang or British flair or any language for that matter, the point is, they all understood what was being said as if it was being spoken in their own language.

They are the opposite of the one-language, tower-building Babel project. At Babel, God scattered the pretentious human race. And at Pentecost, God reunites the scattered people into a new beloved community, made one not by their own hands or by a shared, single language but by the Spirit of God.

They are the new sign of God's Spirit—a community that is as diverse as creation itself, as unique as the fingerprints we leave and the DNA we're made of. But it is a community that understands each other amid our diversity, each one as a child of God. Unity doesn't mean uniformity. It doesn't mean we are all the same. It just means we learn to celebrate our differences. I don't want to be "color-blind"; I want to see color. I want to know people and their stories and their cultures.

TONY: And note, the Bible doesn't say that on the day of Pentecost everyone spoke the same language. It says the people *heard* what others were saying, each of them in his or her own language. Every language was preserved. In the unity of the Spirit that was created on that miraculous day, people didn't lose their own languages. What a beautiful contradiction Pentecost is to the Tower of Babel. On that day, God created mutual understanding without obliterating the ethnic uniqueness embodied in the language of each of the ethnic groups gathered together.

Dialogue on Missions

*Go and make disciples of all nations, baptizing
them in the name of the Father and of the Son
and of the Holy Spirit, and teaching them to
obey everything I have commanded you.*

MATTHEW 28:19–20

TONY: So many Red Letter Christians are committed to the poor in the name of Christ. I am amazed at how many of them live out their commitments by going to developing countries to help needy people. I admire their zeal, but the time has come to take a good look at how we do missionary work.

The 2009 earthquake in Haiti drew an immediate response from many Christians who wanted to rush to that suffering country to help. What followed, however, exposed some practices to which we, as a helping people with all the right intentions, had failed to pay attention. Our major error in Haiti was that we had done for the Haitian people what the Haitian people were quite capable of doing for themselves. If they needed an orphanage, Haitians could count on Christians from North America or a European country to construct one for them. If they needed a school to be built, there always seemed to be some church group that would come to Haiti and build it in a week. If some Haitians needed a church, it was likely that some foreigners would build it. I won't hazard a guess as to how many of the churches, orphanages, and schools in Haiti have been built by religious groups from the United States, but the question is, could the Haitians have built these schools, orphanages, and churches themselves? Of course they could have.

Granted, the poor of Haiti might not have had the building materials they needed or the financial resources to buy the building materials. However, with just a third of the money that was spent to send work groups to Haiti, there would have been enough dollars to buy the building materials and pay Haitian workers to do the building. Perhaps it would have been useful for foreigners to provide some technical assistance or even architects to help design buildings that would withstand an earthquake, but we should have let the Haitians do for themselves what Haitians can do. Stop to think about how many Haitian workers, who desperately needed work, would have had employment if only we had given them the materials to do what needed to be done and let them do the work themselves. In trying to help, we may have done the Haitians a great disservice.

Many critics of missionary work say that well-intentioned work groups have disempowered indigenous people and rendered them reluctant to try to solve their own problems. When I was part of the Clinton Global Initiative, I heard an astounding thing about Haiti from Dr. Paul Farmer, who had been doing magnificent work there, providing medical care, building hospitals and clinics, and training Haitian doctors. Dr. Farmer had been asked to list the number of nongovernmental agencies (NGOs) operating out of Port-au-Prince, of which many were faith based. He reported at the gathering of the Clinton Global Initiative in September of 2010 with the names of 9,943, which is when he stopped counting. These are the ones that are officially registered. Dr. Farmer said that there probably are a lot more NGOs that are not registered, mainly church groups.

So in a country of 9 million people, there are 9,943 NGOs. In most cases, instead of empowering people and giving Haitians what they needed to solve the problems of their country, such groups have done things that may have actually hurt the Haitian people by disempowering them.

Ivan Illich, a missiologist who served in Brazil, said essentially, "Keep your church groups home. We don't want them. If you do come, please come to enjoy the culture, get to know our people, worship with them, listen to them, and learn from them. But stop doing for them what they could and should do for themselves. Stop disempowering them."

One of the things I discovered in the red letters of the Bible is that Jesus doesn't do for us what we can do for ourselves. Instead he says, "The work that I do, you shall do. And you will do even greater works than I have done because I am empowering you to do it" (John 14:12, paraphrased). That emphasis, the empowerment of people, should become the new direction of missionary work because the old ways, in so many instances, have proven to be counterproductive.

SHANE: The words *missions* and *missionary* are never really used by Jesus. Even though Jesus' great "commission" was sending the disciples into the world to live out the mission of God, it's as if he isn't willing to confine missions to special people or special trips. Our whole life is missional. All of us are missionaries. So when it comes to the word *missions*, I say we go big or go home. Either we need to stop using the word, or we need to start commissioning everybody out as missionaries—nurses, carpenters, taxi drivers, school teachers, engineers, and the guy that cleans up elephant poop at the zoo. We are all disciples on a mission. Let's make everyone a minister and missionary and send them out to share God's love and change the world.

The way we think about missions and some of the ways we have traditionally done missions, as outsiders coming in, have done harm to people. It looks very different from the incarnation, from Jesus, who moves into the neighborhood.

Our friend John Perkins, who is a civil rights activist, often recites this great proverb: "Go to the people. Live among them. Learn from them. Love them. Start with what they know. Build on what they have. In the end, you want the people to be able to say, 'We've done it ourselves.'"

Charity can be a good place to start, but it's a terrible place to end. Charity must lead us to justice. That's what holistic mission is all about. Saving souls is part of it, but so is making sure families can eat and have adequate health care and a good education.

That's something we have to build together. Real transformation takes time. It takes learning from the people and making their pain and problems our own. We earn the right to speak into each other's lives.

Every person has something to offer. All of us have something to teach and something to learn. In the Christian Community Development Association, we talk about how restoring a neighborhood takes three groups of people all working together. First, remainers—folks from the neighborhood who could leave as many of their peers do, but who intentionally remain in order to participate in the restoration. Next are the returners—these are people indigenous to the neighborhood who go off to school and job training to acquire skills and bring them back to the neighborhood to help restore it. Finally, there are the relocators—these are folks who move to the neighborhood deliberately, missionally, to be a part of the transformation. All three are heroic in their own ways. But we often put an unfair amount of emphasis on the last, the relocators, which is so sad because it communicates that you have to go somewhere else to live missionally. This mentality is also problematic because it makes relocators out be the heroic, sacrificial missionaries who have given up all comfort and privilege to live in the ghettos or slums, and it can be terribly disempowering if you are from the ghettos or slums.

As we discussed in our dialogue on racism, one of my good friends is an incredible indigenous leader—a remainer—in Philadelphia. He said something a while ago that has deeply formed my consciousness on this: "When folks like you move into this neighborhood, all of your peers think that you are a hero. When folks like me don't move out of this neighborhood, all of my peers think I'm a failure." This is a reality we have to battle. We have to combat the romanticism and sentimental-ity that spins missions in a way that celebrates the privileged, relocating "missionaries," and we have to combat the com-pelling pressure on indigenous folks to move out and forget where they came from. We need to celebrate everyone, and recognize that we all are a part of the solution.

So if you're from outside the neighborhood, you've got something to offer. If you're from inside the neighborhood, you've got something to offer. That kind of missional frame-work allows everybody to feel empowered, and fulfills vital functions.

This also affects the way we do Bible study. Folks with seminary degrees and book knowledge aren't the only teach-ers. Everyone is a teacher and everyone is a learner. Wisdom that comes from the streets is as valuable as wisdom that comes from books.

We've got a little thing going in Philly called the Alternative Seminary. This is the whole concept: everyone is a teacher, and everyone is a learner. We have some classes for a few weeks and some for an entire year. You don't get degrees or credit, and the classes tend to be small and really diverse. You may have someone who's been homeless sitting next to someone who's a CEO. I've been in classes with folks who don't know how to read alongside folks who have written books and read the Bible in the original Hebrew and Greek. It makes for a deep learning experience.

We had one class in an abandoned house we were fixing up. The class was on the economy of God, studying different passages of Scripture that deal with money. It's incredible to read the story of the rich man and Lazarus with someone who's been rich and someone who's been a beggar. We all see the text with different eyes. We hear different things because of who we are. You start to get a sense of what life was like with Jesus as he had a little circle with prostitutes and Pharisees, tax collectors and Zealots, fishermen and teachers of the law—there must have been some good conversations and some fiery debates!

That's a different model of education. It's a different model of missions. We may come in to missionize people, but we sure have got to be ready to learn too. On the other hand, we also have to be careful not to paralyze folks who come from so-called privilege. They, too, have something to give, but sometimes we have to be deliberate to make sure we give special honor to those who may have felt disempowered for whatever reason. For instance, when we think of a Bible study, we don't always think of organizing things in a way that someone who doesn't know how to read feels welcome and invited to actively participate.

TONY: Recently, I've seen many important changes in the way missions organizations are operating. In Haiti, for instance, where education is a big problem, instead of bringing teachers from America, Red Letter Christian workers down there have set up extensive teacher training programs. Instead of simply bemoaning that the teachers in the schools of Haiti lack teaching skills and that some are barely literate, they are helping those teachers to become more literate and teaching them the best pedagogical techniques so they can do a better job. The response has been incredible. Every year literally hundreds and hundreds of teachers go through these training programs—programs that empower Haitians to teach.

Here at Eastern, we started a graduate program to train students to go to developing countries and impoverished sections of American cities to foster the creation of small businesses and cottage industries that people can own and run themselves. We direct our graduates not to own the businesses, or even to start the businesses, but rather to help the indigenous people organize the businesses and own them themselves. But you don't have to go to third-world countries to go to the third world. Third-world conditions exist right here in America. For instance, in some inner-city situations, our graduates might look for people who have building skills and bring them together to encourage them to use those skills. Those who know how to do electrical work, carpentry, or plumbing can be brought together and encouraged to dream and perhaps imagine setting up a construction company. Our graduates know how to ask the questions related to whether or not these potential entrepreneurs have gone through the necessary hoops to be licensed by the city and/or state, know how to access microloans, have a viable business plan, and understand what equipment may be necessary to set up an office. We teach our students to shy away from giving answers and to concentrate on asking the right questions. That way, fledgling entrepreneurs will be able to say, "This is the company that *we* created. We did it ourselves."

Shane, what you said about all the skills that exist unused in your neighborhood is a great commentary on what's wrong with the system. In the long run, the only way to solve the problems of poverty is through job creation, but we cannot disempower people in the process. We've got to inspire people to use their own assets and skills.

SHANE: You know, what I would love to see is the economics professors from fine schools like Eastern University come down and meet with the drug dealers. I think it could be a powerful interaction. Studies have shown that the drug economy is the largest economy in the inner city, and studies have also shown that it is one of the most resilient and innovative.[1] Without a doubt it is a vicious, destructive force, but many of the dealers are unbelievably gifted. Can you imagine if their gifts are channeled toward a different mission? I know of one dealer who was taken in by a friend of mine who noticed her gifts and was able to imagine the possibilities. Before long they started a T-shirts business together that has now made tens of thousands of dollars.

And the mural arts project in Philly has shown us what can happen when graffiti artists simply have an outlet for their skills. They are painting murals now that are some of the finest art installations in the country, and Philly is becoming famous for them. You can do a special mural tour of Philly now. This is exactly the kind of thing we should be looking for—how people can use their gifts to do something beautiful and redemptive!

TONY: I know of a T-shirt factory that was created by some young people in a poor neighborhood in Camden, New Jersey. They designed a shirt that sold well among antiwar activists. The front said, "Old soldiers never die," and on the back it read, "Only the young ones do!" What a message those shirts sent about what happens in wars. And they were made in a T-shirt factory that neighborhood people owned and ran themselves.

Jesus sent his Spirit to empower people to realize their potential, and that should be the model for all of us in doing missionary work (Acts 1:8). When confronting the desperate situations we find in third-world countries and in troubled urban and rural areas here in America, we must realize that our objective must be to empower people and challenge them to use *their* gifts and actualize *their* potential. We have to join with them in such a way so that, as you said a moment ago, when they succeed, they can say, "We did it ourselves."

Dialogue on Resurrection

I am the resurrection and the life.

JOHN 11:25

SHANE: The vision of the New Jerusalem is all about resurrection. The brokenness of our cities is healed. It is not a return to the garden. It is a vision of the garden meeting the city. The city is brought back to life. The gardens take over the concrete.

I like how urban theologian Ray Bakke says, "The story of salvation begins in a garden and ends in a city."[1] The story ends with the healing of creation, the healing of civilization—of the city. The river of life flows right through the middle of the New Jerusalem. And I'm pretty sure you can eat the fish out of that river and swim in it, unlike the Delaware River here in Philly. And the Tree of Life is growing in New Jerusalem; it's healing the nations. Revelation says the gates of the city will never be shut (Revelation 21:25). We can live without fear, and no one is locked out or illegal. Oh, and one of the subtle verses says, "I did not see a temple in the city" (Revelation 21:22). You can hear the echoes of the ripping of the temple veil. There's no need for a temple in the New Jerusalem. God dwells with us again as he did in the garden. No need for a church—God lives in the streets of the New Jerusalem.

TONY: There are many who believe that the end of history is fire, and that on that final day the earth will be consumed. We live in an age of two kinds of doomsday sayers. There are those religionists who believe, according to their dispensationalist theologies, that the world is going to be destroyed because of sin. They believe that the perversities of the human race will become so great that the Lord will have to return and bring an end to it all. On the other hand, there are secularists and New Agers who are saying, "No, we ourselves are going to destroy the planet because of our environmental irresponsibility or our engagement in nuclear war." There is no shortage of doomsayers out there, both on the religious Right and on the secular Left.

SHANE: There are two ways to see the end times: One of those is the story of death and the other is a story of resurrection. One of those is of fire and the other is a feast. The story I see in Revelation proclaims, through Jesus' words and teachings, that everything is going to be restored. A theology of general resurrection proclaims that God is restoring not just human beings but everything that was ever made.

TONY: I grew up believing that you live and then you die, and after you die, if you're a Christian, you go to heaven, where all God's people will live together lovingly and harmoniously. There are, however, many evangelical, Bible-believing, inerrantists who contend that this is not the way it will be. These Christians believe there will be a new heaven *and a new earth.* After Christ returns, this latter group of Christians claims, the world will be renewed and the harmony of nature will be restored. The lion and the lamb will lie down together, and the violence that marks nature today will be no more (Isaiah 65:25). They believe that when Christ returns, all the people of God will be resurrected to live eternally in loving community here on earth. Note that all this will not happen up in heaven; it will be here on earth.

This good news about the future of the earth is an increasingly prevalent message within the evangelical community. There is a growing number of evangelicals who believe that, when Christ returns, the earth will be restored, and there will be a new society made up of faithful people who will live on this planet in love and justice. Then the world will be as God intended it to be when he created it.

SHANE: If faith is believing in what we don't yet see, as Hebrews says, and if we really believe in the New Jerusalem, in God's kingdom coming, that affects the way we live. Our friend Jim Wallis says, "We believe despite the evidence and watch the evidence change." We know the end of the story, so we start living it into being. Like a kid at Christmas sleeps on the couch and puts out Oreos and milk, you *do* things if you really believe that something is coming.

And so it is for us. If we know that the story ends with folks beating swords into plows, we start now. And we sure don't keep building more swords.

When we know that the earth is going to be healed, then we don't want to keep creating new wounds. Thy kingdom come on earth. Today. "Today is the day of salvation. The kingdom of God is now" (2 Corinthians 6:2, paraphrased).

We don't have to wait. We get to begin to live that vision now and to be people who practice resurrection. As Robert Kennedy said, "Some men see things as they are and say 'why'? I dream of things that never were and say, 'Why not?'"[2]

TONY: Philippians 1:6 says that God, who starts a good work in us and through us, will complete it on the day of Christ's return. The Bible suggests that, through people who are committed to Christ in the here and now, God is at work rescuing nature, restoring the planet, working toward social justice, and alleviating the suffering of the poor and the oppressed. Knowing that we are participating with God in an enterprise that will be brought to complete fruition when the trumpet sounds and the Lord returns, makes us into people of hope as we seek to win the lost and change the world.

We are not like those old-time social-gospelers who believed they could create the kingdom of God on their own. Nor are we like the fundamentalists who say we can accomplish nothing lasting in our efforts to make this world a better place. Rather, we Red Letter Christians are a people who say that, through us, God is initiating change in this world, but that the completion of what we are called to change will not occur until Christ comes and joins us in these efforts.

When I'm explaining what we are called to do in anticipation of Christ's coming, I have often used as an illustration what the French underground was doing during World War II. If you could have asked the members of the French underground, "What are you try-ing to accomplish with your ragged handful of saboteurs and your haphazard attempt to be freedom fighters?" they would have said, "It's obvious! We're trying to defeat the Nazi armies who have been occupying our land."

"But you're a small group of untrained soldiers with a few hand grenades and a few machine guns," you would have protested. "You are up against the greatest military machine ever assembled in the history of the human race. You don't stand a chance against them."

No doubt, the members of the underground would have responded, "We're going to go on fighting to liberate our land because we know that one day the signal will be given and a huge invasion force, that is even now being assembled on the other side of the English Channel, will get on ships and come across to join up with us. That invasion force will link up with what we are doing and carry us to victory."

I always have contended that, figuratively speaking, we are God's underground, struggling for justice and working for the rescuing of the planet. And when people scoff and say, "You're far too few and your resources are far too limited," I simply respond, "But we are going to win! We know it doesn't look good right now, but beyond the sky there is a huge invasion force being assembled. We don't know when the signal is going to be given and the trumpet sounded, but one day the Church Militant (that's who we Christians are here and now) will be joined by Christ and the Church Triumphant (those who will be resurrected at his coming) and together we will march to victory." We labor, as Paul says so eloquently, not as those without hope, because we believe in this great coming event that we call the Second Coming of Christ. "Behold," says Scripture, "I make all things new!" (Revelation 21:5 KJV). Our God will come again to reenter history and make everything new again. What a vision of the future!

To go back to Scripture again, I refer you to the thirteenth chapter of Matthew, where Jesus describes what leads up to his second coming. It is important for us to get our eschatology from Jesus rather than from pop culture books or movies. In Matthew 13:24 to 30 and verses 38 to 43, he says that his kingdom is like a sower who goes out and sows wheat. The wheat, Jesus tells us, is really symbolic of the kingdom of God. He then says that, while the wheat is growing, the evil one comes and sows weeds or, as it reads in the King James Version of the Bible, "tares." It is clear from what Jesus says that the one who comes and sows the weeds is Satan, and that the weeds represent his evil kingdom. These two kingdoms, we are told, will grow up together.

In this parable, Jesus tells how the servants come to their master and ask, "What shall we do? Shall we go and try to pull out the weeds?" The master says, "No! If you do that you will destroy a lot of the wheat along with the weeds. If you try to pull up the weeds, you will mess up the wheat. Instead," he tells them, "let the wheat and the tares grow up together until the end. Then we will separate the wheat from the tares" (paraphrased).

What Jesus made very clear is that the kingdom of evil (the weeds) is growing stronger and more manifest every day. Never has evil been more prominently observed in history than it is in today's world, but we are not to be dismayed. Not only is the kingdom of evil growing stronger and more evident every day, but so is the kingdom of God.

In addition to the fantastic growth of Christianity in the third world, consider the incredible progress that Christians have helped to bring about on behalf of the world's impoverished nations. According to reports from Bradley Wright at the University of Connecticut, extreme poverty in developing countries has been cut in half since the 1980s, life expectancy has doubled around the world over the last 100 years, literacy rates have soared from 25 percent to over 80 percent over the last three decades, the percentage of people starving worldwide has dropped from 38 percent in 1970 to 18 percent in 2001.[3] I could go on and on citing statistics of progress in eliminating world hunger, providing decent housing, upgrading education, improving the health of the world's people; and, in almost all of the instances cited, it has been Christians who have played a major role in making these good things happen.

These are all evidence that God is at work in the world, winning people into citizenship in God's kingdom and transforming the world's socioeconomic conditions. God is raising ecological awareness so that more and more people are turning away from carbon energy to solar energy. Today, China is the greatest solar energy nation on the planet. We have to start catching up with China, and we will. Denmark is using thermal energy and building wind turbines at a fantastic rate. The whole world is learning how to create a new earth without depleting its nonrenewable resources. When we are generating energy from the wind, when we are figuring out how to use thermal energy, when the oceans are being harnessed to give us energy, and when there is a growing use of solar energy, we are seeing a new kingdom breaking loose in the midst of the here and now.

SHANE: It's been said that before every revolution, it seemed impossible, and after every revolution, it seems inevitable. Perhaps Jesus is asking us today: "Do you have the eyes to see it? Do you have the ears to hear it? Do you have the imagination to create it?"

I am reminded of that passage in Romans that speaks of how all creation is groaning for the kingdom, as in the pains of childbirth (Romans 8:22). It continues by saying that "we ourselves groan inwardly as we wait: (verse 23). It's an image of groaning, aching, longing. Our waiting is not a passive waiting; we wait expecting, like when a pregnant mother waits on her baby to come. You prepare, you start exercising, breathing, practicing for it. Labor is an interesting image because it's something that happens to you, but it's also something that you are participating in. This world is pregnant with another world. And we get to be the midwives.

Indian activist Arundhati Roy said, "Another world is not only possible, she's on her way. Maybe many of us won't be here to greet her, but on a quiet day, if I listen very carefully, I can hear her breathing."[4]

TONY: When I was a little boy, my mother and I were walking in Philadelphia's Fairmount Park on a quiet summer afternoon. The birds were singing, and we could hear the bugs buzzing. My mother asked me, "Do you hear those sounds?" I said, "Yes," and she went on to say, "Listen to them carefully. Do they make you happy or do they make you sad?"

I thought for a while, and then I said, "Mom, to be perfectly honest, they make me sad." She then explained to me that I felt that way because all the sounds of nature were in a minor key, and whenever music is in a minor key, it creates a feeling of sadness. When Jesus comes back, all the music of nature will move from a minor key to a major key. "And that," my mother said, "will make for joyful music throughout the planet."

The idea that the return of Jesus will change creation from its present suffering into joyful sounds came across as a thrilling hope for the future. The groaning of nature will be no more. Nature will be raised from groaning to rejoicing (Psalm 148).

SHANE: I think of one old Catholic activist I know who's been going for decades and decades. He's gone to jail, gone to protests, formed communities, done everything. One time somebody said, "Don't you look at all the pain and just get over-whelmed sometimes? How do you keep going?" And he said something beautiful: "Every morning I curl up in a little ball. I crawl into the lap of Jesus and hear him whisper how much he loves me." I think that's part of this. As you read Scripture, and especially as you read the red stuff, you get the sense that there is a God who really loves us, and loves the whole world enough to send his Son and enough to resurrect it.

TONY: John 3:16 has all kinds of meaning in what we have been talking about. When we read, "For God so loved the world," we should know that in the original language of the Bible, the word for "world" is *cosmos*, which means literally everything that is in the universe. God's salvation is not just for individuals. His salvation is for everything in this world—for everything in the whole universe. God loves chickens; he loves the trees; he loves the mountains. He looks on everything he has made and says, "It is good!" He declares, "I love the world, and everything that's in the world that I created." This world that God loves will not be destroyed! Instead, it will be renewed, and the people of God will be resurrected to live in this new world.

A Red Letter Future

In wrapping up a book like this, it is important for some predictions to be made about the future of Red Letter Christianity. What does the future hold in store for this effort to take Jesus seriously and to take an honest shot at living out his desires for life?

First of all, there is a great deal of evidence that there is a hunger for this kind of Christianity. For example, the author of a featured article in *Newsweek* magazine observed that people had become tired of the ongoing arguments over such issues as gay marriage and abortion (as important as we believe these arguments to be), and want to focus instead on the things Jesus talked about.[1] The author made a major point in raising up Saint Francis of Assisi as a heroic figure whom more and more religious people are considering an ideal to be imitated. The simplicity of the beliefs and practices of this medieval saint who tried to live out the teachings of Jesus as he articulated them in the Sermon on the Mount (Matthew 5 and 6), are viewed as a contrast to the theological complexity of religious leaders. A Christianity that makes giving to the poor the primary way in which followers of Jesus should use their money, rather than spending it on expensive buildings they call churches in order to honor One who said that he did not dwell in temples made with hands (Acts 7:48).

The attraction of this mendicant monk of another era seems to be growing among those Christians who find something irrelevant about the bureaucracies and hierarchies of institutionalized religion. There is an authenticity in the life of Saint Francis that is attracting a growing host of Christians.

Second, I believe that Red Letter Christians increasingly will become activists for social justice. Because they are taking the words of Jesus literally, they will be led into personal relationships with poor and oppressed people. Not only will they endeavor to respond to the immediate needs of these children of God but also they will be drawn into the social movements that are committed to changing those social structures that contribute to poverty and oppression.

As they feed and clothe the homeless on city streets, these Christ-followers will inevitably become involved with activist groups that are trying to change the political and economic systems that have failed to address the needs of the homeless. Their growing contact with Palestinian Christians will lead them to participate with those who want to end the illegal occupation of Palestinian land, even as they affirm and work for Israel to have safe and secure borders. Friendships with gay, lesbian, bisexual, and transgender individuals will soften their attitudes, and render them less likely to support prohibitions that the religious establishment has long legitimized against LGBT persons.

Seeing the physical and psychological sufferings of military combatants will generate a strong antipathy to war and an increasing commitment to peace efforts. Awareness of the ill effects of environmental degradation will cause these Red Letter Christians to join organizations that challenge those who are skeptical of global warming, and to support many of the regulations of the Environmental Protection Agency.

There is no doubt that living out the red letters on the micro level will lead many of these people to involvement in changing social structures on the macro level.

Finally, we expect that Red Letter Christians will become significantly more oriented to spiritual disciplines. Those who once as evangelicals used to question the practices of Roman Catholics, will come to embrace with enthusiasm the spiritual exercises of the likes of Saint Ignatius, Catherine of Siena, and Saint John of the Cross. It is not surprising that the book *Common Prayer*, which Shane coauthored with Jonathan Wilson-Hartgrove and Enuma Okoro, has not been looked upon with favor by some very orthodox evangelicals, who deem it "too Catholic." Red Letter Christians, nevertheless, are finding crucial guides to intensive spirituality as practiced by many of the Catholic mystics, along with the spiritual disciplines they discover in Protestant sources such as the German pietists and Pentecostal revivalists.

We may not think that this Red Letter Christian movement will ever become a dominant form of religious life; however, we are convinced that in one form or another it will continue to be a positive irritant to a church that has the tendency to become complacently conformed to cultural values. We hope that what we have written will be a part of that and invite all our readers, both young and old, to join this movement. Go to our website, *www.redletterchristians.org*, and find out how. We need you as partners in this Red Letter Revolution.

Acknowledgments

There is no way this book would be a reality without our editor, Angela Scheff, who took the ramblings of the two of us, got our wordy conversations into a size that would fit into these pages, organized our ideas, challenged us to support our assertions with careful referencing, and encouraged us in believing that we had some important things to say. We're grateful for the rest of the team at Thomas Nelson as well—Bryan Norman, Jennifer McNeil, and Janene MacIvor. We're thankful for Peggy Campolo, Katie Jo Claiborne, and Brett Anderson, who gave this book its first reading, corrected the grammar and syntax of sentences, and questioned many of our assumptions. We'd also like to thank Christine Murrison, Brian Ballard, and James Warren, who spent hours doing research and taking care of the hundred and one details that go along with preparing a manuscript for publication.

We appreciate Sarah Blaisdell, who spent many hours transcribing the recorded conversations that went on between the two of us that became the first stages of this book. Her work was brilliant and right on schedule.

Finally, mention must be made of Mark Sweeney who served as our agent. He negotiated the contracts and handled the various business matters that are required in the publication business. He has played an important role, and we are thankful for him.

To everyone cited above, we offer not only our appreciation but also our love.

—Tony Campolo and Shane Claiborne

Notes

Introduction: Why This Book?

1. Some of the leading religious commentators have called Sider's book one of the most important written in the latter half of the twentieth century.

Chapter 1: On History

1. Charles Moore, ed., *Provocations: Spiritual Writings of Kierkegaard* (Farmington, PA: Plough Publishing, 2003), 201.
2. "Beliefs, Vision & History," *Willow Creek Community Church Website*, www.willowcreek.org/chicago/about/beliefs.
3. Greg L. Hawkins and Cally Parkinson, *Reveal: Where Are You* (Chicago: Willow Creek Association, 2007).
4. Here's a glimpse of a few of the things Willow Creek has done in the period of a year: They have distributed 2.8 million pounds of food to neighbors in need; opened 11 clinics in Latin America sharing over 3.1 million dollars; installed 28 solar-powered water systems and dug 106 wells in Africa, providing water access for 200,000 people; hosted one of the largest fair-trade expos in the United States; mobilized 16,000 folks to sort seeds for half a million seed packs sent to Zimbabwe; had 16,000 people pack 3.6 million meals for kids in Africa; filled 18 forty-foot shipping containers to be sent to some of the toughest corners on earth; packed 13,000 hope packs, including mosquito nets, to save lives in Zambia; provided free legal counsel for 893 folks from a volunteer team of lawyers; visited 5,000 inmates at 8 local prisons; and gave away 10,728 coats to folks who are cold. More than 35,000 volunteer opportunities were filled in 2010 at Willow. No doubt these are some stunning examples of compassion, which makes their confession all the more powerful.

Chapter 2: On Community

1. Leo Maasburg and Michael J. Miller, *Mother Teresa of Calcutta: A Personal Portrait* (San Fransico: Ignatius Press, 2010), 36.

2. Eberhard Arnold, *The Early Christians in Their Own Words* (Rifton, NY: Plough Publishing, 1997).

3. *The Works of John Wesley*, vol. 11, *An Earnest Appeal to Men of Reason and Religion*, ed. Gerald Cragg (Nashville: Abingdon Press, 1987), 31.

4. Lenny Bruce, *How to Talk Dirty and Influence People: An Autobiography* (New York: Fireside, 1992), 58.

5. Quoted in Edward W. Bauman, *Where Your Treasure Is* (Arlington, VA: Bauman Bible Telecasts, 1980), 74.

Chapter 3: On the Church

1. For one recent study, see the Pew Foundation's "Religion Among the Millennials," 17 Feb. 2010, www.pewforum.org/Age/Religion-Among-the-Millennials.aspx.

2. Paul Sabatier, *Life of St. Francis of Assisi*, trans. Louise Seymour Houghton (London: C. Scribner's Sons, 1917), 317.

3. Adolf Holl, *The Last Christian*, trans. Peter Heinegg (Garden City, NJ: Doubleday, 1980).

Chapter 4: On Liturgy

1. Shane Claiborne, Jonathan Wilson-Hartgrove, and Enuma Okoro, *Common Prayer* (Grand Rapids: Zondervan, 2010).

2. Emile Durkheim, *The Elementary Forms of Religious Life*, trans. Joseoph W. Swain (New York: The Free Press, 1947).

3. See www.haitipartners.org.

Chapter 5: On Saints

1. Adolf Holl, *The Last Christian*, trans. Peter Heinegg (Garden City, NJ: Doubleday, 1980).

2. Lawrence Cunningham, *Francis of Assisi: Performing the Gospel Life* (Cambridge: William B. Eerdemans Publishing Co.), 146.

3. Omer Englebert, *Saint Francis of Assisi: A Biography* (Cincinnati: St. Anthony Messenger Press, 1979), 95.

4. G. K. Chesterton, *St. Francis of Assisi,* (New York: George H. Doran, 1924).

5. Holl, *The Last Christian.*

Chapter 6: On Hell

1. Viktor E. Frankl, *Man's Search for Meaning* (Boston: Beacon, 2005).

2. Bill Bright's *Have You Heard of the Four Spiritual Laws?* is a classic evangelical text disseminated by Campus Crusade for Christ. The first law is "God loves you and has a wonderful plan for your life."

3. Shane Claiborne, The Irresistible Revolution (Grand Rapids, Zondervan, 2006).

4. Karl Barth, "Evangelical Theology" (The Warfield Lectures, Princeton Theological Seminary, Princeton, NJ, May 2–4, 1962).
5. "Larry King Live," CNN, June 16, 2005.

Chapter 7: On Islam

1. Anne Lamott, *Bird by Bird* (New York: Random House), 22.
2. Jitsuo Morikawa, "My Spiritual Pilgrimage," (lecture to the Ministers and Missionaries Benefit Board, American Baptist Churches, Lincoln, NE, May 23, 1973).
3. Shane Claiborne, *Iraq Journal 2003* (Indianapolis: Doulos Christou Press, 2006).
4. My friend Greg Barrett has written a book about this entitled *The Gospel of Rutba* (Maryknoll, NY: Orbis Books, 2012), and word on the street is there may be a film in the works. See www.thegospelofrutba. com.
5. Luke 7:2, Mark 7:26, John 4:7, and Matthew 9:10, respectively.
6. C. S. Lewis, *Mere Christianity* (New York: HarperCollins, 2001), 208–209.

Chapter 8: On Economics

1. Edward Mote, "My Hope Is Built," 1834.

Chapter 10: On Being Pro-Life

1. Colleen Curry and Michael S. James, "Troy Davis Executed after Stay Denied by Supreme Court," *ABC News Website*, http://abcnews. go.com/US/troy-davis-executed-stay-denied-supreme-court/ story?id=14571862#.T3OS4tV7mSo. Accessed March 28, 2012.
2. Amnesty International, "Death Penalty in 2011: Alarming Levels of Executions in the Few Countries that Kill," *Amnesty International Website*, March 27, 2012, www.amnesty.org/en/news/death-penalty-2011-alarming-levels-executions-few-countries-kill-2012-03-27. Accessed March 28, 2012.
3. See www.deathpenaltyinfo.org. On this site, there is a section titled "Botched Executions," which lists dozens of executions that have gone very wrong with detailed documentation. It is very disturbing, especially for those of us who follow Jesus, who suffered such horror from an imperial execution on the cross.
4. See "Wide Ideological Divide over Death Penalty" by the Pew Research Center (Nov. 9–14, 2011).
5. Joseph Cardinal Bernardin, "A Consistent Ethic of Life," (lecture, William Wade Lecture Series, St. Louis University, St. Louis, MO, March 11, 1984).
6. Joerg Dreweke and Rebecca Wind, "Expanding Access to

Contraception Through Medicaid Could Prevent Nearly 500,000 Unwanted Pregnancies, Save $1.5 Billion," Guttmacher Institute, 2000, http://www.guttmacher.org/media/nr/2006/08/16/index.html.

7. Mother Teresa, Address at the National Prayer Breakfast (The Washington Hilton, Washington, DC, Feb. 3, 1994).

8. See www.consistent-life.org for a great resource dedicated to the consistent life ethic.

Chapter 11: On Environmentalism

1. Erik Reece, Wendell Berry, John J. Cox, *Lost Mountain: A Year in the Vanishing Wilderness: Radical Strip Mining and the Devastation of Appalachia* (New York: Riverhead Books, 2006), 227.

2. Michele Ver Ploeg, et al., "Access to Affordable and Nutritious Food— Measuring and Understanding Food Deserts and Their Consequences: Report to Congress," *United States Department of Agriculture Website*, www.ers.usda.gov/Publications/AP/AP036/. Accessed March 29, 2012.

3. There are a lot of good books out there about the environment, from theology to gardening tips. I'd recommend anything by Wendell Berry, books by Matthew and Nancy Sleeth, Stephen Bouma-Prediger, Norman Wirzba, Scott Sabin, and Jonathan Merritt—all wonderful voices connecting Christianity to environmentalism. *The Green Bible* (New York: HarperOne, 2008), which talks about the "green letters," much as we talk about the red letters, has verses in green that relate to the environment.

4. Stephen Bouma-Prediger, *For the Beauty of the Earth: A Christian Vision for Creation Care* (Grand Rapids: Baker Academic, 2010), 118.

5. See my book *How to Rescue the Earth without Worshiping Nature* (Nashville: Thomas Nelson, 1992).

6. See a video of my visit to Claudio's urban farm at www.youtube/AVUGuDttq5Pg.

7. You can see the aquaponics completion here: www.youtu.be/fodxcnNsEEo.

8. John Robbius, *Diet for a New America* (Tiburou, CA: H. J. Kramer, 1987), 351.

Chapter 12: On Women

1. Rena Pederson, *The Lost Apostle* (San Francisco: Jossey-Boss, 2006), 29.

2. Christians for Biblical Equality, www.cbeinternational.org.

3. He continues, "You won't find a single statement in Genesis 1–2 about the silence or subordination of women to men. Eve is simply the necessary compliment and suitable companion to Adam. What you will find are statements making clear the inadequacy of the man without woman who is the crown of creation, for the text says 'it is not good

for man to be alone.' Patriarchy is not an inherently good thing, an inherently God thing, and it should not be repristinized and set up as a model for Christian ministry." Ben Worthington, "John Piper on Men in Ministry, and the Masculinity of Christianity," Patheos website, www.patheos.com/blogs/bibleandculture/2012/02/12/john-piper-on-men-in-ministry-and-the-masculinity-of-christianity. Ben has also written some other very helpful material on this issue, such as women in the ministry of Jesus.

4. See G. E. Lessing, *The Education of the Human Race,* trans. F. W. Robertson (London, 1872), chapters 1 and 3.

5. Quoted by Zoe Moss, "It Hurts to Be Alive and Obsolete: The Aging Woman," in *Sisterhood Is Powerful,* ed. Robin Williams (New York: Vintage Books, 1970), 170ff.

6. George H. Mead, *Mind, Self, and Society* (Chicago: University of Chicago Press, 1934), 134ff.

7. "10 Surprising Statistics on Women in the Workplace," College Blog, www.collegetimes.us/10-surprising-statistics-on-women-in-the-workplace.

Chapter 13: On Racism

1. I borrowed this definition from Beverly Daniel Tatum, who wrote the national bestseller *Why Are All the Black Kids Sitting Together in the Cafeteria?* (New York: Basic Books, 2003).

2. Steven Levitt and Stephen Dubner, *Freakonomics: A Rogue Economist Explores the Hidden Side of Everything* (New York: William Morrow, 2009), chapter 6.

3. www.naacp.org/pages/criminal-justice-fact-sheet.

4. A couple of good books on this are *The New Jim Crow* by Michelle Alexander (New York: The New Press, 2012) and *Slavery by Another Name* by Douglas Blackmon (New York: Anchor Books, 2008). And my good friend and fellow Red Letter Christian brother Chris Lahr writes extensively about race at www.missionyear.org/blog/chrislahr.

5. Find more in Sophia Kerby, "1 in 3 Black Men Go To Prison? The 10 Most Disturbing Facts About Racial Inequality in the U.S. Criminal Justice System," AlterNet, March 17, 2012, www.alternet.org/drugs/154587/1_in_3_black_men_go_to_prison_the_10_most_disturbing_facts_about_racial_inequality_in_the__u.s._criminal_justice_system?page=1.

6. For more on this, see Douglas Blackmon, *Slavery by Another Name* (New York: Anchor, 2008). See also Michelle Alexander and Cornel West, *The New Jim Crow* (New York: The New Press, 2012).

7. Sara Flounders, "The Pentagon and Slave Labor in U.S. Prisons," Centre for Research on Globalization, June 23, 2011, www.globalresearch.ca/index.php?context=va&aid=25376.

8. See Howard Thurman, *Jesus and the Disinherited* (New York: Abington-Cokesbury Press, 1949).
9. Frederick Douglass, *Narrative of the Life of Frederick Douglass, an American Slave, Written by Himself* (New York: Signet, [1845] 1968), 120.
10. Malcolm X with Alex Haley, *The Autobiography of Malcolm X* (New York: Ballantine Books, 1973), chapter 9.
11. While there are scores of books on race and reconciliation, we recommend *Radical Reconciliation: Beyond Political Pietism and Christian Quietism,* by Allen Boesak and Curtiss Paul DeYoung (New York: Orbis, 2012).

Chapter 14: On Homosexuality

1. George W. Bush, "State of the Union," Feb 2, 2005. Transcript of the speech is available at http://transcripts.cnn.com/ TRANSCRIPTS/0502/02/lkl.01.html.
2. Over a ten-year period while teaching and doing research as a faculty member at the University of Pennsylvania, I interviewed scores of gay men but had only a few in-depth interviews with lesbians.
3. Billy Graham, quoted in Andrew Marin, *Love Is an Orientation* (Downers Grove: IVP Books, 2009), 108.
4. S. T. Russell and K. Joyner, "Adolescent Sexual Orientation and Suicide Risk," *American Journal of Public Health,* 2001: 1276–81.
5. Released as a book titled *UnChristian* by Gabe Lyons and David Kinnaman (Grand Rapids: Baker, 2007).
6. The Barna Group, "A New Generation Expresses Its Skepticism and Frustration with Christianity," The Barna Group Website, September 24, 2007, www.barna.org/barna-update/ article/16-teensnext-gen/94-a-new-generation-expresses-its-skepticism-and-frustration-with-christianity.

Chapter 15: On Immigration

1. Bob Ekblad, *Conspire* magazine Issue 8: Walls and Borders (www.conspiremagazine.org).
2. New Sanctuary Movement of Philadelphia Website, www.sanctuaryphiladelphia.org. See also *Welcoming the Stranger: Justice, Compassion, and Truth in the Immigration Debate* by Matthew Soerens and Jenny Hwang (Downers Gove: IVP Books, 2009).

Chapter 16: On Civil Disobedience

1. Elaine Pagels, *Revelations* (New York: Viking Press, 2012), chapter 4.
2. John Howard Yoder, *The Politics of Jesus*, 2nd ed. (Grand Rapids: Eerdmans, 1994), 162.
3. Martin Luther King Jr., *A Testament of Hope: The Essential Writings and*

Speeches of Martin Luther King, Jr., ed. James M. Washington (New York: HarperOne, 1990), 256–57.

4. We recommend Jacques Ellul and Leo Tolstoy for further reading. Tolstoy's 1886 essay "Writings on Civil Disobedience and Nonviolence" is a classic.

Chapter 17: On Giving

1. See "New Study Shows Trends in Tithing and Donating," Barna Group, April 14, 2008. www.barna.org/congregations-articles/41-new-study-shows-trends-in-tithing-and-donating.
2. Ray Mayhew, "Embezzlement: The Sin of the Contemporary Church," Relational Tithe Website, www.relationaltithe.com/pdffiles/EmbezzlementPaper.pdf. Accessed March 29, 2012.
3. In the spirit of the ancient biblical concept of Jubilee: Leviticus 25:10.
4. Mother Teresa and Lucinda Varney, *A Simple Path* (New York: Random House, 1995), xxxi.

Chapter 18: On Empire

1. Depending on whether we are talking oil or water or diapers, the stats vary, but it's safe to say we are using way more than our fair share. Two websites that break down consumer trends are www.mindfully.org and www.worldwatch.org.
2. George W. Bush, "State of the Union," www.washingtonpost.com/wp-srv/onpolitics/transcripts/bushtext_012803.html.
3. Elaine Pagels, *Revelations* (New York: Viking, 2012), chapter 12.
4. Bill and Gloria Gaither, "There's Just Something About That Name" (Hanna Street Music, 1970).
5. Wes Howard-Brook and Anthony Gwyther, *Unveiling Empire: Reading Revelation Then and Now* (Maryknoll, NY: Orbis Books, 1999).
6. Research conducted by the Club of Rome, a research group at the Massachusetts Institute of Technology. See *The Limits to Growth* (New York: Universe Books, 1972.)
7. Stephen Decatur, as quoted in Max Boot, *The Savage Wars of Peace* (New York: Basic Books), 6.
8. American Exceptionalism is the theory that the United States is different from other countries and has a specific and unique role to play. Often there is a theological undertone similar to Rome. For more on this, see *Jesus for President* (Grand Rapids: Zondervan, 2008).
9. Jack Healy, "Exodus from North Signals Iraqi Christians' Slow Decline," *The New York Times*, March 10, 2012.

Chapter 19: On Politics

1. For instance, *Jesus for President* (Grand Rapids: Zondervan, 2008).

2. No doubt there is much more to this interaction. Many of the coins had Caesar's image on them with the caption "Son of God," which was deeply problematic for Jews and Christians. Jesus continually challenges the ways we attribute Godlike power to money. At one point Jesus even personifies money, giving it a name, "Mammon," and telling us we cannot serve both it and God. Things are more convoluted in our world where we try to make them one and the same, so our money says "In God We Trust" while our economy reeks of the seven deadly sins.

3. Worldwatch Institute, *State of the World 2011: Innovations that Nourish the Planet*, (New York: W. W. Norton and Company, 2011).

4. Sean Kennedy, "Bush Led on AIDS Funds: Will Obama?" CNN Website, July 23, 2010, http://articles. cnn.com/2010-07-23/opinion/kennedy.aids.bush. obama_1_pepfar-aids-funds-plan-for-aids-relief?_s=PM:OPINION).

Chapter 20: On War and Violence

1. Armen Keteyian, "Suicide Epidemic Among Veterans," CBS News Website, February 11, 2009, www.cbsnews.com/stories/2007/11/13/ cbsnews_investigates/main3496471.shtml. See also Pia Malbran, "Veteran Suicides: How We Got the Numbers," CBS News Website, February 11, 2009, www.cbsnews.com/8301-500690_162-3498625.html.

2. Jamie Tarabay, "Suicide Rivals the Battlefield in Toll on U.S. Military," NPR News Website, June 17, 2010, www.npr.org/templates/story/story. php?storyId=127860466. Accessed March 29, 2012.

3. See for example a good compilation of essays addressing the best critiques of pacifism entitled *A Faith Not Worth Fighting For,* ed. Tripp York (Eugene, OR: Cascade Books, 2012).

4. Walter Wink, "The Third Way," Chicago Sunday Evening Club Website, Sermon Archives, www.csec.org/csec/sermon/wink_3707.htm.

5. In the orderly Jewish culture, hitting someone was done with the right hand (in some Jewish communities hitting with the left hand meant exclusion for ten days). And in order to hit someone on the right cheek with the right hand required a backslap. It is clear that Jesus is describing a backhand, like an abusive husband to a wife or a master to a slave. It was a slap to insult, degrade, and humiliate, not meant for an equal but an inferior—a slap to "put them in their place." By turning the cheek, the person made the abuser look them in the eye, and could only hit them as an equal. By turning the cheek, the other person is saying, "I am a human being, in the image of God. And you cannot destroy that."

6. It can be argued that Jesus' command for the disciples to *flee* the city and "run to the hills" on the day of Israel's disaster (70 CE) is a nonviolently prudent idea, lest they all be slaughtered in fighting against the Romans. Following Jesus' teachings, the Christians in the

sixties and seventies indeed did not fight in the Jewish War but fled to cities like Pella.

7. Walter Wink, *The Powers That Be* (New York: Doubleday, 1998 Doubleday), 111.

8. A phrase coined by Walter Bruggeman in his book *The Prophetic Imagination* (Minneapolis: Fortress Press, 2001).

9. See www.centurionsguild.org. Our friend Logan Mehl-Laituri, an Iraq veteran, has written an incredible book called *Reborn on the Fourth of July* (Downers Grove, IL: IVP, 2012). Logan also recommends these films on war: *The Ground Truth* (NBC Universal, 2006, DVD), *Why We Fight* (Sony Pictures Home Entertainment, 2006, DVD), *The Conscientious Objector* (Cinequest, 2010, DVD), *Soldiers of Conscience* (New Video Group, 2009, DVD), *The Fog of War* (Sony Pictures Home Entertainment, 2004, DVD), *This is Where We Take Our Stand* (thisiswherewetakeourstand.com), and *Winter Soldier* (Oscilloscope Laboratories/Milestone Films, 2009, DVD).

Chapter 21: On National Debts

1. Jeanne Sahadi, "Taxes: What People Forget about Reagan," CNN Money Website, September 12, 2010, http://money.cnn. com/2010/09/08/news/economy/reagan_years_taxes/index.htm.

2. Mark J. Penn, "The Pessimism Index," *Time,* June 30, 2011, www.time. com/time/nation/article/0,8599,2080607,00.html.

3. Hans Blommestein and Perla Ibarlucea Flores, "OECD Statistical Yearbook on African Central Government Debt," *OECD Journal* 2011 (2011), issue 1: 1–4.

4. Mercedes Alvaro, www.dowjones.com/djnewswires.asp.

5. Charlayne Hunter-Gault, "Uganda's Successful Anti-AIDS Program Targets Youth," CNN World Website, September 3, 1999, http://edition.cnn.com/WORLD/africa/9909/03/uganda.aids/.

6. Martin Luther King, Dec. 24, 1967, Ebenezer Baptist Church, "A Christmas Sermon on Peace," 1967.

7. For a video that illustrates where the stuff we consume comes from, see www.youtube/gLBE5QAYXp8 and www.storyofstuff.org.

8. Ellyn Ferguson, "House Panel Juggles Competing Interests to Write Farm Bill," *USA Today* website, July 17, 2007, http://www.usatoday. com/news/washington/2007-07-15-farm-bill_N.htm.

9. Dom Hélder Câmara, *Dom Helder Camara: Essential Writings,* ed. Francis McDonagh (Maryknoll, NY: Orbis Books, 2009), 11.

Chapter 22: On the Middle East

1. See more of "Tearing Down the Walls" from the West Bank at www. vimeo.com/38585835.

2. An interview with Alex Awad, dean of students, Bethlehem Bible College, March 8, 2012.
3. Central Intelligence Agency, "The Middle East: West Bank," in *The World Factbook*, March 21, 2012, *CIA Website*. www.cia.gov/library/publications/the-world-factbook/geos/we.html.
4. See *Jesus and the Land* by Gary M. Burge (Grand Rapids: Baker Academic, 2010).
5. Russell Nieli, "The Marriage of a One-State and Two-State Solution," *Tikkum,* July/August 2009, 33.
6. For more on Shane's visit with the Nassar family, see www.youtu.be/3TkPkxDj8Kl.
7. Our friend Porter Speakman has made a few films about the conflict in the Middle East. *Tent of Nations*: www.vimeo.com/37434264; *Checkpoint*: www.vimeo.com/37416952; *Wall*: www.vimeo.com/36911218.

Chapter 23: On the Global Church

1. People like Diana Butler Bass in *Christianity after Religion* (San Francisco: HarperOne, 2012), Jimmy Dorrell in *Dead Church Walking* (Downers Grove: IVP Books, 2011), and Phyllis Tickle in *The Great Emergence* (Grand Rapids: Baker Books, 2008)—for starters.
2. The Crystal Cathedral in California has a building with ten thousand windows; a fifty-two-bell carillon; gigantic, ninety-foot-high doors that open electronically behind the pulpit; a seventeen-foot, 18-karat-gold cross; and an outdoor movie screen for "drive-in" worshipers. See www.crystalcathedral.org.
3. Our friend Chris Haw, who coauthored *Jesus for President* with Shane, has written a brilliant book about his faith journey, growing up at Willow Creek (where he and Shane met), and now ending up Catholic. It's entitled *From Willow Creek to Sacred Heart* (Notre Dame, IN: Ave Maria Press, 2012).
4. A good book on this topic is *Unlearning Protestantism* by Gerald Schlabach (Grand Rapids: Brazos Press, 2010).

Chapter 25: On Missions

1. Based on an estimate of how much money goes through the drug corners in North Philadelphia, the drug trade as an economy is only second to welfare. See more from our friend Coz Crosscombe and Common Grace, Inc., at www.crosscombe.com.

Chapter 26: On Resurrection

1. Raymond J. Bakke and Jim Hart, *The Urban Christian* (Downers Grove: IVP Academic, 1987), 78.

2. Robert Kennedy, quoted in Edward Moore Kennedy, *True Compass: A Memoir* (New York: Hachette, 2009).
3. Bradley R. E. Wright, *Upside: Surprising Good News About the State of Our World* (Ada, MI: Bethany House, 2011), chapter 1.
4. Arundhati Roy, *War Talk* (Cambridge: South End Press, 2003), 75.

Conclusion: A Red Letter Future

1. Lisa Miller, "The Religious Case for Gay Marriage," *Newsweek* (Dec. 5, 2008).

About the Authors

Photo by Gabe Wicks

TONY CAMPOLO, best-selling author, is professor emeritus of sociology at Eastern University, a former faculty member at the University of Pennsylvania, and the founder and president of the Evangelical Association for the Promotion of Education. Tony speaks about three hundred times a year in the United States and around the globe. He has been a media commentator for a wide variety of outlets, has written more than thirty-five books, and blogs regularly at one of his websites, redletterchristians.org.

SHANE CLAIBORNE is a best-selling author, renowned activist, sought-after speaker, and self-proclaimed "recovering sinner." Shane writes and speaks around the world about peacemaking, social justice, and Jesus. He is the author of numerous books, including *The Irresistible Revolution* and *Jesus for President*. He is the visionary leader of The Simple Way in Philadelphia, and his work has been featured in Fox News, *Esquire*, *SPIN* magazine, the *Wall Street Journal*, NPR, and CNN. (thesimpleway.org).